MCSE
WINDOWS NT®
WORKSTATION 4
FOR
DUMMIES®

MCSE WINDOWS NT® WORKSTATION 4 FOR DUMMIES®

by Mike Kendzierski

Foreword by Eckhart Boehme
Marketing Manager Certification and Skills Assessment,
Microsoft Corporation

IDG BOOKS WORLDWIDE™

IDG Books Worldwide, Inc.
An International Data Group Company

Foster City, CA ♦ Chicago, IL ♦ Indianapolis, IN ♦ New York, NY

MCSE Windows NT® Workstation 4 For Dummies®

Published by
IDG Books Worldwide, Inc.
An International Data Group Company
919 E. Hillsdale Blvd.
Suite 400
Foster City, CA 94404
www.idgbooks.com (IDG Books Worldwide Web site)
www.dummies.com (Dummies Press Web site)

Library of Congress Catalog Card No.: 98-85836

ISBN: 0-7645-0402-9

Printed in the United States of America

10 9 8 7 6 5 4 3 2 1

1O/RW/QX/ZY/IN

Distributed in the United States by IDG Books Worldwide, Inc.

Distributed by Macmillan Canada for Canada; by Transworld Publishers Limited in the United Kingdom; by IDG Norge Books for Norway; by IDG Sweden Books for Sweden; by Woodslane Pty. Ltd. for Australia; by Woodslane (NZ) Ltd. for New Zealand; by Addison Wesley Longman Singapore Pte Ltd. for Singapore, Malaysia, Thailand, Indonesia and Korea; by Norma Comunicaciones S.A. for Colombia; by Intersoft for South Africa; by International Thomson Publishing for Germany, Austria and Switzerland; by Toppan Company Ltd. for Japan; by Distribuidora Cuspide for Argentina; by Livraria Cultura for Brazil; by Ediciencia S.A. for Ecuador; by Ediciones ZETA S.C.R. Ltda. for Peru; by WS Computer Publishing Corporation, Inc., for the Philippines; by Unalis Corporation for Taiwan; by Contemporanea de Ediciones for Venezuela; by Computer Book & Magazine Store for Puerto Rico; by Express Computer Distributors for the Caribbean and West Indies. Authorized Sales Agent: Anthony Rudkin Associates for the Middle East and North Africa.

For general information on IDG Books Worldwide's books in the U.S., please call our Consumer Customer Service department at 800-762-2974. For reseller information, including discounts and premium sales, please call our Reseller Customer Service department at 800-434-3422.

For information on where to purchase IDG Books Worldwide's books outside the U.S., please contact our International Sales department at 650-655-3200 or fax 650-655-3297.

For information on foreign language translations, please contact our Foreign & Subsidiary Rights department at 650-655-3021 or fax 650-655-3281.

For sales inquiries and special prices for bulk quantities, please contact our Sales department at 650-655-3200 or write to the address above.

For information on using IDG Books Worldwide's books in the classroom or for ordering examination copies, please contact our Educational Sales department at 800-434-2086 or fax 317-596-5499.

For press review copies, author interviews, or other publicity information, please contact our Public Relations department at 650-655-3000 or fax 650-655-3299.

For authorization to photocopy items for corporate, personal, or educational use, please contact Copyright Clearance Center, 222 Rosewood Drive, Danvers, MA 01923, or fax 978-750-4470.

is a trademark under exclusive license to IDG Books Worldwide, Inc., from International Data Group, Inc.

About the Author

Michael Kendzierski, MCSE, MCT, works as a Systems Engineer, splitting time between the Midwest and New England doing consulting, development, and project management for Fortune 100 clients. He received his bachelor's degree from Providence College and has completed graduate work at Boston University. Michael is a contributing writer for *MCP Magazine* and has written several articles on both Microsoft BackOffice and Computer Networking. Michael has also spoken at several technical conferences regarding ways to reduce the Total Cost of Ownership in the Enterprise. When he's not spending his time consulting and writing, he can be found roaming around the country searching for a local Starbucks. He welcomes e-mail and can be reached at MKendzierski@Worldnet.att.net.

Syngress Media is a Boston-area firm that creates books and software for Information Technology professionals seeking skill enhancement and career advancement. Syngress Media's products are designed to comply with vendor and industry standard course studies and are geared especially to certification exam preparation.

About the Contributors

Kevin O'Neal (MCSE, MCPS, MCP+Internet) is a Systems Integrator for Sprint located in Kansas City. He currently works on the Server Team as an NT and Banyan administrator supporting more than 5,000 total users. His current duties include supporting multiple NT servers located across the country. He has been a systems administrator for 4 years. Kevin achieved the (MCSE, MCPS, MCP+Internet) certifications in less than eight weeks.

Jason Nash currently lives in Raleigh, North Carolina, with his wife Angie (another CNE and MCSE!) and works for Advanced Paradigms, Inc. (www.paradigms.com) Advanced Paradigms is one of the top Microsoft Solution Providers in the country. His certifications include MCSE, MCT, Novell CNE, and CNP (Certified Network Professional). He is currently finishing his MCSD and working on a bachelors of computer science. He welcomes comments from readers; his e-mail address is jnash@intrex.net, and his home page is at www.intrex.net/nash.

ABOUT IDG BOOKS WORLDWIDE

Welcome to the world of IDG Books Worldwide.

IDG Books Worldwide, Inc., is a subsidiary of International Data Group, the world's largest publisher of computer-related information and the leading global provider of information services on information technology. IDG was founded more than 25 years ago and now employs more than 8,500 people worldwide. IDG publishes more than 275 computer publications in over 75 countries (see listing below). More than 90 million people read one or more IDG publications each month.

Launched in 1990, IDG Books Worldwide is today the #1 publisher of best-selling computer books in the United States. We are proud to have received eight awards from the Computer Press Association in recognition of editorial excellence and three from *Computer Currents'* First Annual Readers' Choice Awards. Our best-selling *...For Dummies*® series has more than 50 million copies in print with translations in 38 languages. IDG Books Worldwide, through a joint venture with IDG's Hi-Tech Beijing, became the first U.S. publisher to publish a computer book in the People's Republic of China. In record time, IDG Books Worldwide has become the first choice for millions of readers around the world who want to learn how to better manage their businesses.

Our mission is simple: Every one of our books is designed to bring extra value and skill-building instructions to the reader. Our books are written by experts who understand and care about our readers. The knowledge base of our editorial staff comes from years of experience in publishing, education, and journalism — experience we use to produce books for the '90s. In short, we care about books, so we attract the best people. We devote special attention to details such as audience, interior design, use of icons, and illustrations. And because we use an efficient process of authoring, editing, and desktop publishing our books electronically, we can spend more time ensuring superior content and spend less time on the technicalities of making books.

You can count on our commitment to deliver high-quality books at competitive prices on topics you want to read about. At IDG Books Worldwide, we continue in the IDG tradition of delivering quality for more than 25 years. You'll find no better book on a subject than one from IDG Books Worldwide.

John Kilcullen
CEO
IDG Books Worldwide, Inc.

Steven Berkowitz
President and Publisher
IDG Books Worldwide, Inc.

Eighth Annual
Computer Press
Awards ≥1992

Ninth Annual
Computer Press
Awards ≥1993

Tenth Annual
Computer Press
Awards ≥1994

Eleventh Annual
Computer Press
Awards ≥1995

IDG Books Worldwide, Inc., is a subsidiary of International Data Group, the world's largest publisher of computer-related information and the leading global provider of information services on information technology. International Data Group publishes over 275 computer publications in over 75 countries. More than 90 million people read one or more International Data Group publications each month. International Data Group's publications include: **ARGENTINA:** Buyer's Guide, Computerworld Argentina, PC World Argentina; **AUSTRALIA:** Australian Macworld, Australian PC World, Australian Reseller News, Computerworld, IT Casebook, Network World, Publish, Webmaster; **AUSTRIA:** Computerwelt Osterreich, Networks Austria, PC Tip Austria; **BANGLADESH:** PC World Bangladesh; **BELARUS:** PC World Belarus; **BELGIUM:** Data News; **BRAZIL:** Annuario de Informática, Computerworld, Connections, Macworld, PC Player, PC World, Publish, Reseller News, Supergamepower; **BULGARIA:** Computerworld Bulgaria, Network World Bulgaria, PC & MacWorld Bulgaria; **CANADA:** CIO Canada, Client/Server World, ComputerWorld Canada, InfoWorld Canada, NetworkWorld Canada, WebWorld; **CHILE:** Computerworld Chile, PC World Chile; **COLOMBIA:** Computerworld Colombia, PC World Colombia; **COSTA RICA:** PC World Centro America; **THE CZECH AND SLOVAK REPUBLICS:** Computerworld Czechoslovakia, Macworld Czech Republic, PC World Czechoslovakia; **DENMARK:** Communications World Danmark, Computerworld Danmark, Macworld Danmark, PC World Danmark, Techworld Denmark; **DOMINICAN REPUBLIC:** PC World Republica Dominicana; **ECUADOR:** PC World Ecuador; **EGYPT:** Computerworld Middle East, PC World Middle East; **EL SALVADOR:** PC World Centro America; **FINLAND:** MikroPC, Tietoverkko, Tietoviikko; **FRANCE:** Distributique, Hebdo, Info PC, Le Monde Informatique, Macworld, Reseaux & Telecoms, WebMaster France; **GERMANY:** Computer Partner, Computerwoche, Computerwoche Extra, Computerwoche FOCUS, Global Online, Macwelt, PC Welt; **GREECE:** Amiga Computing, GamePro Greece, Multimedia World; **GUATEMALA:** PC World Centro America; **HONDURAS:** PC World Centro America; **HONG KONG:** Computerworld Hong Kong, PC World Hong Kong, Publish in Asia; **HUNGARY:** ABCD CD-ROM, Computerworld Szamitastechnika, Internetto online Magazine, PC World Hungary, PC-X Magazin Hungary; **ICELAND:** Tolvuheimur PC World Island; **INDIA:** Information Communications World, Information Systems Computerworld, PC World India, Publish in Asia; **INDONESIA:** InfoKomputer PC World, Komputek Computerworld, Publish in Asia; **IRELAND:** ComputerScope, PC Live!; **ISRAEL:** Macworld Israel, People & Computers/Computerworld; **ITALY:** Computerworld Italia, Macworld Italia, Networking Italia, PC World Italia; **JAPAN:** DTP World, Macworld Japan, Nikkei Personal Computing, OS/2 World Japan, SunWorld Japan, Windows NT World, Windows World Japan; **KENYA:** PC World East African; **KOREA:** Hi-Tech Information, Macworld Korea, PC World Korea; **MACEDONIA:** PC World Macedonia; **MALAYSIA:** Computerworld Malaysia, PC World Malaysia, Publish in Asia; **MALTA:** PC World Malta; **MEXICO:** Computerworld Mexico, PC World Mexico; **MYANMAR:** PC World Myanmar; **NETHERLANDS:** Computer! Totaal, LAN Internetworking Magazine, LAN World Buyers Guide, Macworld Netherlands, Net, WebWereld; **NEW ZEALAND:** Absolute Beginners Guide and Plain & Simple Series, Computer Buyer, Computer Industry Directory, Computerworld New Zealand, MTB, Network World, PC World New Zealand; **NICARAGUA:** PC World Centro America; **NORWAY:** Computerworld Norge, CW Rapport, Datamagasinet, Financial Rapport, Kursguide Norge, Macworld Norge, Multimediaworld Norge, PC World Ekspress Norge, PC World Nettverk, PC World Norge, PC World ProduktGuide Norge; **PAKISTAN:** Computerworld Pakistan; **PANAMA:** PC World Panama; **PEOPLE'S REPUBLIC OF CHINA:** China Computer Users, China Computerworld, China InfoWorld, China Telecom World Weekly, Computer & Communication, Electronic Design China, Electronics Today, Electronics Weekly, Game Software, PC World China, Popular Computer Week, Software Weekly, Software World, Telecom World; **PERU:** Computerworld Peru, PC World Profesional Peru, PC World SoHo Peru; **PHILIPPINES:** Click!, Computerworld Philippines, PC World Philippines, Publish in Asia; **POLAND:** Computerworld Poland, Computerworld Special Report Poland, Cyber, Macworld Poland, Networld Poland, PC World Komputer; **PORTUGAL:** Cerebro/PC World, Computerworld/Correio Informático, Dealer World Portugal, Mac*In/PC*In Portugal, Multimedia World; **PUERTO RICO:** PC World Puerto Rico; **ROMANIA:** Computerworld Romania, PC World Romania, Telecom Romania; **RUSSIA:** Computerworld Russia, Mir PK, Publish, Seti; **SINGAPORE:** Computerworld Singapore, PC World Singapore, Publish in Asia; **SLOVENIA:** Monitor; **SOUTH AFRICA:** Computing SA, Network World SA, Software World SA; **SPAIN:** Communicaciones World España, Computerworld España, Dealer World España, Macworld España, PC World España; **SRI LANKA:** Infolink PC World; **SWEDEN:** CAP&Design, Computer Sweden, Corporate Computing Sweden, Internetwelt Sweden, it.branschen, Macworld Sweden, MaxiData Sweden, MikroDatorn, Natverk & kommunikation, PC World Sweden, PCaktiv, Windows World Sweden; **SWITZERLAND:** Computerworld Schweiz, Macworld Schweiz, PCtip; **TAIWAN:** Computerworld Taiwan, Macworld Taiwan, NEW ViSiON/Publish, PC World Taiwan, Windows World Taiwan; **THAILAND:** Publish in Asia, Thai Computerworld; **TURKEY:** Computerworld Turkiye, Macworld Turkiye, Network World Turkiye, PC World Turkiye; **UKRAINE:** Computerworld Kiev, Multimedia World Ukraine, PC World Ukraine; **UNITED KINGDOM:** Acorn User UK, Amiga Action UK, Amiga Computing UK, Apple Talk UK, Computing, Macworld, Parents and Computers UK, PC Advisor, PC Home, PSX Pro, The WEB; **UNITED STATES:** Cable in the Classroom, CIO Magazine, Computerworld, DOS World, Federal Computer Week, GamePro Magazine, InfoWorld, I-Way, Macworld, Network World, PC Games, PC World, Publish, Video Event, THE WEB Magazine, and WebMaster; online webzines: JavaWorld, NetscapeWorld, and SunWorld Online; **URUGUAY:** InfoWorld Uruguay; **VENEZUELA:** Computerworld Venezuela, PC World Venezuela; and **VIETNAM:** PC World Vietnam.

5/7/98

Dedication

To my parents for putting up with me all of these years and wondering where I was going to end up. Well . . . it looks like I landed on my feet once again. Thank you.

Author's Acknowledgments

One of the more pleasurable tasks of being an author is being able to publicly thank all of the people that have stood behind me over the past couple of weeks, months, and years before I started writing this book. It was a long and arduous process, but an experience that teaches you something about yourself that isn't worth giving up for anything in the world. A little piece of you that gets put down on a combination of bytes and papers that hopefully opens up a little window to those around you.

For my first heartfelt thank you, I would like to thank the folks at Syngress Media (especially Amy Pedersen), for giving me such a wonderful opportunity and handing off enough advice to fill up three hard disks. I'd also like to thank the editorial and production staff, and all of the people who worked so hard to help put this book together.

I'd like to thank Dr. Norma Kroll and Arnold Cohn for getting me moving in the right direction. I owe you more than I can put in a simple paragraph.

To those who have helped foster my burning desire for computers: Matt Meservey, Bruce Backa, John Hollinger, Ken Barfield, Pat Barton, and David Vernon. Hopefully, one day I'll catch up to you guys.

To the "three musketeers" (Laura, Lorna & Charli) and Jim for being such entertaining distractions and making life enjoyable in the heartland.

And to Michael Macone, Holly Mohney, Amy Carroccia, Stephen Sullivan, Gary Noyes, Dr. Ford, Providence College, Boston University, the guys in the "lab," Colleen, Murph, Corey, and the Galops.

We would like to thank the people at IDG Books who worked to bring this book to market. They include Diane Steele, Jill Pisoni, Mary Corder, Mary Bednarek, Robert Wallace, Pat O'Brien, Constance Carlisle, and Phil Worthington.

Publisher's Acknowledgments

We're proud of this book; please register your comments through our IDG Books Worldwide Online Registration Form located at http://my2cents.dummies.com.

Some of the people who helped bring this book to market include the following:

Acquisitions, Editorial, and Media Development

Project Editors: Robert Wallace, Pat O'Brien

Acquisitions Editor: Jill Pisoni

Copy Editors: Diane L. Giangrossi, Constance Carlisle

Technical Editor: Steve Loethen

CD-ROM Technical Editor: Mark Kory

CD-ROM Exam Reviewers: Joe Wagner, MCSE, Systems Engineer, ST Labs, Inc.; Steven A. Frare, MCP, Network Engineer, ST Labs, Inc.

Media Development Technical Editors: Marita Ellixson, Joell Smith

Associate Permissions Editor: Carmen Krikorian

Media Development Coordinator: Megan Roney

Editorial Manager: Mary C. Corder

Media Development Manager: Heather Heath Dismore

Editorial Assistants: Darren Meiss, Donna Love

Production

Project Coordinator: E. Shawn Aylsworth; Regina Snyder

Layout and Graphics: Lou Boudreau, J. Tyler Connor, Angela F. Hunckler, Brent Savage, Maridee V. Ennis, Drew R. Moore, Anna Rohrer, M. Anne Sipahimalani, Kate Snell

Proofreaders: Christine Berman, Kelli Botta, Rachel Garvey, Henry Lazarek, Nancy Price, Janet M. Withers

Indexer: Sharon Hilgenberg

Special Help

Mary C. Corder, Pat O'Brien, Kathleen Dobie, Stephanie Koutek, Rev Mengle; Joyce Pepple, Barry Pruett; Publications Services, Inc.; Development of the QuickLearn Game by André LaMothe of Xtreme Games, LLC; CD-ROM Exam authored by Pablo Zeitlin, MCSE

General and Administrative

IDG Books Worldwide, Inc.: John Kilcullen, CEO; Steven Berkowitz, President and Publisher

IDG Books Technology Publishing: Brenda McLaughlin, Senior Vice President and Group Publisher

Dummies Technology Press and Dummies Editorial: Diane Graves Steele, Vice President and Associate Publisher; Mary Bednarek, Director of Acquisitions and Product Development; Kristin A. Cocks, Editorial Director

Dummies Trade Press: Kathleen A. Welton, Vice President and Publisher; Kevin Thornton, Acquisitions Manager

IDG Books Production for Dummies Press: Michael R. Britton, Vice President of Production and Creative Services; Beth Jenkins Roberts, Production Director; Cindy L. Phipps, Manager of Project Coordination, Production Proofreading, and Indexing; Kathie S. Schutte, Supervisor of Page Layout; Shelley Lea, Supervisor of Graphics and Design; Debbie J. Gates, Production Systems Specialist; Robert Springer, Supervisor of Proofreading; Debbie Stailey, Special Projects Coordinator; Tony Augsburger, Supervisor of Reprints and Bluelines

Dummies Packaging and Book Design: Robin Seaman, Creative Director; Jocelyn Kelaita, Product Packaging Coordinator; Kavish + Kavish, Cover Design

♦

The publisher would like to give special thanks to Patrick J. McGovern, without whom this book would not have been possible.

Contents at a Glance

Cartoons at a Glance

By Rich Tennant

page 207

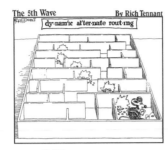

page 291

page 9

page 161

page 23

page 101

page 255

page 333

page 351

Fax: 978-546-7747 • E-mail: the5wave@tiac.net

Table of Contents

· ·

Foreword

• •

*C*ertification makes computer professionals stand out. Technical managers recognize the Microsoft Certified Professional (MCP) designation as a mark of quality — one which ensures that an employee or consultant has proven experience with and meets the high technical proficiency standards of Microsoft products. The ...For Dummies series from IDG Books Worldwide, Inc., really stands out in the marketplace and can help you achieve your goal of certification.

The ...For Dummies series of MCP Approved Study Guides is based on the exam's objectives — and designed to help you meet them. By partnering with Microsoft, IDG Books has develop the MCSE series to ensure that every subject on the exam is covered. Every Microsoft Approved Study Guide is reviewed and approved by an independent third party.

And certification will help you stand out from the crowd as one of the best in your industry. Microsoft training and certification let you maximize the potential of Microsoft Windows desktop operating systems; server technologies, such as the Internet Information Server, Microsoft Windows NT, and Microsoft BackOffice; and Microsoft development tools. In short, Microsoft training and certification provide you with the knowledge and skills necessary to become an expert on Microsoft products and technologies — and to provide the key competitive advantage that every business is seeking.

Research shows that MCP training and certification also provides these other benefits to businesses:

- ♦ A standard method for determining training needs and measuring results – an excellent return on training and certification investments

- ♦ Increased customer satisfaction and decreased support costs through improved service, increased productivity, and greater technical self-sufficiency

- ♦ A reliable benchmark for hiring, promoting, and career planning

- ♦ Recognition and rewards for productive employees by validating their expertise

- ♦ Retraining options for existing employees so that they can work effectively with new technologies

- ♦ Assurance of quality when outsourcing computer services

As an MCP, you'll also receive many other benefits, including direct access to technical information from Microsoft; the official MCP logo and other materials to identify your status to colleagues and clients; invitations to Microsoft conferences, technical training sessions and special events; and exclusive publications with news about the MCP program.

The challenges – both for individuals and for the industry – are out there. Microsoft training and certification will help prepare you to face them. Let this book be your guide.

*— **Eckhart Boehme, Marketing Manager**
Certification and Skills Assessment,
Microsoft Corporation*

Introduction

I wrote this book because I wished that I'd had one available when I prepared to take MCSE Exam 70-73, Implementing and Supporting Windows NT 4.0 Workstation.

I'm probably like you. I'm an IT professional and have been working with networks for a number of years. I decided to pursue my MCSE because I knew it was the right career move. I picked a date to take the exam, and each night I reviewed chapters from my dog-eared copy of the *Windows NT Resource Kit*. I browsed the Web for anything about the exam and usually came away more anxious than before. And I worried that, despite knowing a lot about networks and NT, I wasn't prepared to actually take the exam. What should I focus on? What types of questions would I see? What were the toughest topics? What topics wouldn't be on the exam? No book was available that helped me answer those questions. No book existed that distilled the thousands of pages of information I'd read over the years on NT into a form that helped me effectively study for the exam. As smart as I am, I realized that when it came to taking the exam, I was a "Dummy."

So, if you want to be spared the intellectual preening and chest thumping gymnastics of books that would be best titled "Everything I Ever Knew About NT Workstation, Presented in No Particular Order (The Director's Cut)," this book is for you. It's designed with one goal in mind: to make certain that you pass MCSE Exam 70-73, Implementing and Supporting Windows NT 4.0 Workstation. While other study guides overwhelm you with a lot of extra information about Windows NT 4.0 Workstation *the product,* our primary focus is Windows NT 4.0 Workstation *the exam.*

How This Book Is Organized

Each chapter in the book contains a set of tools built to help you pass the exam. Start with Chapter 1 and work your way to the end. At every step, I show you what to study and what to skip.

This book follows the order of the Microsoft published exam objectives — when that's the best way to study. If you can more easily understand the information by changing the order, I change the order.

I divided this book into parts designed to match the parts of the Microsoft test. The first part is the "before you get started" part containing information on the test and product basics — reviewing before you jump into studying for the exam is a good thing to do. The remaining parts correspond to the sections of the exam: planning, troubleshooting, and so on.

Part I: Getting Ready for the Exam

This part contains information on the Workstation exam, its questions, its structure, and other important information to consider before you begin studying. In addition, Chapter 2 of this part covers some of the more important basics of the product. If you need a refresher course on Workstation, turn to Chapter 2.

Part II: Planning, Installation, and Configuration

Part II prepares you for questions on the fundamentals of planning and deploying your Windows NT 4.0 Workstation installation. Special attention is given to unattended installations, planning strategies for sharing and securing resources, and choosing the correct file system to use in a given situation. The many pages I spend discussing NTFS, FAT, HPFS, security, and dual-boot capabilities accurately reflect the relative importance of these topics on the exam. When it comes to planning, you are likely to encounter scenario questions on the exam. I present information in this section in a way that can help you to analyze these types of questions effectively before answering.

With the planning complete, I carefully walk you through the phases of installation, paying careful attention to dual-boots and upgrades — two areas you're certain to see on the exam.

After you're comfortable installing Windows NT 4.0 Workstation, you'll also be required to know how to remove Windows NT Workstation in a given situation. This includes returning the workstation to its prior configuration and removing Windows NT completely from the workstation, including the removal of all system files.

Installing, configuring, and removing hardware components for different situations can be tedious work. I've created installation labs that can make the process go a bit smoother. As part of installing and configuring hardware devices, you're going to use Control Panel applications to configure a Windows NT Workstation computer in a given situation.

Part III: Managing Resources

In Part III, I go over managing your resources on your Windows NT 4.0 Workstation. This is pretty much about creating and managing local user accounts and local group accounts on your NT Workstation. You'll have to know how to create local groups on your workstation and how to configure, set up, and modify user profiles for your workstation. Expect that several exam questions will test your knowledge of permissions. Be prepared to set up shared folders and permissions for NTFS partitions, folders, and files on your NT 4.0 Workstation. The last section for managing resources is installing and configuring printers in a given environment. This section includes questions about setting up local and network printers for your Windows NT 4.0 Workstation.

Part IV: Connecting Networks

For Part IV, I talk about other types of networks and how they communicate with Windows NT 4.0 Workstation. Because NetWare still owns a large part of the networking market, you need to know how to integrate your NT Workstation as a client in a NetWare environment. You'll be tested heavily on this section, so pay close attention to Client Services for NetWare.

Connecting to other networks requires a network protocol. For this exam, you'll have to know how to use various configurations to install Windows NT Workstation as a TCP/IP client, particularly because this is the protocol that connects to the Internet.

You'll also be tested on adding and configuring the network components of Windows NT Workstation. Make sure that you know where this process takes place and how to add network components and use various methods to access network resources.

Regarding Web publishing, you'll have to know how to configure Microsoft Peer Web Services. I also go over how many concurrent connections are available for users connecting up to Windows NT 4.0 Workstation for this section.

Part V: Connecting to the Internet

This is the smallest tested section on the NT 4.0 Workstation exam, but they're going to test you on configuring your Workstation to install Dial Up Networking in a given situation. You can use this to RAS into an ISP to connect up to the Internet. This is a small section on the exam, but worth noting.

Part VI: Running Applications

Before you take the test, you'll have to know how to start applications on Intel and RISC platforms in various operating system environments. You're probably accustomed to starting applications from your Intel workstation, but I want to make sure that you know how to start applications from a RISC workstation as well.

Besides starting various applications on two different platforms, you also have to know how to start applications at various priorities. You can start any application from the command line by running the application with the Start parameter and the necessary switch at the end.

Part VII: Monitoring, Optimizing, and Troubleshooting

This is the last section of the exam and is usually the hardest to study for. Besides needing to know how to monitor system performance by using various tools that are provided on your workstation, you'll also have to identify and resolve specific performance problems. Besides being able to monitor your system, you'll also have to optimize system performance in various areas. Expect some scenario questions here.

When your computer fails, things get ugly. Be prepared to troubleshoot

- Boot process failures
- Print job failures
- Installation process failures
- Application failures
- Users cannot access a resource
- The system registry

Part VIII: The Part of Tens

This section is really a section of top ten lists on a particular subject. It's a great way to reinforce all the key points in the book and is the part you'll probably have open on the passenger seat next to you as you drive to the exam. Don't spill!

Part IX: Appendixes

Appendixes A and B are complete practice exams that show you whether you're ready to register for the exam. If you don't pass these exams, don't worry; every answer tells you what you need to review and where to find the information. Appendix C is a guide to Microsoft certification and shows how the Workstation exam fits into the big certification picture. Appendix D explains what's on the CD-ROM, which is packed with study aids and other resources.

About This Book

Each chapter in the book contains all the tools you need to study for and to pass the exam. Here's how it works:

Quick Assessment questions

The Quick Assessment quiz assesses what you already know about the exam objectives. In fact, the questions are grouped by objective, and the answers tell you which section to review in the chapter. If you're in a hurry, you can just study the sections of the questions you miss. If you get all of them, skip to the end of the chapter and have at the practice exam.

Labs

Labs guide you through the steps of using the product and solving problems. Step-by-step exercises walk you through a skill that's likely to be an area of focus on the exam. Each lab step is simplified so that you understand the ideas of the process at the same level that they are tested, like this:

Lab 6-1	Correcting a Video Driver Installation with No Display

1. **Start NT Workstation in VGA mode.**

2. **Remove the incorrect video driver that's causing your problems. This is the one currently installed.**

3. **Install a driver that you know works.**

   You'll have to reboot your system for the changes to take effect.

Tables

Sometimes you need just the facts. In such cases, tables provide a simple way to present everything at a glance, like this:

Table 8-1	Basic User Rights
Right	*Description*
Access this computer from network	Connect over the network to a computer.
Add workstations to domain	Add a workstation to the domain, allowing the workstation to recognize the domain's user and global group accounts and the user accounts in trusted domains.
Back up files and directories	Back up files and directories, allowing the user to read all files. This right supersedes file and directory permissions and also applies to the Registry.
Change the system time	Set the time for the computer's internal clock.
Force shutdown from a remote system	This right is not currently implemented. It's reserved for future use.
Load and unload device drivers	Install and remove device drivers.
Log on locally	Log on at the computer itself, from the computer's keyboard.
Manage auditing and security log	Specify what types of resource access (such as file access) are to be audited. View and clear the security log. **Note:** This right does not allow a user to set system auditing with the Policy⇨Audit command of User Manager for Domains; only the Administrators group holds this ability.
Restore files and directories	Restore files and directories, allowing the user to write to all files. This right supersedes file and directory permissions and also applies to the Registry.
Shut down the system	Shut down Windows NT Workstation.
Take ownership of files or other objects	Take ownership of files, folders, and other objects on a computer.

Prep tests

Each chapter ends with a Prep Test. These tests pose questions just like you'll find on the exam. Each questions gauges your understanding of a chapter's topic. If you miss a question, the answer tells you which section of the chapter to review.

Also similar to the exam, the Prep Test questions have circles to mark when only one answer is right. When questions can have more than one answer, the answers have squares to mark.

Icons Used in This Book

Special graphics mark paragraphs that are worth a second look.

Time Shaver helps you to manage and save time while studying or taking the exam.

Instant Answer identifies correct and incorrect exam answers at a glance.

Remember highlights important capabilities and advantages of the technology that may appear on the exam.

Warning points out problems and limitations of the technology that may appear on the exam.

Tip gives information that can come in extra-handy during the exam, like this: *Take your closest someone out to dinner after you pass the exam and reintroduce yourself.*

Where to Go from Here

MSCE Windows NT 4 Workstation For Dummies is all you need to prepare for the exam. So don't waste time; turn the page and get started!

Part I
Getting Ready for the Exam

The 5th Wave — By Rich Tennant

Despite its inclusion on the Hardware Compatability List, Martin shuddered at the thought of having to install Windows NT on the workstation from the early 1950s.

In this part . . .

Back in 1991, when Windows NT appeared on the market, the computer industry had no way of differentiating the various levels of computer professionals — everyone was considered an "expert." No standards or methods were available to tell how knowledgeable someone was in a particular subject. Employers had no protection from lousy work or misrepresentation. Well, those days are gone.

The Microsoft Certified Professional Program offers an official way to measure proficiency in different computer products. Now, does that mean that certified professionals are always the best and most knowledgeable candidates for a job? No, of course not. But certification does allow a way to judge skills and let customers know that they're hiring someone who knows what he or she is talking about.

Hundreds of thousands of smart, creative computer professionals are putting up the money to prove their skill and get certified. The end result of this craze for certification is a legion of experienced, skilled Microsoft Computer Professionals who can support and maintain enterprise-size computer networks.

Part I looks at the ins and outs of the certification process and covers some workstation basics in an exam-prep road map. If you're comfortable with Workstation 101 material, you'll probably get through these chapters in a nanosecond.

Chapter 1

The Workstation 4.0 Exam

· ·

In This Chapter

▶ Taking a look at the Workstation 4.0 exam

▶ Understanding what's being tested

▶ Reviewing the ins and outs of taking the Workstation test

· ·

*T*he NT 4.0 Workstation exam is going to test you on your knowledge of managing your local NT Workstation. You won't see too many questions on configuring domains or trust relationships on this test. The best way to get a good look at the NT 4.0 Workstation exam is to take a detailed look at the Exam Preparation Page that Microsoft provides as a guideline for what to study. This page is your best resource because Microsoft already does all the work for you. You just have to spend time looking up the information before you can take the test.

Appendix C tells you everything you need to know about the various Microsoft certifications and how this exam fits into the big picture.

Your Workstation Exam Blueprint

The following are the exam objectives for the Workstation exam.

Planning

✔ Create unattended installation files.

✔ Plan strategies for sharing and securing resources.

✔ Choose the appropriate file system to use in a given situation. File systems and situations include NTFS, FAT, HPFS, Security, and dual-boot systems.

Installation and configuration

- ✔ Install Windows NT Workstation on an Intel platform in a given situation.

- ✔ Set up a dual-boot system in a given situation.

- ✔ Remove Windows NT Workstation in a given situation.

- ✔ Install, configure, and remove hardware components for a given situation. Hardware components include network adapter drivers, SCSI device drivers, tape device drivers, UPS, multimedia devices, display drivers, keyboard drivers, and mouse drivers.

- ✔ Use the Control Panel applications to configure a Windows NT Workstation computer in a given situation.

- ✔ Upgrade to Windows NT Workstation 4.0 in a given situation.

- ✔ Configure server-based installation for wide-scale deployment in a given situation.

Managing resources

- ✔ Create and manage local user accounts and local group accounts to meet given requirements.

- ✔ Set up and modify user profiles.

- ✔ Set up shared folders and permissions.

- ✔ Set permissions on NTFS partitions, folders, and files.

- ✔ Install and configure printers in a given environment.

Connectivity

- ✔ Add and configure the network components of Windows NT Workstation.

- ✔ Use various methods to access network resources.

- ✔ Implement Windows NT Workstation as a client in a NetWare environment.

- ✔ Use various configurations to install Windows NT Workstation as a TCP/IP client.

- ✔ Configure and install Dial Up Networking in a given situation.

- ✔ Configure Microsoft Peer Web Services in a given situation.

Running applications

- ✔ Start applications on Intel and RISC platforms in various operating system environments.

- ✔ Start applications at various priorities.

Monitoring and optimization

- ✔ Monitor system performance by using various tools.
- ✔ Identify and resolve a given performance problem.
- ✔ Optimize system performance in various areas.

Troubleshooting

- ✔ Choose the appropriate course of action to take when the boot process fails.
- ✔ Choose the appropriate course of action to take when a print job fails.
- ✔ Choose the appropriate course of action to take when the installation process fails.
- ✔ Choose the appropriate course of action to take when an application fails.
- ✔ Choose the appropriate course of action to take when a user cannot access a resource.
- ✔ Modify the Registry by using the appropriate tool in a given situation.
- ✔ Implement advanced techniques to resolve various problems.

Number of questions

The specific Microsoft exam you're about to take will determine how much time you'll be given to finish your exam. For this test, you'll be given 75 minutes to complete 51 questions.

To pass this exam, you need to pass 70 percent of the total exam. That isn't too rough as long as you take your time and read this book!

How questions are structured

For this test, you'll see a variety of questions, such as scenario, multiple choice, and pick the correct answer(s). For the scenario questions, reading through the questions a couple of times before answering is a good idea. For multiple choice questions, it's a good idea to go through the entire scenario for each question in case one question possibly gives away the answer for another question. This doesn't always happen, but sometimes it can help.

The question structure for the Microsoft exams is getting better. The more exams I take, the more questions I see that specify how many correct answers you must have. For example, if you're asked a multiple choice question that specifies that two out of the five possible answers are correct, coming up with those correct answers is much easier than having to guess how many answers are actually correct.

For multiple choice questions, you can usually eliminate a couple of possible answers before you specify your choice. This is great way to sneak in a couple of correct answers that may mean either passing or failing your exam. Usually, a couple of possible answers don't belong in the questions and can be eliminated right away.

Success from Start to Finish

Ready to call up Sylvan Prometric or Virtual University Enterprises (VUE) and schedule your test? Slow down. Take the time to understand what you need to do and how long you need to do it.

Preparation

Study until you're confident in your ability to take the test. This depends on your experience and study time. In general, if you have no experience with Windows NT Server, access to necessary resources and equipment, and plenty of time to study, be ready to take the certification exam in four weeks.

The Introduction of this book explains how to prepare by working through this book from cover to cover.

If you have experience with previous Windows NT Workstation versions and can devote a couple of hours a day for brushing up with this book, you could be ready in a week or two.

When you pass two practice exams in a row, you're ready to try the real exam.

Exam day

The first thing you do when arriving to take your exam is sign in with the Testing Coordinator. You need two forms of identification, one of which must be a photo ID. You aren't allowed to carry anything into the testing area, including

- ✔ Books
- ✔ Bags
- ✔ Papers
- ✔ Cell phones
- ✔ Pagers

Starting with a smile

You're escorted into a closed room and shown to a testing station. Each station contains a computer and is separated from the others by partitions. You're given scratch paper and a pen or pencil. In some cases, you receive a thin white board and an erasable marker instead. All materials should be returned at the end of the exam.

Testing rooms are monitored by sight and sound. Any questions about the integrity of your exam results in termination of that exam.

Keeping your cool

Take your time when you read the questions on this exam. Though I often hear of people running out of time on other exams, I haven't heard of anyone running out of time on the 70-073 exam. Read each question twice just to make sure that you aren't missing anything. You'll see several questions that look exactly the same, but one or two words have been changed.

My strategy for exam taking is to run through and answer all the easy questions first to gain confidence and momentum before I start tackling some of the more difficult scenario questions. I answer all the questions that I can, mark all the questions that pose some trouble, and then come back to them later. I try to leave as much time as possible so that I can double-check my answers before I finish. I know the process sounds long and drawn out, but so far it's worked for me.

Remember the following points as you do some of your practice exams:

✔ Only one or two words may be different in two exam questions.

✔ Terminology may be cited in a very precise manner.

✔ Some questions are deliberately ambiguous.

The testing software makes skipping questions easy. Just click the *Mark* checkbox on all the questions you have not answered. You can go back to all the marked questions as many times as you want.

Don't leave any questions unanswered. If you don't know the answer, guess. There is no penalty for wrong answers. If you leave it blank, you miss it.

Leaving with the results

The exam program stops automatically when your time is up. (If you decide to quit before the end of the allotted time, click the *End Exam* button.) Your test is graded immediately, and the results appear on the screen. The results are printed for you, too. The Testing Coordinator notarizes the printout and stamps it.

The notarized printout is your official report. Don't lose it!

If you pass, the testing organization sends the results to Microsoft. Congratulations! Your MCP kit will arrive in a few weeks!

If you come close, but fail, don't feel too bad. These tests are *tough*. I don't know any MCSE who passed every exam on the first try. If you missed by a hair, review your weak areas and try again. You'll know your weak areas by the percentage you score for each category on the exam report.

Chapter 2

Mapping an Exam Prep Strategy

● ●

In This Chapter

▶ Overview of Windows NT 4.0 Workstation features

▶ Comparing Windows NT 4.0 and the Windows operating systems

▶ Rundown of Windows NT 4.0 characteristics and new technologies

● ●

*Y*ou need to become "one" with Windows NT Workstation so that you can best prepare for the exam. You have to eat, breathe, and sleep NT Workstation — it's the only way to fully prepare for the exam. Part of getting comfortable with the product is knowing the basic, fundamental characteristics of Windows NT — stuff that you won't be tested on directly but that will give you the foundation to understand the questions better.

Windows NT 4.0 is a powerhouse operating system. It is fully 32-bit, stable, secure, and very robust in performing tasks on your network. NT 4.0 is much different from previous versions of Windows in that it is designed with both security and stability in mind. MS-DOS, Windows 3.11, and Windows 95 perform well and are great with legacy applications, but by no means do they match Windows NT in power and performance on the desktop.

Comparing NT . . .

Windows NT may look like other versions of Windows on the surface, but underneath, Windows NT is a whole different system. It's designed to be secure, stable, robust, portable, fast, and easy to use — you honestly can't say that about any other operating system on the market. Basically, NT doesn't crash unless you do something that you probably shouldn't be doing.

What separates Windows NT from all other operating systems is security. NT has many features that take advantage of security, such as NTFS security, fault tolerance, and the Windows NT network model.

. . . And Windows 95

Windows 95 is made up of mainly 16- and 32-bit code and isn't designed with security and stability in mind. Windows 95 may have the same fancy GUI as NT, but is not nearly as secure, stable, or tweaked for speed as NT.

. . . And MS-DOS and Windows 3.x

Yep, people still use MS-DOS for legacy applications, so Windows NT must be able to interact with MS-DOS clients on the network, as well as the many different Windows 3.x clients out in the world. Windows NT handles these 16-bit applications differently than it does 32-bit applications because MS-DOS wants to access hardware directly — something that NT isn't a big fan of.

. . . And NT Server

Windows NT Server is like a stronger big brother to Windows NT Workstation. NT Workstation can do almost everything that NT Server can do, but on a smaller scale. Windows NT Server can have as many clients as a license can support; Windows NT Workstation is limited to ten concurrent network connections. NT Server is also different because of its capability to support multiple clients — it's designed as a server, not as a workstation.

For the exam, remember that NT Workstation can do anything that NT Server can do except that NT Server does it on a higher level. Think locally instead of in a domain state of mind. Most of the exam questions pertain to your local workstation as a client. You may see a couple of domain questions, but such questions are very rare.

Windows NT Feature Set and Architecture

Many features are unique to Windows NT. The following sections give you the lowdown to prepare you for references to these features elsewhere in this book (and on the exam).

Windows NT is made up of many different subsystems. These subsystems are used to emulate other operating environments so that many different applications can run effectively on your NT Workstation. The environmental subsystems that are part of Windows NT include POSIX, MS-DOS, and WIN32.

Portability

Portability? What does that mean? Although most Windows NT computers usually run on an Intel platform, you can port Windows NT to other platforms, such as RISC or the Macintosh PowerPC. Portability is running the operating system on other platforms and making NT as universally available as possible.

Most of the source code for Windows NT is written in C or C++, which allows NT to be compiled for many different platforms. The same source code can be recompiled to build versions of Windows NT that are specific to each processor's instruction set.

Just remember that you can run NT on other types of computers, such as Alpha (RISC processors) or Macintosh (PowerPC).

Multitasking

Have you ever had 12 applications open at the same time? That's the kind of multitasking that Windows NT allows because of its ability to handle multiple applications at once with relatively little performance degradation. NT takes advantage of *symmetric multiprocessing* — the ability to use more than one processor in a symmetrically balanced manner.

Multithreading

In addition to being a preemptive, multitasking operating system, Windows NT is also *multithreaded,* meaning that more than one thread of execution can execute in a single task at once. Multithreading allows every thread access to the same memory address space, thus providing very fast communication among threads. Because threads don't require a separate address space, threads are also easier to create than are processes.

Processes own resources; threads execute code. Two typical examples of using multiple threads include using a background thread to print a Word document or to execute an Internet Explorer request. A single-threaded application can't respond to user input until it's finished printing or downloading or whatever process it's carrying out.

File systems

Chapter 3 gets into all the details of file systems; for now, just remember that Windows NT 4.0 supports multiple file systems and that your system setup (dual-boot or single-boot) determines the file system you use and the type of security you want.

New to Windows NT 4.0 is the dropping of support for HPFS, which is where OS/2 and NT can officially part ways. If you have HPFS on your system, NT will make you delete it or convert it to NTFS before you can proceed.

Security

With all the security options that Windows NT offers — such as NTFS partitions, account policies, auditing, user profiles, and system policies — you can really secure your NT Workstation.

Of course, NT Workstation is only as secure as you make it. Turning on all these security options is your choice and your responsibility.

Client support

Windows NT allows connectivity with a multitude of clients. Here's a brief list:

- MS-DOS
- Banyan VINES
- Windows 3.*x*
- Windows 95
- Novell NetWare
- UNIX

Whatever your client, you can probably find some way to make NT communicate with it.

Multiprocessor support

Windows NT can take advantage of multiple processors — even up to 32 with an OEM build of Windows NT. Now that processors are becoming relatively cheap, adding a second processor may not be a bad idea. Because

NT is a preemptive, multitasking operating system, the more processors you have loaded on your workstation, the better NT performs. Instead of one application hogging up all the processor's time, Windows NT schedules different thread priorities so that all your applications have access to the processor.

Connectivity

To support different types of connectivity, Windows NT supports many different types of protocols. The networking world is made up of many diverse computers, and Windows NT tries to communicate with them all. For the exam, you mainly need to know about connectivity with Novell NetWare.

NT memory architecture: Virtual memory and demand paging

Windows NT handles memory a lot differently than Windows 95 and its predecessors. Windows NT wants to make sure that as much memory as possible is available to all the applications and at the same time that the memory is secure and cannot be accessed by any promiscuous code running on the workstation.

If you run out of physical memory, Windows NT uses part of your hard disk to help run applications or store dynamic data. That's called *virtual memory* (VM). VM is slower than conventional physical memory and, if you use a lot of VM, causes a great deal of paging on your hard disk.

To be as secure as possible, Windows NT does not allow memory to access certain parts of the kernel or let applications directly access the hardware. This memory protection keeps Windows NT up and running and prohibits it from crashing all the time. You can also secure 16-bit MS-DOS applications by running them in their own memory spaces so that they won't be able to crash other 16-bit applications.

Kernel mode is the most secure part of the operating system. Anything running in Kernel mode has direct access to the heart of the operating system. Kernel mode is also the most dangerous mode because if a process or thread goes bad in Kernel mode, it crashes the operating system. Ouch!

Part II
Planning, Installation, and Configuration

The 5th Wave   By Rich Tennant

Before installing Windows 95, Dwayne prepares to partition the hard drive.

©RICHTENNANT

In this part . . .

So where to start preparing for the exam? How about hardware requirements and other areas involved with planning for an installation? Do you know how to upgrade to Windows NT 4.0? Are you comfortable with the issues involved in a corporate-wide rollout of Windows NT Workstation?

After rolling out the workstations, you have to configure them. The first place to start is security; Microsoft hammers you on the exam if you don't understand share or file security. You need to know how to securely share resources with other computers on the network, which gets into choosing the appropriate file system to use — NTFS, FAT, or even dual-boot systems.

Just look over the tables in the following chapters to check out the subtle differences between the file systems and all the other details of planning, installing, and configuring workstation systems.

Chapter 3

File Systems and Disk Administration: Setting Up Shop

Exam Objectives

▶ Choosing the appropriate file system to use in a given situation

*T*he Windows NT Workstation exam tests your knowledge in several areas pertaining to file systems. For example, you should be knowledgeable about the following:

- ✔ The best file system to choose in the given circumstances regarding user-access needs
- ✔ The best file system to choose to improve performance with a given configuration
- ✔ NTFS security on local drives
- ✔ Creation and deletion of partitions in Disk Administrator

Most of the file-system questions on the exam focus on NTFS.

The first half of the chapter discusses the file systems covered on the exam, and the second half discusses the utilities used to manage those file systems. *Note:* This chapter assumes that you're familiar with the MS-DOS commands used to partition and format disks.

You may not see questions concerning NTFS fault-tolerance features, POSIX support, CDFS (Compact Disc File System — a read-only file system that Windows NT uses for CD-ROMs), or supported network file systems from other vendors. Nevertheless, we touch on these subjects briefly in the chapter — just in case a question about one of these topics sneaks into your exam.

Quick Assessment

Choose the appropriate file system. File systems and situations include NTFS, FAT, HPFS, Security, dual-boot systems

1 If you move a compressed folder from an NTFS partition to a FAT partition, will the folder be compressed or uncompressed?

2 You have a computer with three IDE drives. Would you use a stripe set or a volume set to enhance performance?

3 Use the _____ file system if you want to set up a dual boot between MS-DOS and NT Workstation on the same volume.

4 Are NTFS permissions more restrictive or less restrictive when logging on to a machine remotely?

5 The _____ file system allows you to set security on individual files and folders.

6 Does FAT allow you to compress individual files and folders?

7 The _____ file system is preferred for disks that are smaller than 400MB, if security is not a concern.

8 The _____ file system is preferred for disks that are larger than 400MB.

9 The _____ file system has fault tolerant features built into it.

10 A folder on an NTFS partition has been shared. The NTFS permissions are set for the accounting group to have full access and the users group to have no access. Kevin calls you and says he can't access the folder. You see that he is a member of the accounting group and the users group. Why can Kevin not access the folder?

Answers

1 *Uncompressed.* See "Compression."

2 *Stripe set.* See "Volume sets" and "Stripe sets."

3 *FAT.* See "Compatibility: FAT is king."

4 *More restrictive.* See "Security: NTFS rules."

5 *NTFS.* See "Security: NTFS rules."

6 *No.* See "Compression."

7 *FAT.* See "FAT versus NTFS: Choosing the right system."

8 *NTFS.* See "FAT versus NTFS: Choosing the right system."

9 *NTFS.* See "NTFS fault tolerance."

10 *Because he is a member of the users group, which has no access permission to the folder.* See "Security: NTFS rules."

FAT and NTFS File-Storage Systems: A Place for Everything

Windows NT supports three systems for storing and handling files on a workstation: FAT (file-allocation table) file system, NTFS (Windows NT file system), and CDFS (Compact Disc Filing System).

The exam doesn't cover CDFS; so as you study, focus on contrasting the features of FAT and NTFS (you can also use a combination of FAT and NTFS).

These three options give you the flexibility to run multiple operating systems as well as the ability to use all the features offered with each operating system. (It also means that you have a little more material to study for the exam!)

Windows NT 4.0 no longer supports the high-performance file system (HPFS), the primary file system for IBM's OS/2 operating system. HPFS was previously supported in Windows NT 3.5*x*. If you have a computer that you want to install NT on with HPFS, either you have to convert the partition to NTFS, or you can backup all of your data, remove (as in delete) the HPFS partition, and restore your data.

FAT32, an updated version of FAT on Windows 95 (OSR2), is not compatible with Windows NT. Be careful reading the questions. You will probably see a couple of questions from this chapter that say the same thing except that *FAT* will be replaced with *NTFS*.

FAT versus NTFS: Choosing the right system

FAT, which is supported by a wide variety of operating systems and was originally designed for small disks, consists of five pieces:

- **Partition boot sector:** Houses the information that lets FAT know whether the disk is bootable.
- **FAT1:** Holds information about clusters, such as which clusters are unused, which clusters are being used by files, which clusters are bad, and which cluster is the last in a file.
- **FAT2:** Duplicate of FAT1.
- **Root folder:** Has an entry for each folder and all files that reside in the root directory; can handle only 512 entries.
- **Other files and folders:** Contains entries for all the other files and folders on the partition; can handle more than 512 entries.

NTFS, a more advanced file system than FAT, offers enhanced security, manages large volumes more efficiently, and is a recoverable file system. But its volumes can be accessed only by the Windows NT operating system. NTFS consists of four parts:

- **Partition boot sector:** Houses the information that lets NTFS know whether the disk is bootable.

- **Master File Table:** Keeps records of the 16 NTFS system files that make up the NTFS file system structure.

- **System files:** Houses the 16 NTFS system files that make up the NTFS file system structure.

- **File area:** Location where your data is kept.

Table 3-1 gives you a quick summary of how FAT and NTFS differ. (The following sections go into more detail.)

Table 3-1	Comparing FAT and NTFS	
Characteristic	*FAT*	*NTFS*
Compatibility	MS-DOS, Windows 3.*x*, Windows 95, and Windows NT	Windows NT
Security	None	Full file- and directory-level permissions tied to Windows NT logon security
Maximum file size	4GB	64GB
Maximum partition size	4GB	2TB (in practice)
File compression	None	File- and directory-level compression
Filenames	8.3 (255 characters with Windows NT)	255 characters

Which file system is appropriate in a given situation?

- **Partitions greater than 400MB:** Use NTFS because it uses disk space more efficiently than FAT.

- **Partitions smaller than 400MB:** Use FAT because it uses less system overhead than NTFS.

- **Security:** Regardless of disk size, NTFS is the only correct choice if security is required on the partition.

Note that you can't format a floppy disk with NTFS because the file system would take up too much space.

Keep these thoughts in mind as you see questions involving FAT:

- ✔ FAT is the best choice for partitions greater than 400MB if security is not an issue.
- ✔ FAT offers compression only on an entire volume, not on individual files and folders.
- ✔ FAT is required if you'll be using any operating systems other than Windows NT.

Compatibility: FAT is king

FAT is the most widely accepted file system; it is compatible with Windows NT, Windows 95, MS-DOS, and OS/2. NTFS is compatible with Windows NT only. Therefore, if you have any questions that speak of a dual boot with Windows NT and another operating system, you know that the other operating system has to reside on a FAT partition.

Security: NTFS rules

For any question concerning security as a requirement, the answer is most likely NTFS. Only NTFS allows you to set file and directory permissions; no security is available with FAT.

Security relates mostly to NTFS:

- ✔ **FAT:** You can add permissions to a share only; any subfolders and files within that share all contain the same permissions. (With NTFS, each file in the share can have different permissions.)
- ✔ **NTFS:** You can assign different permissions to individual files and folders. Also, you can assign permission to a folder and assign more-restrictive permissions to files in that folder, which means that a user may have permission to access the folder but not necessarily to access all the files in the folder. So you can give someone access to a particular file or folder without creating a whole new share for it.

  For example, if I have a share on an NTFS volume called Documents, the share permissions can be set up to allow everyone full control. If I put a file called Review.doc in the Documents folder and set the NTFS permissions to allow no access to anyone, then everyone can access all the folder's files except for Review.doc. When you choose to restrict everyone from a file, you still have access to it because you are the creator or owner of the file.

With NTFS, folder files that have not been given specific permissions inherit the permissions of the folder they reside in.

Note that NTFS can have different security depending on whether you're logging on to the machine locally or remotely, as Chapters 7, 8, and 11 discuss. NTFS permissions are more restrictive when logging on to a machine remotely.

When you see a question asking what rights someone has to an NTFS file or folder, read the question carefully. With NTFS permissions, if you are a member of a group that has been granted no access to the file or folder, you have no access, even though you may have permission to access a file or folder with your user account. With NTFS security, *no access* always overrules any other permissions.

Hard disk structure

You may not see any questions about hard disk structure, but here's the scoop, just in case.

Sector and cluster sizes

Both FAT and NTFS use sectors (the smallest storage unit on a hard disk; usually 512 bytes) and clusters (one or more adjoining sectors). Each cluster has a default number of sectors, depending on the cluster size.

File and partition sizes

You may see a question that deals directly with file and partition sizes. Here's a little information on file and partition sizes:

- ✔ **NTFS partition size:** NTFS can support up to a 2TB (terabyte) partition size using today's industry-standard 512K cluster size. Theoretically, NTFS can support up to a 16-exabyte partition, but no hardware is currently available to test that limitation. (Remember also that NTFS is not recommended on small partitions because it takes more overhead than FAT does.)

- ✔ **NTFS file size:** The maximum NTFS file size is between 4GB and 64GB.

- ✔ **FAT partition and file size:** The maximum size of a FAT file or partition is 4GB.

Volume size

The exam may not cover volumes directly, but understanding volumes is important because some of the questions do reference volumes.

A *volume* is a single drive letter that can be accessed by the file system. The space for a volume can come from a single partition, or it can come from free space on several disks that have been formatted to be a volume set. (See "Volume sets," later in this chapter.)

You can extend a volume set on NTFS, but not on FAT. If you're using the FAT file system, the only way to extend the volume set is to convert the file system to NTFS first.

NTFS allows larger file volumes than other file systems. It can handle up to a 2TB (terabyte) file volume using the industry-standard 512-byte sector size. If the industry standard changes, NTFS can theoretically handle up to 16 exabytes on a file volume. FAT can handle only up to 4GB (gigabyte) on a file volume.

Compression

Here's how partition compression works in FAT and NTFS:

- ✓ **FAT:** You can compress only the entire partition.
- ✓ **NTFS:** You can compress individual files, folders, or the entire partition.
  - • To use NTFS compression, your cluster size cannot be larger than 4K.
  - • The file compression generally compresses text files about 50 percent and executable files about 40 percent.
  - • NTFS uncompresses the file when an application accesses the file, and then recompresses the file when the file is saved or the application is closed.

The exam tests your knowledge of whether a file keeps its compression attribute when moved or copied from one location to another. Table 3-2 gives you the different scenarios.

Table 3-2 Compression Attributes of a Moved or Copied File	
If You Do This	**The File Will Be . . .**
Copy a compressed file to an uncompressed folder on the same partition	Uncompressed
Move a compressed file to an uncompressed folder on the same partition	Compressed
Copy or move an uncompressed file to a compressed folder on the same partition	Compressed

If You Do This	The File Will Be . . .
Copy or move a file from a compressed partition to an uncompressed folder on a different partition	Uncompressed
Copy or move a file from an uncompressed partition to a compressed folder on a different partition	Compressed

These compression rules apply to NTFS only. A folder or file will not be compressed if it moves to a FAT partition because FAT does not support NTFS compression.

You can compress files from Windows Explorer by

- ✔ Selecting the file, folder, or partition and opening the Properties dialog box. Figure 3-1 shows the Properties dialog box of an NTFS volume with the compression option checked to compress the drive.

- ✔ Using Compact.exe from the command line.

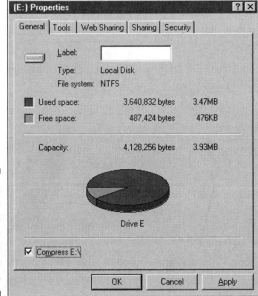

Figure 3-1: Compressing an NTFS volume through the Properties dialog box.

Supported filenames

In Windows NT, FAT supports long filenames of up to 255 characters, including the path. Here are the rules for FAT:

- ✔ Filenames can start with letters or numbers.
- ✔ The only characters that cannot be in a filename are

  ? [ ] / \ | : ; = , ^ *

- ✔ Filenames can have multiple periods in them; the three characters after the last period are the file extension.
- ✔ FAT preserves any capital letters that you use in names, but FAT is not case-sensitive.

Converting between NTFS and FAT

Windows NT supports a utility called Convert.exe that lets you convert a FAT partition to NTFS. To convert from FAT to NTFS, go to the command line and type

```
convert c: /fs:ntfs
```

where C is the drive letter of the partition that you want to convert. Figure 3-2 shows this conversion command.

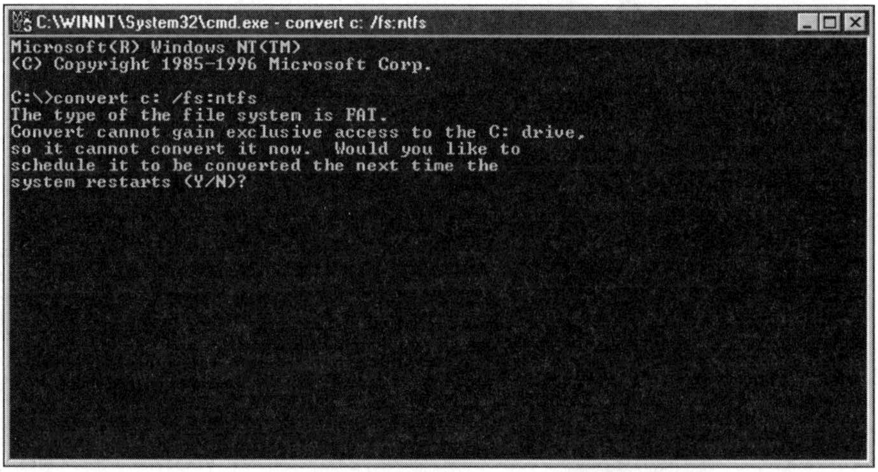

```
C:\WINNT\System32\cmd.exe - convert c: /fs:ntfs                  _ □ X
Microsoft(R) Windows NT(TM)
(C) Copyright 1985-1996 Microsoft Corp.

C:\>convert c: /fs:ntfs
The type of the file system is FAT.
Convert cannot gain exclusive access to the C: drive,
so it cannot convert it now.  Would you like to
schedule it to be converted the next time the
system restarts (Y/N)?
```

Figure 3-2:
Converting
from FAT to
NTFS.

However, no conversion utility can convert from NTFS to FAT; the FAT-to-NTFS conversion is a one-way process. Lab 3-1 shows you the steps you need to take to change an NTFS partition to FAT.

Lab 3-1 **Converting from NTFS to FAT**

1. **Back up all the data on the drive.**

2. **Boot to DOS and run fdisk to delete the NTFS partition.**

3. **Reformat the drive to FAT.**

4. **If Windows NT resides on the drive being converted, reinstall it.**

5. **Restore the data on the drive.**

NTFS fault tolerance

You may see a question concerning NTFS fault tolerance. The two types of fault tolerance that NTFS uses are

- ✔ **Transaction logging:** This type is a combination of lazy-writes and a volume-recovery technique. Transaction logging typically takes only a second or two to verify an NTFS volume.

- ✔ **Cluster remapping:** With cluster remapping, NTFS automatically checks your SCSI disks for bad sectors each time it reads and writes. If Windows NT tells NTFS that NTFS is trying to write to a bad sector, NTFS automatically finds a new sector to write the data to. NTFS then stores the address of the bad sector so that the sector isn't used again. If Windows NT tells NTFS that NTFS is trying to read from a bad sector, NTFS stores the address of the bad sector, but the data in that sector is lost.

Disk Administrator: NT's Answer to DOS Disk Operations

Disk Administrator has taken the place of fdisk and format from MS-DOS. Format is still available from the command line; however, partitioning is allowed only from Disk Administrator in Windows NT. Disk Administrator also has new enhanced features that were not available in previous operating systems: partitions, volume sets, and stripe sets.

Partitions

Disk partitioning enables you to break up a single hard disk into multiple drive letters. A partition is created from free space on a hard disk.

The two supported types of partitions are as follows:

- ✔ **Primary partition:** The part of the hard disk that starts the computer. In Windows NT, this partition includes Boot.ini and Ntdetect.com. The primary partition is assigned a drive letter; your first primary partition is C.

- ✔ **Extended partition:** Another part of the hard disk. The extended partition is not assigned a drive letter; instead, you create logical drives in the extended partition, which allows you to have multiple drives in this single partition. For example, if you have a 2GB drive, you can create a 512MB primary partition (drive C) and a 1536MB extended partition and then create several logical drives in the extended partition — a 256MB drive D, 256MB drive E, 512MB drive F, and so on.

Here are a couple more partition-related terms that you need to know:

- ✔ **Active partition (also known as the *system partition*):** The startable partition in the computer, where Windows NT loads its boot files from. These files include Ntldr, Ntdetect.com, Boot.ini, and sometimes Bootsect.dos (for dual-boot systems) and Ntbootdd.sys. These files may vary, depending on the hardware configuration of the computer system.

- ✔ **Boot partition:** The partition that houses the Windows NT operating system files (in the Winnt directory). The boot partition can be either a primary partition or an extended partition. This partition is not where the computer itself boots from; it's just the partition that the Windows NT operating system boots from.

The Windows NT files can reside on the active partition. However, you need to understand that the active partition and the boot partition are *not* the same thing. You can set your NT boot files (The "\Winnt" directory) on any partition you want. If you remember during Windows NT installation, they ask you (only if you have more than one partition) which partition you would like to install the Windows NT source files onto.

Windows NT allows you to have up to four partitions on a disk. You can have either four primary partitions or three primary partitions and an extended partition. To create or delete a partition, choose Partition⇨Create or Partition⇨Delete in Disk Administrator. Figure 3-3 shows the format option.

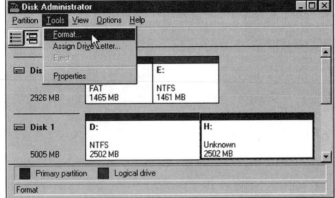

Figure 3-3:
Formatting in Disk Administrator.

Volume sets

A *volume set* is free space taken from one or multiple disks to create one logical drive. You can have up to 32 disks in a volume set. For example, if you have two hard disks, you can take 200MB of free space from the first disk and 500MB of free space from the second disk and create a 700MB volume set that appears as one drive letter.

You're likely to see a situational question asking you how to speed up disk access, with creating a volume set being one of the possible answers. You don't see any performance gain from a volume set. You do see a performance gain from a stripe set, which we discuss in the next section. The answer to any performance-gain question involving volume sets and stripe sets is, therefore, stripe set.

If you're using NTFS, you can extend a volume set. To create a volume set, choose Partition⇨Create Volume Set, as Figure 3-4 shows.

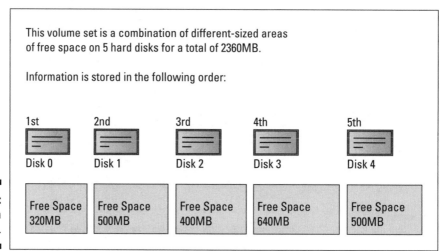

Figure 3-4:
Creating a
volume set.

You cannot extend a volume set if you're using FAT. Remembering this fact may at least help you eliminate an incorrect answer or two.

See "Volume size," earlier in this chapter, for more about volumes.

Stripe sets

A *stripe set,* like a volume set, is free space combined to create one logical drive. To understand the difference between stripe sets and volume sets, consider these characteristics of a stripe set:

- ✔ A stripe set cannot reside on one disk. You need a minimum of two disks to create a stripe set.
- ✔ A stripe set can handle up to 32 disks.
- ✔ The free space needs to be about the same size on each disk to create a stripe set.
- ✔ A stripe set offers performance enhancements over a volume set.

To create a stripe set, choose Partition⇨Create Stripe Set, as Figure 3-5 shows.

Formatting partitions, volumes, and stripe sets

To format, select the partition, volume, or stripe set and then choose Tools⇨Format.

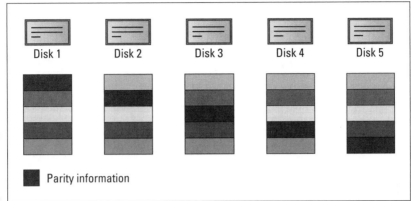

Figure 3-5:
Creating a
stripe set.

Parity information

Drive letters

You can change the drive letters for partitions, volumes, volume sets, stripe sets, and CD-ROM drives by choosing Tools⇨Assign Drive Letter, as Figure 3-6 shows.

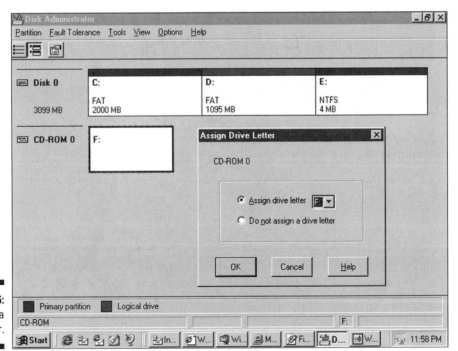

Figure 3-6:
Changing a
drive letter.

Prep Test

1 You are asked to improve disk performance on a Windows NT Workstation computer that has four 1GB SCSI hard drives. Each drive is formatted with a single FAT partition. The first hard drive contains the system and boot partitions and the paging file.

Which answer allows you to increase disk performance?

A ○ Create a stripe set with parity.

B ○ Create a volume set.

C ○ Create a stripe set.

D ○ The computer is already configured for optimal performance.

2 During the holidays, you add some temporary employees who will be using your NT Workstation. You want to secure your individual files. Which file system allows you that level of security?

A ○ FAT

B ○ FAT32

C ○ NTFS

D ○ HPFS

3 You move a folder from an NTFS partition on your Windows NT Workstation to a shared NTFS folder on a remote Windows NT Server. What will be the permissions of the folder on the NT Server?

A ○ The same permissions as the original residing on the user's workstation

B ○ The same permissions as the target folder

C ○ Full Access permission

D ○ No Access permission

4 Currently, you're running NT Workstation 3.51 with an HPFS partition. You want to upgrade to NT Workstation 4.0 and preserve all file and security settings. How can you do this?

A ○ Install Windows NT 4.0 and then convert the file system to NTFS.

B ○ Convert the file system to NTFS and then install Windows NT 4.0.

C ○ Install Windows NT 4.0 and then convert the file system to FAT.

D ○ Convert the file system to FAT and then install Windows NT 4.0.

5 You have not set any specific permissions on files in a folder that resides on an NTFS partition. What would the permissions be on those files?

   A ○ The files would have full-access permission.

   B ○ The files would have no-access permission.

   C ○ The files would have read permission.

   D ○ The files would inherit the permissions of the folder they reside in.

6 What will the permissions be of a folder that you copy to another folder on the same NTFS partition?

   A ○ The permissions will remain the same as the source folder.

   B ○ The permissions will change to the permissions of the target folder.

   C ○ The permissions will automatically be set to read-only.

   D ○ The permissions will automatically be set to full-control.

7 How do you convert an NTFS partition to FAT?

   A ○ Use the Convert.exe command at the command prompt.

   B ○ Format the drive as NTFS from Disk Administrator and restore all data from a backup tape.

   C ○ Use the convert option in Disk Administrator.

   D ○ First boot to DOS, run fdisk, and format the drives as FAT; then restore the data from a backup tape.

8 You have a 3GB drive that you will be storing sensitive information on. You will be using only one partition on the drive. Why should you choose NTFS? (Pick two.)

   A ❏ Only NTFS offers security on individual files and folders.

   B ❏ NTFS is more efficient on drives smaller than 400MB.

   C ❏ NTFS is more efficient on drives greater than 400MB.

   D ❏ NTFS is universally accepted by all Microsoft operating systems.

9 You copy a folder from an NTFS partition on your workstation to an NTFS partition on a remote server. What will the permissions of the folder be?

   A ○ The permissions will be the same as the folder it is copied to.

   B ○ The permissions will remain the same as they were on your local workstation.

   C ○ The permissions will be set to default read-only.

   D ○ The permissions will be set to full control.

10 What would the security permissions be on a folder that you moved from an NTFS partition to a FAT partition?

A ○ The permissions would remain the same.

B ○ The folder would inherit the security permissions of the FAT partition.

C ○ FAT does not support security, so the permissions would be lost.

D ○ The folder cannot be moved from a FAT partition to an NTFS partition.

11 What file systems does Windows NT 4.0 support? (Choose all that apply.)

A ❑ FAT

B ❑ NTFS

C ❑ CDFS

D ❑ HPFS

12 You are setting up an NT Workstation, and each user needs to have access to his or her own files but not each other's files. Which file system would you choose?

A ○ FAT

B ○ FAT32

C ○ NTFS

D ○ HPFS

Answers

1 *C.* Stripe sets increase disk performance by writing data across multiple disks. Stripe sets with parity are not supported on NT Workstation, only on NT Server. A volume set will not increase performance. *See "Volume sets" and "Stripe sets."*

2 *C.* In Windows NT, NTFS is the only file system you can use that supports security. FAT does not support security. Windows NT does not support FAT32 or HPFS. *See "Security."*

3 *B.* If you move a folder to another NTFS partition, the folder inherits the attributes of the folder it is moved to. *See "Security."*

4 *B.* You must convert the file system to NTFS before you install NT 4.0 to preserve all file and security settings. You cannot convert the file system to FAT without formatting the drive and restoring from a tape backup (and even so, FAT would not recognize any security settings). *See "Security."*

5 *D.* If you have not specifically assigned permissions to files, the files inherit the permissions of the folder that the files reside in. *See "Security."*

6 *B.* When you copy a folder from one location to another on the same NTFS partition, the folder inherits the permissions of the new folder. *See "Security."*

7 *D.* Don't confuse converting NTFS to FAT with converting FAT to NTFS. *See "Converting between NTFS and FAT."*

8 *A and C.* NTFS is the only NT 4.0–supported file system that supports security. NTFS is also more efficient on drives greater than 400MB. *See "FAT versus NTFS: Choosing the right system."*

9 *A.* When you copy a folder from a remote workstation, the permissions are inherited from the folder's new location. *See "Security."*

10 *C.* All NTFS security permissions would be lost. *See "Security."*

11 *A, B, and C.* Windows NT 3.51 was the last version to support HPFS. *See "Compatibility: FAT is king."*

12 *C.* Only NTFS allows you to set permissions for individual files. (Remember that NT 4.0 does not support HPFS or FAT32.) *See "Security."*

Chapter 4

Installing and Uninstalling NT Workstation

• •

Exam Objectives

▶ Installing Windows NT Workstation on an Intel or a RISC platform

▶ Creating unattended installation files

▶ Setting up a dual-boot system

▶ Removing Windows NT Workstation

▶ Configuring server-based installation for wide-scale deployment

• •

*M*icrosoft has a definite focus on installation in all its exams, and Workstation is no different. The Microsoft exam goals for installation that you must know are

✔ Install Windows NT Workstation on an Intel platform.

✔ Set up a dual-boot system.

✔ Remove Windows NT Workstation.

✔ Install, configure, and remove hardware components (such as network adapter drivers, SCSI device drivers, multimedia devices, and so forth).

✔ Use the Control Panel applications to configure a Windows NT Workstation computer.

✔ Upgrade to Windows NT Workstation 4.0.

✔ Configure server-based installation for wide-scale deployment.

The important things to remember about installation are hardware requirements, including decisions about which operating system to use; planning, including the implications of your installation decisions; the installation itself, including the different ways to install NT and the parameters of Winnt.exe and Winnt32.exe; automated installation, including the purposes of the different files involved; and the boot process. But don't get too worried about "information overload!" You have plenty of tables and labs to go over, before you take this exam. Just what you wanted!

Quick Assessment

Installing Windows NT Workstation

1 What parameter for Winnt.exe is used to create the three boot disks that ship with Windows NT?

2 Do you use the three startup disks to install Windows NT on to a RISC based computer?

3 What Windows NT Setup Utility should you use if you are doing an upgrade from a previous version of Windows NT?

Setting up a dual-boot system

4 If you're not sure of the hardware in your computer, you can use the _____ tool, which can be found in the _____ folder on your NT CD-ROM.

5 What file can you edit to change your dual-boot information?

6 The HCL is included on the Windows NT CD-ROM in the _____ folder.

Creating unattended installation files

7 How many UDF files will you need to create in order to install Windows NT Workstation on four different types of computers?

8 You use the _____ file to convert long filenames.

9 Which application helps you create snapshot files for automatic installations?

10 The first step in installing Windows NT from a network is to create the _____ from which they will be installed.

Removing Windows NT Workstation

11 What must you do differently when removing Windows NT from an NTFS partition than from a FAT partition?

Configuring server-based installations

12 Quick. . . . Name a file that's needed to rollout Windows NT Workstation along with pre-installed applications.

Answers

1   */OX*. See Table 4-2.

2   *No.* You use the menu option in BIOS. See "Installing Windows NT."

3   *Unattend.txt, Sysdiff.exe, Unique Database File.* See "Performing an unattended installation (server-based deployment)."

4   *NTHQ; Support/Hqtool.* See "NT Hardware Qualifier (NTHQ)."

5   *Boot.ini.* See "Setting up a dual-boot system."

6   *Support.* See "Hardware Compatibility List (HCL)."

7   *One.* See "Answer files and Uniqueness Database Files (UDFs)."

8   *$$Rename.txt.* See Lab 4-3.

9   *Sysdiff.exe.* See Lab 4-3.

10   *Share.* See "Starting the setup with or without the CD-ROM."

11   *You must delete the NTFS partition and restore all data.* See "Removing Windows NT."

12   *Winnt32.exe.* See "Upgrading to NT."

Planning the Installation

The exam questions reinforce the notion that the key to a successful Windows NT installation is planning. If you plan well, you need to install Windows NT once only. (Which is a good thing!) The following sections go over some aspects of installation that you should think about before you actually install. Remember the motto . . . Be Prepared!"

Meeting hardware requirements

Three key tools are at your disposal during the installation process. The exam asks you about at least one of them: minimum hardware requirements, the Hardware Compatibility List (HCL), and the NT Hardware Qualifier (NTHQ) utility.

Minimum requirements for Intel and RISC systems

Before beginning your Windows NT installation, you must be sure that your computer meets the minimum system requirements. Windows NT supports Intel-compatible processors and RISC processors. Table 4-1 shows the requirements for Intel systems as set by Microsoft and the Digital Alpha requirements, respectively. You'll see more questions relating to Intel computers on this exam, so make sure that they don't trick you by mentioning RISC instead.

The tables show the minimum requirements; in the real world, not too many servers run on the minimum. But for the exam, you need to commit the minimum requirements to memory.

Table 4-1	Minimum Windows NT System Requirements for Intel Computers	
Hardware Component	**RISC**	**Intel Requirements**
Processor	Compatible RISC Processor	80486, 33 MHz
Memory	16MB RAM	16MB RAM
Hard disk space	110MB	110MB
Display	VGA	VGA
Floppy disk	3½-inch floppy	3½-inch floppy
CD-ROM drive	Supported CD-ROM	Supported CD-ROM
Network adapter	Optional	Optional
Mouse	Supported mouse	Supported mouse

Although the Windows NT CD-ROM includes software for Intel, Digital Alpha, MIPS, and PowerPC, you should know that support for MIPS and PowerPC has been discontinued. The exam doesn't ask about these two.

Remember to read the exam question carefully: Is it asking about an Intel or a RISC system?

Hardware Compatibility List (HCL)

In addition to knowing the minimum requirements, you also need to know whether Windows NT supports your particular hardware. The one and only sure way to check is to use the Hardware Compatibility List (HCL), the results of tests that Microsoft has performed on many different pieces of hardware to see whether the hardware works with Windows NT.

Hardware that's on this list should function fine under Windows NT. If your hardware is not listed on the HCL, that doesn't mean the hardware is incompatible. It just means that Microsoft has not tested that specific piece of equipment. The best thing to do is to check with a manufacturer before you buy a piece of hardware to make sure that the hardware has a driver (if needed) for Windows NT. Nothing's more depressing than getting a new toy that doesn't work under your favorite operating system.

The Hcl.hlp file in the Windows NT CD-ROM's Support folder contains the HCL. This list is constantly changing. To make sure that you always work from the current version, obtain the latest copy from www.microsoft.com/hwtest.

NT Hardware Qualifier (NTHQ)

If you're not certain what hardware is in your computer, you can run the NT Hardware Qualifier (NTHQ), which is in the Support\Hqtool folder on the Windows NT CD-ROM. To use this tool, you must make a bootable floppy by using the Makedisk.bat command.

Partitioning the hard drive

When installing Windows NT, one of the first decisions you have to make is how to set up your hard drive partitions. Be sure that the partition you plan to use has enough available disk space; see Chapter 3 for the space requirements and for more information about partitions.

The names of two important types of partitions — the system partition and the boot partition — confuse many people. Remember that Windows NT boots from the *system* partition, not the *boot* partition.

Many times, the system partition and the boot partition are on the same drive. If you install the Windows NT system files onto the same partition that your computer boots from, the system files and the boot files coexist fine.

Choosing a file system

After choosing the partition to install Windows NT on to, you must decide on the file system to use. Your choice is essentially between FAT and NTFS (Windows NT 4.0 does not support HPFS). See Chapter 3 for more about these file systems. Although picking the file system with the most features may seem obvious, that's not always the best choice. Not all operating systems support all file systems.

Here's what you need to know about FAT and NTFS in the context of installation:

- ✔ **FAT:** MS-DOS, OS/2, Windows 3.*x,* Windows 95, and Windows NT support the FAT file system. If you need to dual-boot between Windows NT and MS-DOS or Windows (and have Windows NT on the same drive as the other operating system), you need to use the FAT file system.

- ✔ **NTFS:** NTFS is the native file system for Windows NT. It is not supported by any other major operating system. NTFS supports much larger drives than FAT and also supports extended attributes and permissions. If you're setting up a computer that runs only Windows NT, NTFS is definitely the file system for you. Just think of NTFS and you think of security.

Windows NT does not support the new FAT32 file system. If you see this as an answer on the exam, you can immediately strike it from your possible answers list.

Also remember that FAT can be converted to NTFS, but NTFS cannot be converted to FAT.

Setting up a dual-boot system

Several questions on the exam are likely to involve dual-boot systems. If the Windows NT setup finds another operating system, Windows NT automatically installs a very nice system for booting to other operating systems. With this dual-boot system, you see a menu that enables you to choose the operating system each time you boot your computer. See Lab 4-1. Even if you have only Windows NT installed, this menu shows two options for booting to Windows NT: the normal boot and the VGA-only boot.

You can control and change this boot menu easily either by using the System applet in the Control Panel or by editing the Boot.ini file.

Lab 4-1   Setting Up a Dual-Boot System with Windows 95

1. **Our first step is to make sure that we can dual-boot with Windows NT 4.0 Workstation! Make sure that we have a FAT-16 partition to begin with. Remember that Windows 95 cannot recognize NTFS.**

2. **Setting up a dual-boot system is nothing more that installing Windows 95 into another directory off your hard disk. After you finish installing Windows 95 and boot up, Windows NT Boot sector recognizes the change and adds the necessary changes to Boot.ini.**

Upgrading to NT

Here's what you need to do to upgrade from other Microsoft operating systems:

- ✔ **From Windows 3.x,** install Windows NT into the same folder that Windows 3.x was in, and Windows NT automatically converts your program groups, application settings, and desktop information into the new Windows NT installation.

  If you want to keep Windows 3.x on your system, tell the Windows NT setup to put the new Windows NT into a different folder. Windows NT then automatically sets up a menu to let you choose which operating system to use when you boot.

- ✔ **From Windows NT 3.x,** you have the option of completing a new installation or upgrading. If you choose to upgrade, NT 4.0 keeps the following settings intact:

  - User and group accounts
  - Network settings
  - Network configuration
  - Desktop
  - Administrative tool preferences

- ✔ **From Windows 95,** upgrading from Windows 95 isn't so simple. Windows NT and Windows 95 use different registry settings and hardware-device support. The only way to upgrade to Windows NT from Windows 95 is to install NT in a different folder and then reinstall all your applications.

> ✔ **From Windows NT** you're required to remember one important point. When upgrading your Windows NT Workstation from a previous version of Windows NT, you have to use the 32-bit Windows NT setup utility, Winnt32.exe. Otherwise, you can expect a lot of headaches when you try to upgrade NT with Winnt.exe! Remember, NT loves 32-bit applications!

Installing Windows NT

The following sections show you the various ways in which you can install Windows NT. Knowing these different methods is very important for the exam because you will definitely see them. Be sure to note when to use each method and how.

Practice installing NT as many times as possible. Pay close attention to the different methods and options and write down the choices you make during setup. This practice can help you on the exam.

Starting the setup with or without the CD-ROM

You can go the traditional route and install from the Windows NT CD-ROM, or you can copy the necessary files from the CD-ROM to a hard disk to install straight from the hard disk or across a network.

From the CD-ROM

Windows NT supports almost all CD-ROM drives sold today — SCSI, IDE, and ATAPI all put you in good shape for a simple installation. All you need are the Windows NT CD-ROM and three floppy disks that are provided. To begin the installation for an Intel computer, just pop the boot disk into drive A and boot your computer.

To install Windows NT to a RISC-based computer, you only need the CD-ROM. The three boot floppies are not used. Simply select the "Install Windows NT from CD-ROM" option in the RISC computers BIOS to begin.

From the hard disk or a network

To start the Windows NT setup if NT doesn't support your CD-ROM drive or you want to install from across a network, you use the Winnt.exe or Winnt32.exe program from the command line. (Winnt32.exe serves the same purpose as Winnt.exe, but it's for Windows NT only; it does not run under MS-DOS or Windows 95.)

When you install from a hard disk, you need more hard disk space than you do with a normal installation. The setup process begins in MS-DOS or Windows 95 (assuming that you can get to your CD-ROM drive from there) and copies the Windows NT files from the CD-ROM to the hard disk. Then the setup program accesses the files from the hard disk instead of from the CD-ROM.

The first step in installing Windows NT from a network is to create the share from which the installation files will be installed. You have two ways to create this share:

✔ Use the XCOPY command to copy the \I386, \MIPS, and/or the \ALPHA folders from the CD-ROM to a shared folder on a server. Be sure to use the /S parameter for XCOPY so that all subfolders are also copied.

✔ Share out the \I386, \MIPS, and/or the \ALPHA folders directly from the Windows NT CD-ROM. Although this method is slower than sharing the data off a hard disk, it is simpler to set up.

After sharing the folders, you can connect to them from the computer that you want to install Windows NT on. Use the /S parameter for Winnt.exe or Winnt32.exe to point to the shared files.

The exam tests you on the various switch options available with Winnt.exe. Table 4-2 shows the parameters that you can expect to see on the exam; you probably won't be tested on the parameters shown in Table 4-3. *Note:* Winnt32.exe supports all the same parameters as Winnt.exe except for /F and /C.

Table 4-2	Winnt.exe Parameters You Can Expect to See on the Exam
Parameter	*Function of the Switch*
/S[:]sourcepath	Specifies the source location of Windows NT files. Must be a full path of the form *x:\[path]* or *\\server\share[\path]*. The default is the current folder.
/OX	Creates boot floppies for CD-ROM installation.
/B	Allows floppyless operation (requires /S).
/U	Allows unattended operation and optional script file (requires /S).

Table 4-3	Winnt.exe Parameters You Probably Won't See on the Exam
Parameter	**Function of the Switch**
/T[:]tempdrive	Specifies a drive to contain temporary setup files. If not specified, the setup program attempts to locate a drive for you.
/I[:]inffile	Specifies the filename (no path) of the setup information file. The default is Dosnet.inf.
/X	Does not create the setup boot floppies.
/F	Does not verify files as they're copied to the setup boot floppies.
/C	Skips the free-space check on the setup boot floppies you provide.
/R	Specifies an optional folder to be installed.
/RX	Specifies an optional folder to be copied.
/E	Specifies a command to be executed at the end of the GUI setup.

Tip: If you can practice the process of installing Windows NT on a computer with an unsupported CD-ROM drive, do it — it's well worth the time and effort.

Going through the setup

The Windows NT Workstation setup process is very simple. The beginning section is a text-based menu system; the second section is a GUI. Lab 4-2 quickly guides you through the steps.

Lab 4-2   **Setting Up Windows NT**

1. **Hardware Identification:** This listing of detected hardware is a bare-minimum scan; normally, you just leave this list as it is.

2. **File Systems and Partitions:** Choose the file system and partition scheme that you want to use (see "Partitioning the hard drive" and "Choosing a file system," earlier in this chapter).

3. **NT Directory Location:** The default folder for installing Windows NT is \Winnt, but feel free to put it anywhere you want.

4. **Hard Disk Examination:** The setup program checks your hard disks for any type of corruption; you can have it do a secondary check as well.

   You now move to the GUI part of the setup.

5. **Options: Decide how you want to install Windows NT Workstation.**

   Custom setup is usually the best choice because it enables you to pick and choose.

6. **Computer Name: Choose a descriptive name for your computer.**

   If you're in a company, respect your company's naming standard, but if you're at home, use your imagination.

7. **Emergency Repair Disk (ERD): Create an Emergency Repair Disk, which saves you from having to reinstall Windows NT if anything bad happens to your computer configuration.**

8. **Common Components: Choose the components that you need and deselect the ones you don't, to save disk space.**

9. **Network Adapter Configuration: Windows NT can detect your network adapter for you, or you can manually specify one. (Letting NT try to detect it first is always worth a shot.)**

10. **Protocols: Install the protocols that you want to use.**

    If you already have other computers on the network, choose a protocol or protocols that they all use.

11. **Workgroups and Domains: Depending on the rest of your network, you may join a domain or simply belong to a workgroup.**

    If you choose a workgroup, pick one to which others in your group or team belong, to make locating resources easier.

12. **Miscellaneous Settings: Configure other components that you've installed, such as the Inbox.**

Performing an unattended installation (server-based deployment)

Because of the exam's focus on proper planning, you need to understand the advantages of server-based deployment for installing Windows NT Workstation to multiple computers at the same time. At the same time that you install NT Workstation to your workstations via server-based deployment, you can install applications as well. To automate the setup process, you use two files: Unattend.txt (the answer file) and the UDF (Uniqueness Database File).

Unattended installation is likely the correct answer to any question that asks you the best way to install NT Workstation to multiple computers.

Answer files and Uniqueness Database Files (UDFs)

Answer files are normal text files that contain answers to the many questions you encounter while installing Windows NT. The default name for this file is Unattend.txt, though you can name it what you want. The answer file is pretty simple to use; it *can* become tricky when you get to such things as networking and protocol.

Here's what an answer file looks like, with examples of answers that you need to provide on the right side of the equal signs:

```
[Unattended]
OemPreinstall = no
ConfirmHardware = no
NtUpgrade = no
Win31Upgrade = no
TargetPath = WINNT
OverwriteOemFilesOnUpgrade = no

[UserData]
FullName = "MCSE Student"
OrgName = "SomeCompany, Inc."
ComputerName = MY_WORKSTATION

[GuiUnattended]
TimeZone = "(GMT-08:00) Pacific Time (US & Canada);
            Tijuana"

[Display]
ConfigureAtLogon = 0
BitsPerPel = 16
XResolution = 640
YResolution = 480
VRefresh = 70
AutoConfirm = 1

[Network]
Attend = yes
DetectAdapters = ""
InstallProtocols = ProtocolsSection
JoinDomain = Domain_To_Join

[ProtocolsSection]
TC = TCParameters

[TCParameters]
DHCP = yes
```

You can directly edit the answer file with any text editor, or you can use the Windows NT Setup Manager (Setupmgr.exe in the \Support\Deptools\I386 folder on the Windows NT CD-ROM for Intel computers or \Support\ Deptools\Alpha for Alpha), which is a simple point-and-click graphical tool to help you create answer files. Figure 4-1 shows the opening screen of Setup Manager.

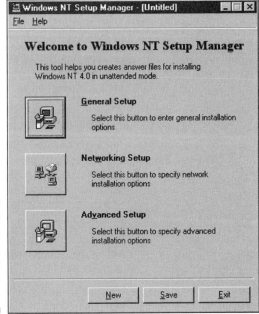

Figure 4-1: Creating an answer file with the Setup Manager.

To start creating an answer file with Setup Manager, click the General Setup button and fill in the settings, which Table 4-4 explains. After you're done with General Setup, you move on to Networking Setup; see Table 4-5. Table 4-6 goes through the Advanced options that you may see on the exam.

Table 4-4   Setup Manager General Setup Tabs and Settings

Tab	Setting	Purpose
User	User Name	The name of the person installing or using this installation of Windows NT.
User	Organization	The name of the company or organization that licensed this copy of Windows NT.

(continued)

Table 4-4 *(continued)*

Tab	Setting	Purpose
User	Computer Name	The NetBIOS name you want to give to the computer that this copy of Windows NT will be installed on.
User	Product ID	The product ID for this version of Windows NT.
General	Confirm Hardware during Setup	Check this box if you want to confirm or change the hardware that Windows NT detects during setup.
General	Upgrade Option	Check this box to let Windows NT setup automatically upgrade any other version of NT that it finds.
General	Run a Program with Setup	Use this option if you want to start another application during setup (such as some sort of customized program to help with your installations).
Computer Role	Select the role of the computer	Choose whether the computer will be a domain controller or server in a domain or workgroup.
Computer Role	Enter the workgroup/ domain name	Enter the name of the workgroup or domain to which this computer will belong.
Install Directory	Use Default Directory	Use the normal installation directory of \Winnt.
Install Directory	Prompt user for installation directory	Prompt the user during setup to enter the installation directory.
Install Directory	Specify install directory now	In the field provided, enter the directory you want Windows NT installed into.
Display Settings	Configure the graphics device at logon	Allows the user to manually specify the graphics device settings when logging on after the installation.
Display Settings	Settings	Use this to manually specify the resolution, colors, and refresh rates for the user.

Tab	Setting	Purpose
Display Settings	Automatically use the above settings	Check this box to use the settings you made for resolution, colors, and refresh rates.
License Mode	Per Server	Click this box to use the per server mode of licensing. You also need to enter the number of client licenses you have purchased.
License Mode	Per Seat	Click this box to use the per seat mode of licensing.

Table 4-5 Setup Manager Network Setup Tabs and Options

Tab	Setting	Purpose
General	Manual Network Installation	Click this box to let the user set up the network manually when Windows NT installs.
General	Automatically detect and install first adapter	This option tells setup to detect only one network adapter and then to install the appropriate driver.
General	Specify adapter(s) to be detected	This option tells setup to try to detect only the adapters that you specify. You specify these adapters on the Adapters tab.
General	Specify adapter(s) to be installed	This option is similar to the previous one. It only installs the adapter(s) you specify, whether they're detected or not. You specify these adapters on the Adapters tab.
General	Adapter Section Name	The name of the section to put these adapters under in the Unattend.txt file. You should probably just leave the default setting.
General	Detect Count	This setting specifies the number of detection attempts that setup will make (just leave it at 1).
General	List of Adapters	Add to this list the adapters that you want setup to try to detect or install.

(continued)

Table 4-5 *(continued)*

Tab	Setting	Purpose
Protocols	Protocol Section Name	The name of the protocol section in Unattend.txt. Just leave the default setting.
Protocols	List of Protocols	Add to this list the protocols that you want to install. You can also make any parameter changes.
Services	Services Section Name	The name of the services section in Unattend.txt. Just leave the default setting.
Services	List of Services	Add to this list the services that you want to install. You can also make any parameter changes.
Internet	Parameter Section Name	The name of the section this information will fit under in Unattend.txt. Just leave the default setting.
Internet	Installation Directory	The directory that you want to install Peer Web Services into.
Internet	Services	Check the service you want to install, and enter its root directory into the blank.
Internet	Options	Check the options that you would like installed.
Internet	Guest Account Name and Password	Enter the guest account name and password that will be used for anonymous logons. Normally, this option is set to IUSER_MACHINENAME.
Internet	Do not install Internet Server	Stops setup from installing the Internet services.
Modem	Port Number	The Com Port number that the modem is connected to.
Modem	Modem Description, Manufacturer, and Provider	Modem-specific information to be used during installation. Check with your manufacturer for this information.

Table 4-6	**Setup Manager Advanced Tabs and Options**	
Tab	*Setting*	*Purpose*
General	Install a New HAL	Use this option if you have a special type of computer that requires a specific Hardware Abstraction Layer (HAL). This option is normally used for computers with multiple processors.
General	Specify Keyboard Layout	Use this option if you want to use a foreign or different keyboard layout.
General	Reboot	Use these two checkboxes to force setup to reboot at a specific time.
General	Skip Welcome Wizard and Administrator Password Pages	Check these boxes to skip the appropriate pages to make the setup process more automated.
File System	File System	Choose the appropriate action you want taken when Windows NT is installed. You can either leave the computer's file system as it is or convert it to NTFS.
File System	Extend OEM Partition	Check this box if you have a partition larger than 2GB.
Advertisement	All Options	Use these options to change the text and graphics that you see during setup.

Click the Save button at the bottom of the main Setup Manager screen to save your changes to the Unattend.txt file.

Whether you used Setup Manager or a text editor to edit the answer file, you activate the answer file by setting the /U switch on Winnt.exe or Winnt32.exe, as shown here:

```
WINNT.EXE /U:[name of answer file] /S:[path for
          installation files]
```

An Unattend.txt file works for one type of hardware only. If you have three different types of computers, you need three Unattend.txt files.

A Uniqueness Database File (UDF), which is really just an extension of the Unattend.txt file, provides the setup program with information (such as the computer name) that is unique to each computer, during an unattended installation. By using the appropriate parameter for Winnt.exe or Winnt32.exe, you replace certain sections in the Unattend.txt file with those sections from the UDF file.

UDF files have the same format as Unattend.txt files, with one additional section entitled UniqueIds. A UDF file holds all the information that an Unattend.txt file can hold except for the following sections:

- Unattended
- OEMBootFiles
- MassStorageDrivers
- KeyboardDrivers
- PointingDeviceDrivers

These sections are used during the text portion of the Windows NT setup.

You use a text editor to create UDF files (no neat graphical utility, like Setup Manager, is available for this one). Here's an example of a UDF file:

```
[UniqueIds]
Nash = Nash:UserData
Harris = Harris:Userdata

[Nash:UserData]
FullName = "Jason Nash"
OrgName = "Advanced Paradigms, Inc."    .
ComputerName = NASH-NT
ProductId = "123-1234567"

[Harris:Userdata]
FullName = "Johnathan Harris"
OrgName = "Advanced Paradigms, Inc."
ComputerName = "HARRIS-NT"
ProductID = "123-1234567"
```

The first section, UniqueIds, has lines that show mappings to sections later in the UDF. For example, the ID of Nash refers to Nash:UserData. This mapping helps ease the use of UDFs.

Both users in this sample UDF have the same type of computer, so a single Unattend.txt suffices; the UDF handles all the unique personal information.

Unlike the situation with answer files, you can have just one UDF for hundreds of different users.

Installing other applications along with Windows NT

Lab 4-3 shows how you set up Windows NT to install other applications automatically at the same time that you install NT.

Lab 4-3   Setting Up Automatic Installation of Applications

1. **In the Clients\Winnt\Netsetup folder, create a subfolder called Oem to store the application files.**

2. **Create the following subfolders within Oem:**

   - **Textmode** holds files that are needed during the first phases of setup — the phases with the text look, not the pretty graphical sections that you get to later. If you're installing any type of SCSI drivers, updated HALs, or other drivers that are needed for the GUI setup, you put them here.

   - **$$** is used to replace core system files. Suppose that you download an update to some files for Windows NT, and now you want to install them automatically during setup. You put these files in the $$ folder. The $$ folder needs to duplicate the Windows NT folder structure — for example, if you have an update for a file in the System32 folder, you need to create a System32 subfolder in the $$ folder.

   - **Net** contains other folders that hold files needed for network cards and network software.

   - **Drive letter** corresponds to the letter of the drive that you want applications installed on — for example, create Oem\C if you're installing to drive C. Under this folder, create a subfolder that has the same name and path as where you want the application to be installed. You launch the setup of these applications through the Cmdlines.txt file, as you see in Step 3.

3. **Does the application that you want to install support scripting — that is, can it be installed by using a single command? (You can't make choices while these applications are being installed.)**

   If the application supports scripting: **Use the Cmdlines.txt file to tell the Windows NT setup how to install the application. The syntax for this file is simply a list of commands in the order in which you want them run:**

   ```
   [Commands]
   "command 1"
   "command 2"
   "command 3"
   ```

If the application does not support scripting: Use the Sysdiff.exe program, located in the \Support\Deptools\I386 folder on the Windows NT CD-ROM. This program has three parameters:

- **/snap** takes a snapshot of your system before the applications are installed.

- **/diff** creates a differential file set after all the applications are installed, to note changes to the system.

- **/apply** takes the differential set created with /diff and applies those differences to the new workstation, putting all the files in place like you want. You put this command in the Cmdlines.txt file.

4. **Edit the answer file so that NT looks at the Cmdlines.txt file during installation.**

   See "Answer files and Uniqueness Database Files (UDFs)," earlier in this chapter.

5. **If you're installing Windows NT from a server that doesn't support long filenames, you convert your application's filenames by using the $$Rename.txt file, located in the $$ folder.**

   The format for this file is as follows, where the section name is the path to the folder holding the files that you're referring to:

```
[section name]
short name 1 = "long name 1"
short name 2 = "long name 2"
```

Remember that Sysdiff is used only when you need to install applications that do not support scripting.

Removing Windows NT

Remember these two points, and you'll be well equipped to deal with the exam questions that concern uninstalling Windows NT:

✔ If NT is installed on an NTFS partition, you must delete the partition and reinstall all data. See Lab 4-4 for details.

✔ If NT is installed on a FAT partition, you just delete the Windows NT files and use the Sys command on the drive. See Lab 4-5 for details.

Lab 4-4   Removing an NTFS Volume

1. Start the computer from the Windows NT Setup disk.

2. When you get to the partition options, select the partition with Windows NT installed and press D to delete it.

3. Press F3 to exit setup.

4. Reformat the partition and restore the data.

Lab 4-5   Removing NT from a FAT Partition

1. Boot the computer with an MS-DOS or Windows 95 disk that contains the Sys.com command.

2. From the boot disk, type SYS C: to make drive C boot under the MS-DOS or Windows 95 operating system.

3. Remove the boot disk from drive A. Reboot the computer off the hard disk.

The FAT file system is the easier one to remove Windows NT from. You most often have this situation when you have a dual-boot system and want to make it boot Windows 95 only.

You can now remove the Windows NT files from the computer. Here's a list of files that are safe to remove:

✔ C:\Pagefile.sys

✔ C:\Boot.ini

✔ C:\Nt*.*

✔ C:\Bootsect.DOS

✔ All files and subfolders in the Winnt folder

✔ All files and subfolders in the \Program Files\Windows NT folder

Prep Test

1 What is the minimum hard disk space needed to install Windows NT Workstation?

A ○ 100MB

B ○ 110MB

C ○ 120MB

2 Which partition are the Windows NT system files stored on?

A ○ Boot

B ○ System

3 In which case would you not use Winnt.exe?

A ○ You need to make the three disks that came with Windows NT.

B ○ Windows NT does not support your CD-ROM during installation.

C ○ You are installing from a network share.

D ○ You need to update a driver in the installation share.

4 What do you need to do so that you can install Windows NT from a network server?

A ○ Uncompress the files.

B ○ Create a share point.

C ○ Write an install script.

5 If you have three different types of computers and 200 users, how many Unattend.txt files and UDFs do you need?

6 Which file does Setup Manager help you create?

7 Which subfolder under Oem do you use to add device drivers?

8 Which Sysdiff command do you put in the Cmdlines.txt file?

Answers

1 B. See Table 4-1.

2 A. Don't let the name fool you! The boot files are stored on the system partition, and the actual Windows NT files are on the boot partition. *See "Partitioning the hard drive."*

3 D. Winnt.exe can be used for any of the scenarios except for updating files. *See "Answer files and Uniqueness Database Files (UDFs)."*

4 B. Before you can install from across the network, you need to create a share point from which to get the files. *See "From the hard disk or a network."*

5 *Three Unattend.txt files; one UDF.* You need one Unattend.txt file for each different computer type. But no matter how many users you have, you need only one UDF. *See "Answer files and Uniqueness Database Files (UDFs)."*

6 *Unattend.txt.* See *"Answer files and Uniqueness Database Files (UDFs)."*

7 *Textmode.* See Lab 4-3.

8 */apply.* This line adds to the new workstation all the files that were found when doing the /diff test. *See Lab 4-3.*

Chapter 5

Booting NT Workstation

● ●

Exam Objectives

▶ Install Windows NT Workstation on an Intel platform in a given situation

▶ Optimize system performance in various areas

▶ Set up a dual-boot system in a given situation

▶ Identify and resolve a given performance problem

▶ Choose the appropriate course of action to take when the boot process fails

▶ Choose the appropriate course of action to take when the installation process fails

▶ Choose the appropriate course of action to take when a user cannot access a resource

● ●

*A*lthough the only boot-related objective that Microsoft specifies for the exam is "Set up a dual-boot system in a given situation," the exam does cover other aspects of booting as well. Booting up your Windows NT Workstation is one area that you take for granted until it suddenly doesn't work. But not to worry. Life isn't over as we now know it! To understand how you troubleshoot your NT boot process, you have to understand how it works. That's where I come in! I'll go through each phase of the Windows NT Workstation boot process from beginning to end so that you can get a good feel for how it works.

Understanding the NT boot process gives you a head start when it comes time to discuss editing your Boot.ini and understanding the ARC Naming convention. After we have all the cool computing terminology down pat, we can get more into how to troubleshoot NT's boot process when things go wrong and how to setup a dual-boot environment with your NT Workstation. This chapter prepares you to answer questions about such topics as the following:

✔ The order in which NT boots various parts of the system

✔ What to do if something goes wrong during the boot sequence

✔ The ways in which you customize and optimize the boot process (including how to set up a dual-boot system)

✔ How to edit the Boot.ini file to control what happens during the system boot

Quick Assessment

Install
Windows NT
Workstation
on an Intel
platform

1 Ntldr displays the boot menu that it gets from _____.

2 If you don't want the user to have a choice about the operating system he or she boots to, you can change the timeout value to _____.

3 _____ is the path to the Windows NT Workstation boot files.

4 The best way to modify the settings for the Boot.ini file is in the _____ _____.

5 Quick . . . name the features of both scsi and multi for your boot.ini.

6 The / _____ switch allows you to specify VGA mode during setup.

7 The _____ tells the boot loader which partition on the hard disk your operating system is on.

Set up a
dual-boot
system in
a given
situation

8 If you're going to dual-boot Windows NT and Windows 95, you can't use _____.

9 If you're going to dual-boot between two versions of Windows NT, you can't install NT in the same _____ directory.

Optimize
system
performance
in various
areas

10 You can specify how long you want your NT Workstation to boot by editing your Boot.ini in the _____ _____.

Answers

1   *Boot.ini.* See "Running through the Boot Process for Intel Systems."

2   *0.* See "Boot loader."

3   *multi(0)disk(0)rdisk(0)partition(1)\WINNT.* See "Operating systems."

4   *Control Panel.* See "Editing Boot.ini."

5   *scsi:* SCSI controller that does *not* have its BIOS enabled; *multi:* Controller that *does* have the BIOS enabled. See "ARC naming convention."

6   *BASEVIDEO.* See "Switches" for more information.

7   *Partition parameter.* See "ARC naming convention."

8   *NTFS.* See "Setting Up a Dual-Boot System."

9   *Winnt.* "See Setting Up a Dual-Boot System."

10   *Control Panel.* See "Editing Boot.ini" for details.

Running through the Boot Process for Intel Systems

Each time you load Windows NT, it goes through a complicated process to start itself up. Knowing the steps in this process is helpful when something during the boot goes awry and you need to troubleshoot. (Hopefully, not too often!) Here's the boot process for an Intel system (the exam is unlikely to ask about booting a RISC system):

1. The Power On Self Test (POST) does a quick check of the computer to make sure that everything is running correctly. You can think of it as making sure that you have your car keys and wallet before you leave the house. If you receive an error during this process, you have to fix the problem before trying to install or run Windows NT.

2. The computer tries to find the hard drive and floppy drives in the computer. Your computer tries to boot off one of these devices; which device depends on how you have your BIOS configured. Because Windows NT is installed on the boot partition, the Master Boot Record tells the PC to load the Ntldr file.

   Now Windows NT goes through several load phases. You can determine by the on-screen action when a certain load phase is running.

3. Ntldr is read from the disk and then displays the boot menu that it gets from the Boot.ini file.

   • If the user chooses to boot to Windows 95 or DOS, Bootsect.dos is loaded into memory and executed.

   • If the user chooses to boot to Windows NT (which is the path that the rest of these steps assume), Ntdetect.com is loaded and searches for information to help Windows NT boot. You can see this search happening when the following text comes on-screen:

   ```
   NTDETECT V4.0 Checking Hardware...
   ```

4. Ntdetect.com takes the information it learns and transfers the data to Ntldr, which displays the following text:

   ```
   OS Loader V4.0
   Press spacebar now to invoke Hardware Profile/Last Known
        Good menu.
   ```

You are given about three to five seconds to press the spacebar if you want to boot to the Last Known Good configuration that Windows NT used when you logged on. The Last Known Good is a good tool to use if you have a sudden problem with Windows NT, such as errors with the registry or system files. You can think of this as your last resort or "Uh Oh!" button. Hopefully, you won't have to make it this far. If you don't press the spacebar to implement the Last Known Good, NT assumes that everything is okay.

5. Ntoskrnl.exe loads and starts the Windows NT kernel. Here's more or less what you see on-screen:

```
Microsoft (R) Windows NT (TM) Version 4.0 (Build 1381).
1 System Processor (64MB Memory)
```

While Windows NT is booting, the kernel loads all the device drivers that you've installed and starts the services that you've enabled.

6. The familiar GUI comes on-screen. To initialize your logon process, you must press Ctrl+Alt+Delete to terminate any Trojan horse hacking programs (which mimic the logon process but are actually capturing your logon and password) that may be on your computer.

7. In the logon box, you enter your user name and password and indicate whether you're logging on to your local workstation or domain.

Editing Boot.ini

The best way to modify the settings for the Boot.ini file, which is hidden in the root directory of the boot partition, is through the Control Panel. However, you can make only the most common types of adjustments in the Control Panel; for other modifications, you need to open Boot.ini in Notepad and make your edits there. For your best interests, try and do all your editing with Boot.ini within the Control Panel. Otherwise, you have to be VERY careful and not accidentally input an incorrect entry, or NT won't boot.

Here are a couple of things to remember when editing Boot.ini:

✔ Boot.ini has the System and Read Only attributes set, which you need to turn off before you can edit the file. You change these attributes by using this command:

```
ATTRIB -R -S C:\Boot.ini
```

When you're finished editing the file, use this command to reset the attributes:

```
ATTRIB +R +S C:\Boot.ini
```

✔ If you change the path to the Windows NT boot files, also change the path to the default choice (if it's the same Windows NT installation). If you don't, you add to the boot menu a choice that may not work.

Be careful when altering the Boot.ini file. Have an updated Emergency Repair Disk handy, just in case you make a mistake.

Tip: In preparation for the exam, we recommend that you think up scenarios that call for different settings in the Boot.ini file and try out those variations of the file to see how they affect your system. For example, if a partition on your hard disk fails, you need to change your Boot.ini to reflect the changes to your new boot files.

Structure

Boot.ini consists of two parts: *boot loader* and *operating systems*, both of which use ARC pathnames — something else you need to know about for the exam.

Boot loader

The boot loader section contains two settings that affect the entire boot menu:

✔ **Timeout:** The time limit, in seconds, in which the user has to decide which selection to make. If the user does not make a selection, the default choice is automatically selected.

If you don't want the user to have a choice about the operating system to boot to, you can change the timeout value to 0, which causes the menu to just flash on-screen and automatically boot to the default setting.

✔ **Default:** The path (in the ARC naming convention) for the operating system that's chosen by default if the timeout reaches 0.

You can change the timeout and default settings in the Control Panel System applet.

Operating systems

The second section of Boot.ini contains a list of operating systems that you can choose to boot to. The second Windows NT directive looks like this:

```
multi(0)disk(0)rdisk(0)partition(1)\WINNT="Windows NT
        Workstation Version 4.00 [VGA mode]" /basevideo /
        sos /NoSerialMice:COM1
```

✔ **The path, in ARC format, to that operating system's boot files.** In the example: multi(0)disk(0)rdisk(0)partition(1)\WINNT.

✔ **The name, in quotation marks, shown on the boot menu.** In the example: "Windows NT Workstation Version 4.00 [VGA mode]."

✔ **Any other optional parameters to pass to the operating system.** In the example: /basevideo /sos /NoSerialMice:COM1.

You can change the text displayed on the menu or add or remove any of the optional switches.

ARC naming convention

The ARC (Advanced RISC Computing) naming standard can be used across many platforms, including Intel x86 and the RISC-based computers that Windows NT supports. Here are the syntax for ARC paths and an explanation of what each piece represents (a good candidate for memorization):

```
scsi|multi (x) disk(y) rdisk(z) partition(a)
```

✔ **scsi | multi:** Identifies the hardware adapter. This setting — scsi or multi — depends on the type of hard disk controller used:

- scsi: For a SCSI controller that does *not* have its BIOS enabled

- multi: For a controller that *does* have the BIOS enabled

Whether the disk and rdisk settings are used depends on the scsi | multi setting, as the disk and rdisk descriptions in this bulleted list describe.

✔ *x:* The ordinal number of the hardware adapter.

✔ **disk (y):** SCSI bus number. If the scsi | multi setting is set for scsi, you use only the disk parameter; if the setting is multi, the disk parameter is set to 0.

✔ **rdisk (z):** SCSI LUN number. If the scsi | multi setting is set for multi, you use only the rdisk parameter; if the setting is scsi, the rdisk parameter is set to 0.

✔ **partition (a):** The number of the partition on the hard disk. Tells the boot loader which partition on the hard disk your operating system is on.

The key thing to remember here for the exam is that, unlike the other parameters, the partition parameter has a value that starts at 0, not 1. The partitions are numbered in a certain order; primary partitions are numbered first, and then logical partitions are numbered.

You should know the ARC naming convention in detail in case you ever have to repair a Windows NT system with a bad hard disk. This topic may come up on the exam in a fault-tolerant (such as mirroring or duplexing) scenario, so be prepared.

Switches

The many switches that you can add to Boot.ini — all of which are potential
exam questions — are used for troubleshooting your NT Workstation. They
can be a lifesaver if you ever crash your system. (And believe me, I do this a
lot! Sometimes being curious has its disadvantages!)

- **/NOSERIALMICE=COMx:** Tells Windows NT not to examine a particular
  serial port for a mouse. Useful if you have another piece of hardware —
  not a mouse — attached to the serial port; Windows NT may think that
  the hardware is a mouse and load a driver for it, which means that your
  device's normal software won't work.

  If you don't specify a serial port in the COMx parameter, Windows NT
  doesn't look at any serial ports for a mouse.

  One of this book's authors used the /NOSERIALMICE option to solve a
  real-life problem: Every time he booted to Windows NT, the UPS would
  go to battery power because the signal that NT sent out looking for a
  mouse was interpreted by the UPS (which was connected to a serial
  port) as "go on battery." The /NOSERIALMICE option worked because
  it made Windows NT scan all the serial ports for mice.

- **/BASEVIDEO:** Causes Windows NT to load the default VGA driver at
  640 x 480 resolution.

  Suppose that you install a video driver and something bad happens,
  such as the display becoming scrambled and illegible. The solution to
  the problem is easy and most likely has already been done for you: Use
  the /BASEVIDEO parameter, which allows you to get into Windows NT
  and change your video driver to something else.

- **/CRASHDEBUG:** Enables the Automatic and Restart capabilities. You
  can also turn this setting on in the Control Panel.

- **/SOS:** Displays a list of drivers as they're loaded when Windows NT
  starts up.

  By default, Windows NT displays only a row of dots as drivers are
  loaded. If you've installed several drivers at once and then Windows NT
  locks up when you reboot, you can use the /SOS parameter to determine which driver is causing the problem: The last driver to show up
  before your computer locks up or crashes is usually the culprit.

- **/NODEDEBUG:** Tells Windows NT that there is no debugging information to monitor because NT doesn't try debugging any problems on its
  own. This switch is used by developers and not us normal people.

- **/MAXMEM:*n*:** Limits Windows NT to *n* amount of RAM (in megabytes).

  For example, if you suspect that your second 16MB RAM chip is bad but
  the first chip is fine, you can add /MAXMEM:16.

What you can do in the Control Panel

The Control Panel is the official Microsoft recommendation for editing Boot.ini. Here's what you can change through the Control Panel System applet:

- ✔ Timeout setting in the boot loader section of Boot.ini
- ✔ Default setting in the boot loader section of Boot.ini
- ✔ /CRASHDEBUG switch for Boot.ini

So what *can't* be changed from the Control Panel? Pretty much anything else. If you need to change the ARC paths, optional parameters, or displayed text, you must use a text editor, such as Notepad in Windows or Edit in MS-DOS.

Setting Up a Dual-Boot System

Windows NT has a dual-boot system that you can configure to meet your needs by using the Boot.ini file, which Ntldr uses to display the boot menu. Boot.ini reflects all the operating systems that you currently have loaded on your system. Windows NT is also intelligent enough to recognize when another Windows operating system is installed and will automatically make changes to your Boot.ini to reflect the new setup.

If you're dual-booting Windows 95 and Windows NT, Boot.ini gives you the option of starting either Windows 95 or Windows NT. To default to the Windows 95 operating system, you have to specify in your Boot.ini file that you want to boot to 95 and not Windows NT.

Dual-booting Windows NT is a simple matter as long as you follow a few rules:

- ✔ **Dual-booting with Windows 95 or MS-DOS:** Use a compatible file system, such as FAT.

  - • **NTFS:** You can't convert the file system to NTFS; Windows 95 doesn't recognize NTFS as a file system, and converting to NTFS causes you to lose your Windows 95 Workstation. If it's NTFS, don't even try dual-booting with 95. Previous versions of NT work fine here, but make sure that you don't install in the same %Windows% directory!

  - • **FAT32:** Although Windows 95 runs on FAT32 (a file system that allows Windows 95 to recognize hard disks larger than 2GB), Windows NT 4.0 does not recognize this file system.

  See Chapter 3 for more information about file systems.

✔ **Dual-booting with any previous versions of Windows NT:** Create a separate directory to install for your Windows Directory to ensure that you're dual-booting and not upgrading. Otherwise, you could be in for a BIG surprise when you're done with your installation! OOPS!

Prep Test

1 Which file does Ntldr use to boot to an operating system other than Windows NT?

   A ○ Ntdetect.com

   B ○ Bootsect.dos

   C ○ Boot.ini

   D ○ None of the above

2 How can you limit the amount of memory that is available to Windows NT?

3 If you have a SCSI controller with the BIOS enabled, do you use the multi setting OR the scsi setting in Boot.ini?

4 If you don't want the user to have a choice about the operating system booted to, you can change the timeout value to which of the following?

   A ○ 1

   B ○ 2

   C ○ 0

   D ○ 3

   E ○ 5

5 The _____ file searches for information on the computer to help Windows NT boot.

6 When Windows NT starts to load, it locks up. To find out which driver is responsible, you use what parameter?

   A ○ /SOS

   B ○ /rdisk

   C ○ /CRASHDEBUG

   D ○ /NODEDEBUG

7 You just installed a new SCSI driver on your NT Workstation and rebooted your workstation. Now Windows NT doesn't boot properly. What can you do to fix the problem?

   A ○ Use the Last Known Good.

   B ○ Use your Windows NT boot disk.

   C ○ Add the /SOS switch in Boot.ini to remove the bad driver.

   D ○ Boot to VGA mode and replace the bad driver.

8 You want to dual-boot with Windows NT 4.0 Workstation and Windows 95. What file system can you use for dual-boot purposes?

A ○ NTFS

B ○ HPFS

C ○ NFS

D ○ FAT

9 You just installed a new video driver. After rebooting your system, you can't see anything. What switch can you add to Boot.ini to troubleshoot this problem?

A ○ /BASEVIDEO

B ○ /Drivers

C ○ /SOS

D ○ /NODEBUG

10 Liz is dual-booting between Windows NT Workstation and Windows NT Server. She currently has NT Workstation set to install without a timeout period. What file does she have to edit in order to set the time out period to 15 seconds?

A ○ Ntldr

B ○ Boot.ini

C ○ User.dat

D ○ Timing.sys

11 Melissa is dual-booting between Windows NT 4.0 Workstation and MS-DOS. When she tries to load MS-DOS from the boot process, she receives the following error.

```
Non-System disk or disk error
Replace and press any key when ready.
```

What could be the problem with her computer?

A ○ Using the FAT File system.

B ○ Bootsec.dos is missing.

C ○ She doesn't have permission to load MS-DOS.

D ○ MS-DOS is corrupt.

Answers

1 *B.* If the user chooses to boot to Windows 95 or DOS, the Bootsect.dos file is loaded into memory and executed. *See "Running through the Boot Process for Intel Systems."*

2 *Use the /MAXMEM switch in the Boot.ini file.* MAXMEX is a switch that will signify to NT that you can only use a specified amount of memory when running Windows NT. *See "Switches."*

3 *multi.* You only use scsi on controllers without the BIOS enabled. *See "ARC naming convention."*

4 *C.* Changing the timeout value to 0 causes the menu to just flash on-screen and automatically boot to the default setting. *See "Boot loader."*

5 *Ntdetect.com.* If the user chooses to boot to Windows NT, Ntdetect.com is loaded. *See "Running through the Boot Process for Intel Systems."*

6 *A.* This parameter displays a list of drivers as they're loaded when Windows NT starts up. The last driver to show up before your computer locks up is usually the culprit. *See "Switches."*

7 *A.* When you have a problem booting after you make a change to your system, try using the Last Known Good option during the boot process. The Last Known Good is a snapshot of your last successful logon and gives you a chance at fixing your workstation. *See "Running through the Boot Process for Intel Systems."*

8 *D.* If you're going to be dual-booting with Windows NT and Windows 95, make sure that you're using the FAT file system. Windows 95 doesn't recognize NTFS on the local hard disk. *See "Setting Up a Dual-Boot System."*

9 *A.* To go into VGA mode on your workstation, you can use the /BASEVIDEO switch with Boot.ini. You can then remove the incompatible video driver and change to a compatible video driver on your workstation. This option is a great help when you're trying to troubleshoot a bad video driver. *See "Switches."*

10 *B.* If you want to make any changes to how long your OS will wait before you choose what operating system to install during the boot process, you have to edit Boot.ini. *See "Boot loader."*

11 *B.* If her Bootsec.dos file is missing or corrupt, she won't be able to load MS-DOS. You MUST have this file in order to load MS-DOS in a dual-boot scenario. *See "Running through the Boot Process for Intel Systems."*

Chapter 6

Configuring the Desktop

● ●

Exam Objectives

▶ Installing, configuring, and removing hardware components

▶ Using Control Panel to configure the computer

▶ Modifying the Registry in certain situations

● ●

*T*he Control Panel is the NT Workstation version of Mission Control. If you need to configure any hardware devices or check your system resources, you have only to look in one place: the Control Panel. Here, you can configure hardware devices, check out system settings, or check to see whether services are running. To know the ins and outs of the Control Panel is to rule the desktop! And ruling the desktop means acing exam questions on this topic.

The Microsoft objective that this chapter pertains to is: "Use the Control Panel applications to configure a Windows NT Workstation computer in a given situation." With regard to this objective, the Control Panel questions on the exam focus on which Control Panel applications you use to configure certain items. Follow along on your system as this chapter covers the Control Panel applets. You can probably figure your way through the dialog boxes on-screen, but coming up with the right choices on the exam, when you're not looking at the program, can be more difficult.

This chapter also covers the other tools for configuring and checking out your workstation: the Registry and Windows NT Diagnostics (also known as the WINMSD utility).

Quick Assessment

Use Control Panel applications to configure a workstation

1 You can use the _____ tab in the Control Panel to configure your NT Workstation to create a memory dump in case of a stop error.

2 If you do not have a network card to install, you can install the _____ _____ _____ in place of a real network card.

3 The Telephony service is in charge of _____ _____ _____.

4 What does a UPS do, and why would you want one installed?

Install, configure, and remove hardware

5 If you install a faulty video driver, you can start Windows NT in _____ mode and reinstall a working driver.

6 If you want to configure any type of hardware device, you have to go into the _____ _____.

Modify the Registry by using the appropriate tool

7 Name the three types of User Profiles and characteristics of each: _____, _____, and _____.

8 The _____ Registry utility is used to set security permissions on Registry keys.

9 If you want to search for a specific word located in the Registry, which Registry utility would you use?

Answers

1 *Startup/Shutdown.* See "Startup/Shutdown."

2 *MS Loopback Adapter.* See "Network."

3 *Dial Up Networking.* See "Telephony."

4 *Uninterruptible power supply. You would want a UPS installed in case of power failure to make sure your system is not brought down abruptly.* See "UPS (software settings)."

5 *VGA.* See Lab 6-1.

6 *Control Panel.* See "Configuring Hardware with the Control Panel."

7 *Local: Profile that is specific to the workstation.*

Roaming; Profile that follows the user from workstation to workstation and saves their settings.

Mandatory: User cannot change any settings on the desktop or workstation. See "User Profiles."

8 *Regedit.exe.* See "Searching the Registry" for more information.

9 *Regedit.exe.* See "Searching the Registry."

Configuring Software with the Control Panel

The Control Panel is the backbone of Windows NT Workstation. As you can see in Figure 6-1, you have the luxury of configuring all your NT Workstation settings — such as your services, networking components, video, keyboard, and SCSI device — in one location. The following sections cover the software-configuration applets in the Control Panel; see "Configuring Hardware with the Control Panel" later in this chapter for the hardware-configuration applets.

System

The System Properties dialog box (shown in Figure 6-2) is a small window into how your NT Workstation is performing. You can find useful information on such things as

✔ Performance

✔ Virtual memory

✔ Environment variables

✔ Software and hardware profiles

Figure 6-1: Using the Control Panel to set configurations.

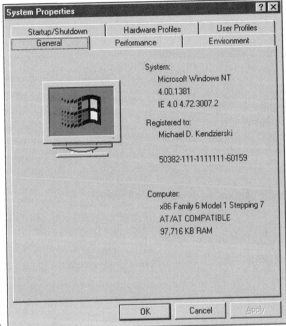

Figure 6-2:
Configuring
system
settings
for NT
Workstation.

The dialog box has tabs for General, Performance, Environment, Startup/Shutdown, Hardware Profiles, and User Profiles.

General

The General tab gives you information about

- Whom your computer is registered to
- How much memory is installed on your system
- What version of Windows NT is installed
- What service packs are installed

Performance

The Performance tab gives you the option of choosing what type of performance you want for Workstation. You can

- Alter the Application Performance to foreground or background
- Change the Virtual Memory settings

Environment

This tab may seem a little confusing at first, but it's just a graphical utility that outlines your System Variables. If you have a problem with a path statement, this tab is where you can fix it. You can also set, edit, or delete system or user variables from this panel as well.

Startup/Shutdown

The Startup/Shutdown tab is pretty useful for configuring Workstation in the case of the Blue Screen of Death, or as I like to call it, Blue Angry. *Tip:* This tab, which Figure 6-3 shows, is one area that you absolutely should memorize because you'll most likely be tested on it. Here, you can

- Configure NT Workstation to create a memory-dump file
- Configure NT Workstation to create the memory-dump file location
- Configure NT Workstation to reboot automatically
- Configure NT Workstation to write to the event log
- Configure the NT Workstation time out to determine which operating system to use in a dual-boot scenario

Hardware Profiles

Hardware profiles are a snapshot of your hardware settings and are commonly used in portable computers where you may be connected to a local area network.

By using a hardware profile for each hardware configuration that you have, you can save yourself time by choosing which hardware profile you want to use instead of changing and stopping services depending on where you are located.

Windows NT tries to determine which hardware profile to use, but if it's having any problems, it prompts you for assistance.

User Profiles

User profiles, which contain desktop settings and other information related to the user's logon, are created on the computer whenever a new user logs on to the workstation. With the use of profiles, users can customize their working environments to a large degree. Part of the beauty of Windows NT is that you can have different types of user profiles depending on your configuration. If you want to keep your user profiles on a server, you have the option of using roaming or mandatory profiles, where a user's profile is downloaded from the server to each workstation that the user works on. If you're not going to be keeping profiles on the server, you can use local profiles on the individual workstations.

- ✔ **Local profile:** Resides on a user's NT Workstation and saves such settings as display configuration, network connections, and most recently used documents. Whenever someone logs on to a different NT Workstation, a new local profile is created from the settings located in the Default_User key of the registry. This profile resides in the \Winnt\Profiles folder of the boot partition.

- ✔ **Roaming profile:** Follows a user around to each workstation that he or she logs on to and saves that individual's settings accordingly. If you're using an NT Server for domain security, you can configure User IDs to have a roaming profile so that no matter which workstation on the network a user is working on, the user's profile is downloaded from the server logon. Personal profiles are configured with the .usr extension.

- ✔ **Mandatory profile:** Never changes and is specific to a user or group. Changes that the user makes to the desktop are not saved with the profile settings; for example, if you log off for the day with new wallpaper, the wallpaper is back to what it was originally the next time you log back on that workstation. A mandatory profile MUST end with a .man extension.

- ✔ **Logon Scripts:** Logon Scripts are used to set up user environments, such as network drive mappings and printers, without having to manage them all the time. When the user logs on to the network, the Logon Script is executed by the computer authenticating the user. Similar to a Roaming profile, a personal profile also ends with the .usr extension.

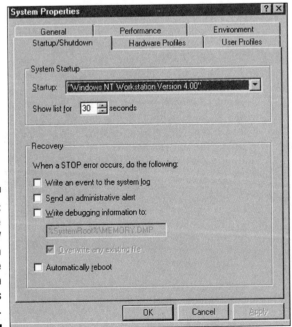

Figure 6-3:
Using the
Startup/
Shutdown
tab in the
System
Properties
dialog box.

Ports

The Ports applet is the place to be if you're having trouble with Dial Up Networking on one of your COM ports. Here, you can

- ✔ Take a look at what ports are available
- ✔ Check the settings of your ports
- ✔ Add or delete ports

Services

The Services applet is where to find out how all your services are performing. If a problem appears in Event Viewer, Services is the place that you check. You can also choose and manipulate the services that begin at startup. Check Event Viewer if you are having trouble with Services. To take greater control over your services, you can set your services to either start automatically, start manually, or even disable the service.

Telephony

You configure your Dial Up Networking properties in the Telephony section. In order for this applet to be visible, you need to have Dial Up Networking installed on the workstation.

UPS (software settings)

You run the UPS service only if you have an uninterruptible power supply. This service is used to monitor whether your workstation is running a UPS. If you lose power for some reason, your UPS signals Windows NT via a special serial cable to shut down the workstation. Then the UPS service kicks in and warns the user that the workstation is going to shut down. As you can see in Figure 6-4, you can configure all UPS properties in the Control Panel with the UPS applet.

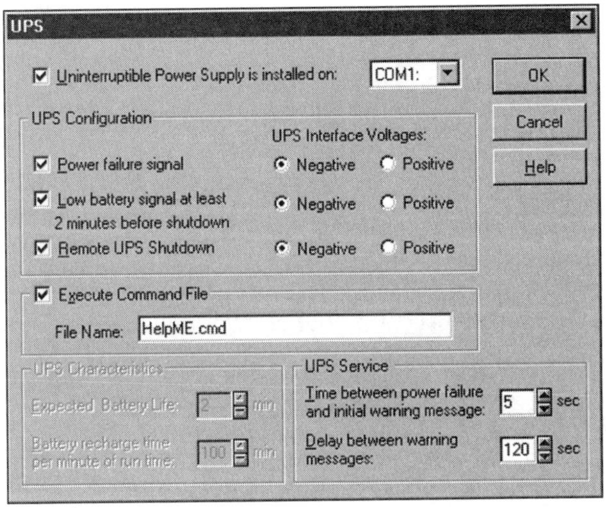

Figure 6-4:
Configuring
your UPS.

Configuring Hardware with the Control Panel

Microsoft doesn't test you on how to install a hard disk, CD-ROM drive, or UPS, but the exam *does* cover how to configure each new hardware device.

Until you let Windows NT know that you've installed a new hardware device on your computer, NT doesn't recognize this device. Before you can use your new piece of hardware, you have to configure it in the Control Panel.

Network

As with other network components, you install your network adapter (and other network components) by using the Network applet in the Control Panel. Here, you can add your network card through the Adapter tab. If Windows NT doesn't have the drivers for your network card, you can install the drivers manually.

Before you even think about installing your network card, you should make sure that you have the necessary drivers. This step eliminates any headaches that you may get later on if Windows NT can't configure your network adapter for you.

If you don't have a network card to install, you can install the MS Loopback Adapter, which takes the place of a network card so that you can install network services. You can use the MS Loopback Adapter to configure and install your network services until you have an actual network card.

SCSI adapters

You can install any type of SCSI adapter by using the SCSI applet. Here, you can see what types of adapters are currently configured, and you can add or remove any new SCSI adapters for your NT Workstation.

Tape devices

You have to add any new tape drivers manually on your NT Workstation so that NT recognizes your drive. With the Tape Devices applet, you can see what tape devices are currently working, and you can add or remove any new devices that you may have.

The Auto-Detect button attempts to identify devices and installs software automatically.

UPS (hardware settings)

A uninterruptible power supply, or UPS, is your last defense in case of a power failure. If, for some reason, you have a power failure, you could lose data that you have on your workstation or fry your hard disk or possibly even your whole motherboard. A UPS keeps NT Workstation running long enough to shut down gracefully, instead of shutting the power off all at once. In the UPS applet, you can configure your UPS.

Display

If you install the wrong video driver and reboot, you may not receive video at all, which is why installing video drivers can be a tricky process. As Figure 6-5 shows, you can install new video drivers from the Display applet.

If you install the wrong driver, reboot, and get no display, you have a fix available, as Lab 6-1 shows. (You'll likely be asked about this process on the exam.)

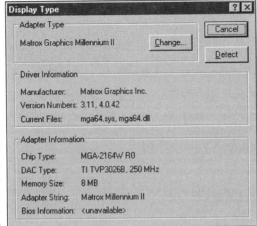

Figure 6-5:
Configuring
your display
adapter.

Lab 6-1   Correcting a Video Driver Installation with No Display

1. Start NT Workstation in VGA mode.

2. Remove the incorrect video driver that is causing your problems. This is the one currently installed.

3. Install a driver that you know works.

4. Reboot your system for the changes to take effect.

Mouse

Windows NT does a pretty good job handling mouse drivers, but if you're using a three-button mouse with automatic scrolling, you want to make sure that it's going to work well.

The Mouse applet enables you to

✔ Change from one mouse to another

✔ Change your mouse pointers

✔ Choose whether the primary mouse button is the left or the right button

Working in the Registry

The Registry is the brain behind your computer. Whatever is configured on your NT Workstation is hidden away someplace in the Registry. It's a good place to know because sometimes you can find out what's wrong with your computer by checking in the Registry.

Microsoft recommends that you try to edit your computer's configuration via the Control Panel instead of editing the Registry directly. But sometimes you have no choice but to edit the Registry.

Registry structure

The Registry is made up of different types of components:

- ✔ At the top are hives. The following six hives are broken up into a hierarchical structure to control individual sections of the Registry:
    - HKEY_LOCAL_MACHINE
    - HKEY_CURRENT_USER
    - HKEY_CLASSES_ROOT
    - HKEY_USERS
    - HKEY_CURRENT_CONFIG
    - HKEY_DYNAMIC_DATA
- ✔ Hives are made up of hundreds and even thousands of different keys.
- ✔ Beneath these keys are many subkeys, depending on what part of the Registry you're looking at.
- ✔ In these subkeys are different types of Registry values, such as Strings, Multi-Strings, Dwords, and Binary entries.

The HKEY_LOCAL_MACHINE hive handles all the settings for your local NT Workstation — all the information about your computer, such as your hardware settings and installed software applications. Changes to your local NT Workstation mean changes to HKEY_LOCAL_MACHINE.

Searching the Registry

You have two utilities to use for searching the Windows NT 4.0 Workstation Registry:

  ✔ **Regedt32.exe:** Lets you search for a specific key or folder that appears in the Registry. Doesn't let you search for a random word. Also lets you set permissions on certain keys in the Registry. Figure 6-6 shows how you can set security permissions with Regedt32.

  ✔ **Regedit.exe:** Lets you search for a specific word or section of a word throughout the entire Registry, as Figure 6-7 shows. You can search for part of a word instead of a key. Does not let you set permissions.

Regedit.exe gives you greater search flexibility than Regedt32.exe does. But with Regedt32.exe, you can set Registry key permissions, which you can't do with Regedit.exe.

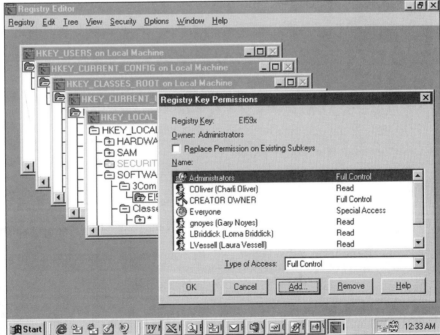

Figure 6-6:
Setting
permissions
on a
Registry key
with
Regedt32.exe.

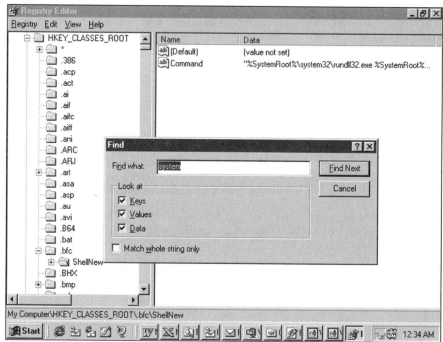

Figure 6-7:
Searching
the Registry
with
Regedit.exe.

Using Windows NT Diagnostics

The Windows NT Diagnostics utility (WINMSD) gives you such information
about your computer as

 ✔ What services are running on your system

 ✔ What type of networking is installed

 ✔ How much memory is currently being used

As you can see in Figure 6-8, the Windows NT Diagnostics utility handles
many of the same functions as the Control Panel applets handle — Display,
System, Services, and Network, for example.

Windows NT Diagnostics are a quick and dirty version of the Control Panel
applets. You can get all your detailed information by opening up WINMSD
instead of four different Control Panel applets.

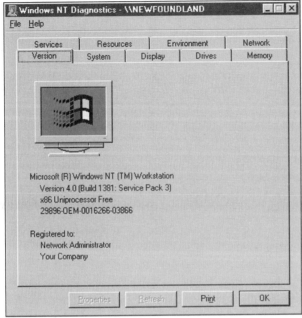

Figure 6-8:
Using the
Windows
NT
Diagnostics
utility.

Prep Test

1 If someone installed a new software application on your local workstation, what registry hive would you look under to see whether someone installed a new software application on your local workstation?

A ○ HKEY_LOCAL_MACHINE

B ○ HKEY_CURRENT_USER

C ○ HKEY_DYNAMIC_DATA

D ○ HKEY_DEFAULT_USER

2 Which utility do you use to find a specific word located in the Registry?

A ○ Regedt32.exe

B ○ FindFast.exe

C ○ Regedit.exe

D ○ RegFind32.exe

3 Where can you configure all your hardware settings and check your system resources?

A ○ Windows NT Diagnostics utility

B ○ Control Panel

C ○ User Manager

D ○ Device Manager

4 Which Control Panel applet lets you configure an uninterruptible power supply for your NT Workstation?

A ○ UPS

B ○ Network

C ○ Telephony

D ○ Services

5 Which Control Panel applet do you have to use to change the startup/shut-down options on your NT Workstation?

A ○ UPS

B ○ System

C ○ Services

D ○ Startup

6 Which utility do you use to find information about your network settings, hard disk, memory, and video?

A ○ Control Panel
B ○ Windows NT Diagnostics
C ○ Display
D ○ User Manager
E ○ Memory

7 Every time Nuala Anne logs on to a different NT 4.0 Workstation, she receives the default settings for the workstation. Which type of profile is she using?

A ○ Mandatory profile
B ○ Roaming profile
C ○ Local profile
D ○ Wandering profile

8 Which two locations can you check to make sure that your services are running on your local workstation? (Choose all that apply.)

A ❑ Disk Administrator
B ❑ Control Panel⇨System
C ❑ Windows NT Diagnostics utility
D ❑ Control Panel⇨Services

9 Richard just installed the wrong display driver on his workstation, and now nothing seems to work. What steps can he take to restore his settings? (Choose all that apply.)

A ❑ Reboot to VGA mode.
B ❑ Last Known Good from the command prompt.
C ❑ Insert the Emergency Repair Disk in Drive A and press Ctrl-Alt-Delete.
D ❑ Install a new video driver.
E ❑ Reboot, using the /SOS switch.

Answers

1 *A.* Any changes to your local NT Workstation are stored in the Registry under the HKEY_LOCAL_MACHINE hive. You can find your system's hardware, software, and security information here. *See "Registry structure."*

2 *C.* Regedit.exe lets you search for either whole or partial words; Regedt32.exe doesn't. *See "Searching the Registry."*

3 *B.* The Control Panel is made up of many different applets and is the gateway to configuring and checking on all your hardware devices, such as SCSI adapters, network adapters, UPS, video, and tape drives. *See "Configuring Software with the Control Panel" and "Configuring Hardware with the Control Panel."*

4 *A.* The UPS applet lets you configure such settings as which port to connect your UPS to, whether to execute a command file, or how much time to set between failure messages. *See "UPS (software settings)" and "UPS (hardware settings)."*

5 *B.* To make sure that your computer begins a memory dump if it encounters a stop error, you can go into Control Panel⇨System to configure these options. *See "Startup/Shutdown."*

6 *B.* You can use WINMSD or Windows NT Diagnostics to get quick information about such areas as Networking, Memory, Video, Environment Variables, and Services. *See "Using Windows NT Diagnostics."*

7 *A.* A mandatory profile exists on a server and is used for default settings. Every time a person logs on to a workstation that's using mandatory profiles, the workstation retains the same settings. *See "User Profiles."*

8 *C, D.* If you need to check and see if all of your services are running on your NT Workstation, you can verify them through the Windows NT Diagnostics utility and the Services applet in the Control Panel. *See "System" and "Services."*

9 *A, D.* Luckily with Windows NT, if you install the wrong display driver, all is not lost. All you have to do is boot to VGA mode and then install the correct display driver. This step will fix your problem. *See "Display."*

Part III
Managing Resources

The 5th Wave · By Rich Tennant

"We sort of have our own way of mentally preparing our people to take the MCSE NT Workstation exam."

In this part . . .

Managing the resources on your NT Workstation is essential to maintaining a secure and stable working environment. Local user and group accounts aren't easy to manage — you have to worry about user profiles and different types of security policies to help lock down your workstation. Your main goal is to make sure that you have a secure environment, but not so secure that users can't get their work done. Knowing how to manage all the resources on your computer — groups, users, permissions, policies, and different types of network services — is crucial to doing well on this exam.

Besides user profiles, you need to know how to set up shared folders and permissions as a fundamental part of security. A secure workstation is a stable workstation, and knowing how to implement permissions on NTFS partitions, folders, and files adds to the overall security of your NT Workstation. If you don't understand the concepts behind locking down your workstation, you may have some trouble on the test. The labs and tables in the following chapters review the basic security guidelines and features that Windows NT is so famous for!

Chapter 7

Users and Groups:
The Digital Commune

. . . .

Exam Objectives

▶ Creating and managing local user and group accounts to meet given requirements

▶ Setting up and modifying user profiles

▶ Planning strategies for sharing and securing resources

▶ Setting up shared folders and permissions

. . . .

*T*o take control of your workstation, you have to manage your users and group accounts. You administer all local user and group accounts — creating, deleting, renaming, and copying accounts and modifying profiles — with the User Manager.

Part of modifying user profiles involves configuring logon scripts, home directories, and group memberships. For more information on configuring the three types of user profiles (mandatory, roaming, and local), you can check out Chapter 6.

For the exam, you need to be concerned not only with how to set up different types of user and group accounts but also with how and when to use permissions on those accounts. After you've set up an effective working environment that complements both your user and group management, you can add permissions and policies where needed to give your users and groups a degree of flexibility, using the various security levels of share permissions and NTFS permissions. See Chapter 8 for more about these permissions.

Quick Assessment

Create and manage local user accounts and local group accounts to meet given require-ments

1 To create an account on your local workstation, you use the _____ _____.

2 By default, the _____ user account is disabled for security reasons.

3 The four options for creating a new user account are: _____, _____, _____, and _____.

4 If you have to create multiple user accounts, you can use a template and _____ the template to create similar accounts.

5 When you delete a user account, the _____ is gone for good — you can't re-create it.

6 Name four default groups on the workstation.

7 True/False: When you remove a group, you remove all the users as well.

8 True/False: You can delete and remove the default groups on your NT Workstation.

Planning stratgies for sharing and securing resources

9 True/False: You place replicate logon scripts in the \Winnt\System32\Replication folder.

10 You can set up both the user's _____ _____ and user profile in the User Environment Profile dialog box of the User Manager.

Setting up shared folders and permissions

11 The _____ group has permission over the entire workstation and can add and remove drivers and create users and groups as well.

12 The _____ _____ group can share both files and printers on the workstation.

Answers

1   *User Manager.* See "Creating and Managing User Accounts."

2   *Guest.* See "Using the default user accounts."

3   *User name; full name; description; password.* See "Creating user accounts."

4   *Copy.* See "Creating user accounts."

5   *SID (Security ID).* See "Disabling, removing, and renaming user accounts."

6   *Administrators; Guests; Replicator; Power Users; Users; and/or Backup Operators.* See "Using default groups."

7   *False.* See "Deleting groups."

8   *False.* See "Deleting groups."

9   *False.* See "Changing user profiles."

10   *Home directories.* See "Changing user profiles."

11   *Administrators.* See "Administrators."

12   *Power Users.* See "Power Users."

Creating and Managing User Accounts

A user must have an account in order to log on locally to an NT Workstation and use the allocated resources. Although NT Workstation comes with two default accounts, you generally need to create a new account for each of your users. You create and configure all user accounts in the User Manager, which is located in Start➪Programs➪Administrative Tools.

Using the default accounts

When you install NT Workstation, it creates two accounts on the workstation by default. These default accounts are enough to get you started on your workstation.

- **Administrator account** is a built-in account for administering the computer; the most powerful account on your workstation.

  - **Full permissions on everything:** With an Administrator account, you have full rights on the workstation and can take ownership of any folder or file. You can do pretty much whatever you want — install and remove drivers, install software applications, and control permissions. Policies and permissions are topics covered in Chapter 8.

  - **Cannot be disabled or deleted:** The Administrator account can't be disabled or deleted. (It can, however, be renamed.)

- **Guest account** is a built-in account for guest access to the computer/domain.

  - **Limited permissions:** Log on locally. Members of the guest group cannot install any software applications, change system time, or change drivers. They have limited permissions on the workstation.

  - **Disabled by default:** The Guest account is disabled by default to prohibit any undesired users from logging on to the local workstation.

If you see a question about using the Guest account for a task, it may be a trick question, to make you look for the answer in the wrong place. Remember that the Guest account is disabled by default.

Creating user accounts

When you create a user account, you need to supply the following information in the New User dialog box (shown in Figure 7-1). Your only information that you are required to provide is the User Name and password:

- ✔ User name
- ✔ Full name
- ✔ Description
- ✔ Password

You can also modify the user account further (see "Changing user profiles" for some of these tasks):

- ✔ Configure the user's profile
- ✔ Add a logon script
- ✔ Add a home directory
- ✔ Specify whether the user can change the password
- ✔ Require that the user change the password
- ✔ Specify whether the user can disable the account

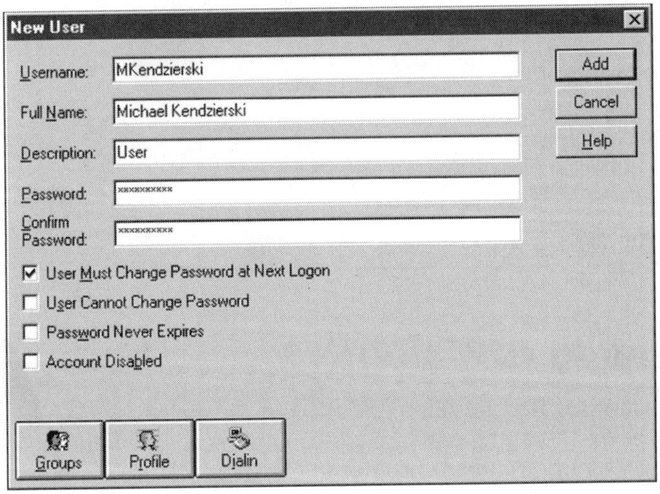

Figure 7-1:
Creating
new-user
accounts
in NT
Workstation.

New User	
Username: MKendzierski	Add
Full Name: Michael Kendzierski	Cancel
Description: User	Help
Password: **********	
Confirm Password: **********	

☑ User Must Change Password at Next Logon
☐ User Cannot Change Password
☐ Password Never Expires
☐ Account Disabled

Groups Profile Dialin

If you're creating a group of users with all the same configurations (members of similar groups or with similar permissions), you can make a single template user account and then make copies of the template, rather than create and configure each user account one by one. Lab 7-1 describes this method.

Lab 7-1	Using a Template for Creating New Users

1. **Create one user account to be the template, configured as you want the entire group to be configured.**

   See "Changing user profiles" for information about configuring accounts.

2. **Create as many copies of this account as you need by pressing F8 and changing the user name and any other information that needs to be adjusted for each account.**

   Figure 7-2 shows what a copied account looks like.

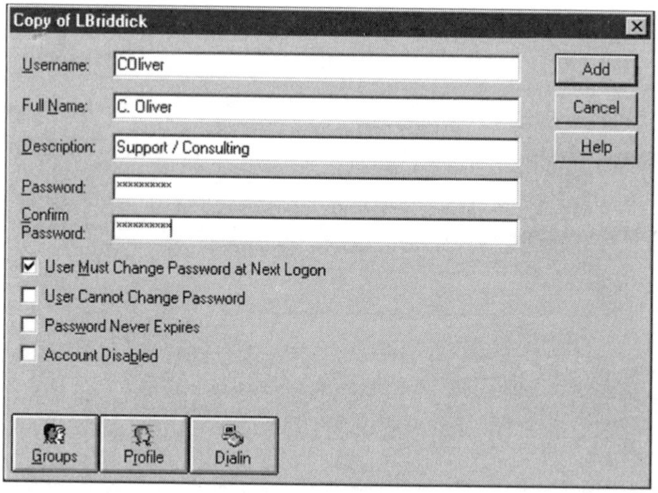

Figure 7-2: Copying user accounts.

Copy of LBriddick

Username:	COliver	Add
Full Name:	C. Oliver	Cancel
Description:	Support / Consulting	Help
Password:	**********	
Confirm Password:	**********	

☑ User Must Change Password at Next Logon
☐ User Cannot Change Password
☐ Password Never Expires
☐ Account Disabled

Groups Profile Dialin

Changing user profiles

Not all users require the same permissions, security access, and profiles. You can make the initial configurations and necessary adjustments by changing user environment profiles in the User Manager. Figure 7-3 shows what you see when you click the Profile button in the New User dialog box (described in the "Creating user accounts" section of this chapter).

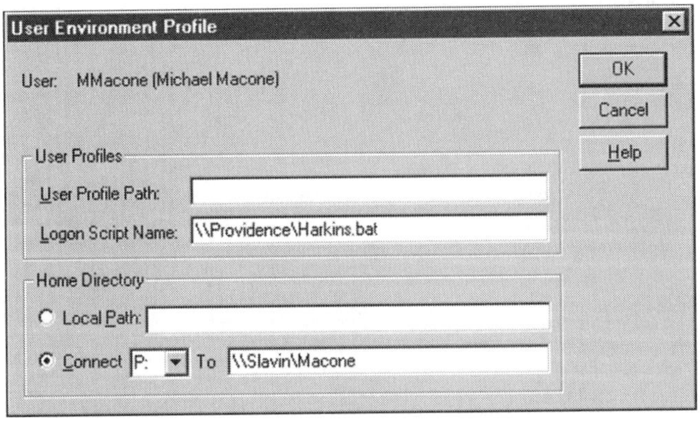

User Environment Profile

User: MMacone (Michael Macone)

[OK] [Cancel] [Help]

User Profiles

User Profile Path: [   ]

Logon Script Name: [\\Providence\Harkins.bat]

Home Directory

○ Local Path: [   ]

● Connect [P: ▼] To [\\Slavin\Macone]

Figure 7-3:
Configuring
user
environment
profiles.

Two of the options that you configure in the profile are as follows:

✔ **Logon scripts:** Used for setting up a user's working environment — such as mapping network drives and mapping printers to certain ports. When a user logs on to his or her workstation, the user's logon script is executed to configure the desktop environment.

To ensure that logon scripts are up-to-date on all domain controllers, you need to replicate the scripts. As Figure 7-4 shows, you replicate the logon scripts from the \Winnt\System32\Repl\Export\Scripts folder on a domain controller to the \Winnt\System32 \Repl\Import\Scripts folder on the other domain controllers. This replication ensures that no matter what domain controller authenticates a user, the user's logon script is always available.

✔ **Home directories** are commonly used as personal storage areas for individual users. You can set up the user's home directory through

1. The User Manager.

2. Double-click the name of the user.

3. Click the Profile button and add the path to the user's home directory.

You should store home directories in a shared or hidden directory on either a domain controller or a Windows NT server to ensure that a user's home directory is always available whenever the user logs on. Figure 7-5 shows an example of how users' home directories are stored in a HomeDirs folder on a shared drive D.

You can customize a user's working environment, such as desktop settings and other information related to the user's logon, by manipulating the User Profiles settings in the System Properties dialog box of the Control Panel. For more information about those settings, check out Chapter 6.

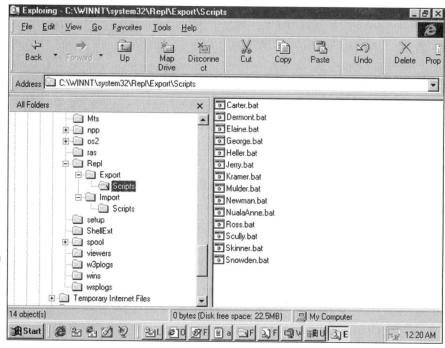

Figure 7-4:
Replicating
logon
scripts.

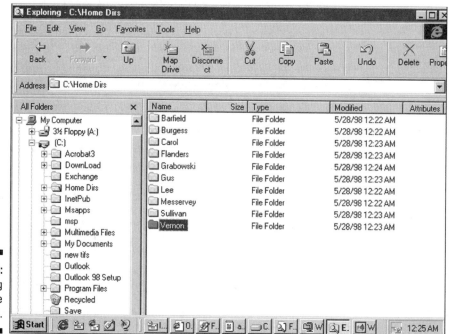

Figure 7-5:
Configuring
users' home
directories.

Disabling, removing, and renaming user accounts

Whenever a new user is created, a Security ID (SID) is created for that user. This SID is unique in the environment and cannot be duplicated. When you delete an account from your workstation, the SID is deleted as well — all the resources, permissions, rights, and ownership that go along with that account are deleted.

Therefore, if you delete a user account, you can't create a new user with the same name and expect the new user with the duplicated name to be able to use the previous user's permissions and shares. The new user has a different SID.

You may see a process question about the best method for replacing a user account. The general rule for removing users from your workstation is to *disable* their accounts rather than *delete* the accounts. Then if someone replaces the former user, you can just rename that disabled account instead of having to reset the NTFS permissions and grant the new user access to existing share points.

For example, suppose that a user named Danielle leaves the company and is replaced by Colleen, who will be doing the same job as Danielle and requires the same NTFS file permissions on all existing shares. Instead of deleting Danielle's account and creating a new one for Colleen, you can just rename Danielle's account as Colleen's, as Lab 7-2 describes. Then you don't have to replace groups, permissions, or anything else.

Lab 7-2   Renaming a User Account

1. **In the User Manager, select the account to be renamed and choose User⇨Rename. See Figure 7-6.**

   The Rename dialog box appears, as Figure 7-7 shows.

2. **Type a new user name in the Change To box.**

If you see a question about deleting user accounts, check to see whether the answer talks about renaming accounts or disabling them instead. Remember, the correct way is to disable user accounts, not delete them! After you delete an account, its SID and account information are deleted forever!!

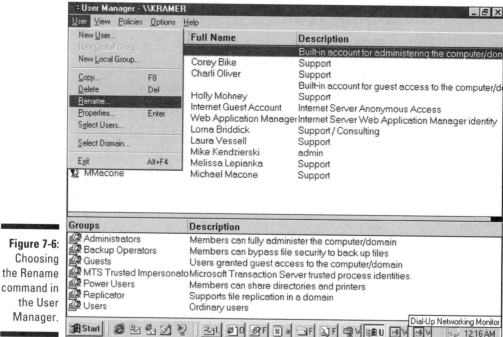

Figure 7-6:
Choosing
the Rename
command in
the User
Manager.

Figure 7-7:
Changing
the name
on a user
account.

Group Accounts

When you need to assign permissions to a number of people, using groups can save you time and effort. A single group has all permissions and policies in common, so you have to administer only the one group rather than each individual user. Just add users to the appropriate group — either one of the NT Workstation built-in groups or a group that you create — instead of assigning each permission or policy individually:

✔ **Local Group** is affected on the "Local" workstation. These users only have permission locally.

✔ **Global Group** is part of the "Domain." These users have permission on any computer that is part of the domain.

| ✔ **Default Group** is a group of users that is created when you install Windows NT 4.0 Workstation for the first time. This group cannot be deleted or renamed.

To assign a user to a group, you simply click the Groups button in User Manager and choose a group when setting up the user profile. See "Creating and Managing User Accounts" earlier in this chapter for details about creating user profiles.

Using Default groups

When installed, NT Workstation creates default, built-in groups representing the common functions of the workstation: administrators, two levels of users, guests, and backup operators. Built-in groups already have permissions and user rights assigned to them, from full run of the workstation (Administrators) to barely any privileges at all (Guests). You can see all the built-in groups in the User Manager, as Figure 7-8 shows.

The following lists shows the restrictions for built-in groups:

| ✔ You cannot delete any "system" groups or default groups on your local workstation.

| ✔ You cannot rename any "system" groups or default groups on your local workstation either.

| ✔ You can make any adjustments to their permissions that you like.

Figure 7-8:
Viewing
descriptions
of the built-
in groups in
the User
Manager.

```
User Manager                                                    _ □ ✕
User  Policies  Options  Help

Username                Full Name              Description
Administrator                                  Built-in account for administering the computer/dom
Guest                                          Built-in account for guest access to the computer/d
MKendzierski            Michael D. Kendzierski  Author



Groups                  Description
Administrators          Members can fully administer the computer/domain
Backup Operators        Members can bypass file security to back up files
Guests                  Users granted guest access to the computer/domain
Power Users             Members can share directories and printers
Replicator              Supports file replication in a domain
Users                   Ordinary users
```

Administrators

Members of the Administrators local group are truly masters of their domain, with full control over the computer. The characteristics of the Administrators group are as follows:

- ✔ **Automatically granted every built-in right and ability, including granting permissions, enabling shared resources, and installing applications and device drivers**

  The Administrators group is the only one on the local workstation to be granted all rights automatically.

- ✔ **Responsible for keeping order on the workstation**

  Administrators need to make sure that everyone using the workstation has the correct permissions and user rights. Be careful that only the appropriate people have Administrators rights, to prevent the unauthorized changing of permissions and user rights. By keeping track of all of your users and groups, you can make sure that you always keep order on the workstation by not allowing users too many permissions on the workstation.

- ✔ **Ability to keep track of the security log in the Event Viewer**

  The security log keeps track of all access for the workstation when you enable auditing on your workstation. Only members of the Administrators group can use this special privilege; however, you can manually add this privilege to the permissions of other users or groups.

  Members of the Users group can use the Event Viewer to look at the system and application logs, but only members of the Administrators local group can view the security log from the Event Viewer.

To specify other users viewing the security log, you have to specify this through User Manager⇨User Rights⇨Advanced User Rights⇨Manage Auditing and Security Log.

Power Users

Think of the Power Users group as the Users group on steroids. Power Users have more workstation flexibility and authority than the ordinary Users group members do, but less than the Administrators group. In addition to the normal functionality that Users have — running applications, accessing network files, and printing — a Power User can do the following:

- ✔ Share resources, such as printers and folders, from his or her workstation
- ✔ Force the shutdown of a remote system

Users

All new users that you create on the workstation become immediately members of the Users group. Users group members don't have any extraordinary privileges on the workstation; they have normal functionality. For example, they can

- ✔ Run applications
- ✔ Access files on the network
- ✔ Print

Guests

The Guests local group is for users who rarely or occasionally log on to a workstation. This group has the most limited permissions on your NT Workstation computer: Members can log on to the workstation but don't have access to any sensitive areas on the machine, can't install software or device drivers, and can't make any system changes unless specified by an administrator.

Backup Operators

Members of the Backup Operators group have the user right to back up and restore files on the local workstation as part of their default privileges. This user right is specifically part of the Backup Operators group, but you can create your own local group and add this user right to that group's set of privileges — that is, a user doesn't have to be a member of the Backup Operators group in order to do backups.

This group is also valuable if you want to add global groups so that the Backup Operators group can back up files on the local workstation.

You can add users to the Backup Operators local group on the workstation if you want specific users to be in charge of backup files. Just make sure that your users know the responsibility that they are being given.

Creating your own local groups

Sometime during the course of administering your NT Workstation, you need to create a new local group. Lab 7-3 shows you how simple the process is.

Lab 7-3	Creating a Local Group

1. In the User Manager, choose User⇨New Local Group.

You see the New Local Group dialog box.

2. Enter the name of your new local group.

There's also a place to add a brief description of how the group is used.

3. Add the users that you want to belong to the new group.

Your new local group now appears in the User Manager.

Just as with new users that you create on your NT workstation, a group that you create is immediately issued a Security ID (SID), which identifies the group for security privileges when a member of that group attempts to access different resources on the network.

Editing your groups

To add members to a group, remove members from a group, or change the description of a local group, select the group in the User Manager and choose User⇨Properties.

In case you need to add or remove User rights for a specific group, you can do this task through the User Manager. Follow these simple steps and you'll be all set!

1. Open the User Manager.

2. Click the User Rights.

3. Find your User Right that you need to modify and either add or remove your local groups.

Deleting groups

Here's what you need to know about deleting groups:

✔ You cannot delete the default, built-in groups that NT Workstation provides. You can delete any group that you created.

✔ When you delete a group, you're removing the local group only. The deletion does not remove any user accounts or global groups that are members of the deleted group.

✔ A deleted group is gone for good; you can't recover it.

As with user accounts, when you delete a group from your workstation, you're deleting the SID for the group account as well. Therefore, you lose all permissions and resources associated with the deleted group and cannot reestablish them by creating another group with the same name. If you want to create a new group, you have to reset all permissions and user rights. So be careful when deciding to get rid of a group!

Prep Test

1 Gary needs to create a new set of user accounts that will all be members of the same groups, with the same permissions. What can Gary do to make his job easier?

A ○ Use the Multp.exe utility.

B ○ Copy a user account in the User Manager.

C ○ Run MakeUser.exe.

D ○ Run Sysdiff.exe.

2 You are instructed to remove Jeff's user account and create an account for Cindy, his replacement, who will be doing the same job and will need the same permissions on network shares. What option do you have instead of deleting Jeff's account?

A ○ Use the Replace.exe utility.

B ○ Rename Cindy's account to Jeff's old account.

C ○ Copy Cindy's user account over Jeff's.

D ○ Use WINMSD.

3 What files are normally placed in the C:\Winnt\System32\Repl\Import\Scripts folder to be replicated?

A ○ .Inf files

B ○ Emergency Repair Disk

C ○ Boot.ini

D ○ Logon scripts

4 Where can you configure a user's environment variables, such as logon scripts and profiles?

A ○ User Manager⇨Profile

B ○ User Manager⇨Password

C ○ Admin Tools⇨WINMSD

D ○ Control Panel⇨Services

5 What default user account cannot be disabled or deleted, for security reasons?

A ○ Guest

B ○ Power User

C ○ Administrator

D ○ Backup Operator

6 Laura has to create a new user in the User Manager on her local workstation. What information does she have to enter to create the account? (Choose all that apply.)

A ❑ User name

B ❑ Location

C ❑ Description

D ❑ Password

E ❑ Logon server

F ❑ Full name

G ❑ Home directory

7 What are the two default user accounts that are created on the workstation? (Choose all that apply.)

A ❑ Power Users

B ❑ Guest

C ❑ Users

D ❑ Administrator

8 Which two groups have access to the default User Rights "Backup File and Directories?" (Choose all that apply.)

A ❑ Power Users

B ❑ Administrators

C ❑ Users

D ❑ Backup Operators

9 Which group(s) can be deleted from the workstation?

A ○ Accounting

B ○ Power Users

C ○ Administrators

D ○ Backup Operators

10 What gets created whenever you create a new group on the workstation?

A ○ Team Leader

B ○ Global Group

C ○ SID

D ○ GUID

11 Which of the following aren't built-in groups on the local workstation? (Choose all that apply.)

A ❑ Power Users

B ❑ Security

C ❑ Administrators

D ❑ Guests

E ❑ Accounting

F ❑ Admins

G ❑ Test Users

H ❑ Backup Operators

12 The network administrator, Jim, has many users who require more permission than ordinary users but don't need full administrative rights on the workstation. What group should he add them to?

A ○ Administrators

B ○ Backup Operators

C ○ Power Users

D ○ Guests

13 Lorna needs to be able to check the security log on her computer to verify that no one is trying to access NT workstation and her secure files. What local group can you add her to so that she has this right?

A ○ Power Users

B ○ Guests

C ○ Supervisor

D ○ Administrators

Answers

1 *B.* If you need to create multiple user accounts, you can copy the user account that you want to re-create instead of creating each account one by one. *See "Creating user accounts."*

2 *B.* If you delete a user account, that account SID cannot be replaced, and all the user settings or share permissions are lost. If you rename the account, you can save all user settings, home drives, and permissions. *See "Disabling, removing, and renaming user accounts."*

3 *D.* Logon scripts are placed in this folder to ensure that no matter what logon server handles the authentication, the user always has his or her logon script available. *See "Changing user profiles."*

4 *A.* If you want to configure a user's environment variables, you have to configure their profile with the User Manager. Through the User Manager, you can configure their user profile, logon scripts, and the path to their home directory. *See "Changing user profiles."*

5 *C.* The Administrator account is created by default during the installation and cannot be deleted or disabled. *See "Using the default accounts."*

6 *A, C, D, F.* You also have the option of configuring more parameters, such as logon script, home directory, and profile, with the Profile button in the User Manager. *See "Creating user accounts."*

7 *B, D.* The two default user accounts that are created on the local workstation are Administrator and Guest. These accounts cannot be deleted from the local workstation but can be renamed. *See "Using the default accounts."*

8 *B, D.* Only members of the Administrators and Backup Operators groups have permission to back up and restore files and folders on the workstation. However, you can add this user right to specific users or groups. *See "Backup Operators."*

9 *A.* You cannot delete any of the built-in groups that are part of the workstation. Accounting is not one of the built-in groups, so you can delete it. *See "Deleting groups."*

10 *C.* Every new user or group is issued a Security ID. Whenever a user tries to access a resource, the user's SID is checked for necessary access permissions. *See "Creating your own local groups."*

11 *B, E, F, G.* Windows NT Workstation comes with a set of default groups that help you administer your NT Workstation. These default groups are: Administrator, Guests, Backup Operators, Replicators, Power Users, and Users. *See "Using Default groups."*

12 *C.* The Power Users local group has more flexibility on the local workstation. By default, members of the Power Users group can share files, folders, and printers on the network as well as remotely shut down a system. *See "Power Users."*

13 *D.* Only members of the Administrators group have the User Rights to access and view the security log on the NT Workstation. *See "Administrators."*

Chapter 8

Security Policies and Tools: NT Lays Down the Law

Exam Objectives

▶ Planning strategies for sharing and security resources

▶ Managing local user and group accounts

▶ Setting permissions on NTFS partitions, folders, and files

Creating a Windows NT Workstation-based security model is essential to a secure network. Security starts with the individual workstation; from there, you branch out to the rest of the system. You have many tools at your disposal to help lock down and secure NT Workstation. The exam tests you on NT security policies (such as enforcement of password security) and workstation-based security functions (such as logon authentication) that you use to enforce your security model.

An essential part of protecting your data is making sure that you have a valid backup of your important files and folders. A good backup strategy should be part of any security model. Be especially attentive to backing up the Registry.

Remember to ask yourself a key question: How secure do you want each workstation to be? Your goal is to create a safe environment for users, not to prohibit users from doing their work. When designing your security model, look for the happy medium that locks down the workstation without preventing users from gaining the access they need.

Here's a general tip for security questions on the exam: Correct answers tend to be the ones that involve the highest level of security — in other words, Microsoft tends to lean toward the most secure answer.

Quick Assessment

1 Account policies deal with _____ security on the workstation.

2 The Backup Files and Directories user right is given only to members of the default _____ and _____ groups.

3 You can track auditing on your NT Workstation from the _____.

4 If you want to view the security log, you have to open up _____.

5 Three of the basic user rights are _____, _____, and _____.

6 To watch what users are doing on your workstation, you can enable _____.

7 You configure user rights, auditing, and account policies from _____.

8 Three of the seven options for account policies are _____, _____, and _____.

9 In Windows NT, every resource is considered a(n) _____.

10 You can edit many features on your NT Workstation, including the logon notice, by editing your _____.

11 True/False: To audit file and object access on your NT Workstation, you must have NTFS installed.

Answers

1 *Password.* See "Account policy: Passwords and automatic account lockout."

2 *Backup Operators and Administrators.* See "Securing Your Data with NT Backup."

3 *Security log.* See "Audit policy."

4 *The Event Viewer.* See "Audit policy."

5 *Access this computer from network; Add workstations to domain; Back up files and directories; Change the system time; Force shutdown from a remote system; Load and unload device drivers; Log on locally; Manage auditing and security log; Restore files and directories; Shut down the system; Take ownership of files or other objects.* See Table 8-1.

6 *Auditing.* See "Audit policy."

7 *User Manager.* See "Controlling the Workstation with Security Policies."

8 *Maximum Password Age; Minimum Password Age; Minimum Password Length; Password Uniqueness; number of lockout attempts; Lockout Duration; User must log on in order to change password.* See "Account policy: Passwords and automatic account lockout."

9 *Object.* See "Applying Security Functions to Objects."

10 *Registry.* See "Customized logons and the Registry."

11 *True.* See "Audit policy."

Controlling the Workstation with Security Policies

Security policies — the network administrator's laws for the local workstation — protect data and the integrity of the workstation from overly curious users. Without carefully implemented security policies, local security on the workstation can be breached, leaving the information on the workstation wide open to potential hackers. These are the guys (and gals) who are trying to break into your workstation and make your life very difficult. The only defense is to secure the workstation in such a way that these hackers eventually get bored and realize that Windows NT can be pretty dang secure, if you know what you're doing!

With policies, you can enforce password security (account policy), manage user rights, and keep an eye on how different users are behaving themselves (audit policy). When you implement all these policies together as a whole, you have more control over who accesses the workstation and which resources users can access and use on the workstation.

Account policy: Passwords and automatic account lockout

Password security is the most common flaw that hackers use to exploit NT security (besides those yellow sticky notes plastered to everyone's computer monitors with all their passwords — and I do believe that you know what I am talking about!). To ensure password security on the workstation, you enforce *account policies*. These account policies, which relate mostly to passwords, apply to anyone who has a local account on the workstation. To configure account policies, open up User Manager⇨Policies⇨Account. The Account Policy dialog box, shown in Figure 8-1, lets you set the following restrictions:

- **Password restrictions:** Stipulating that users need to change their passwords every 21 days (or however long you decide) and must make their passwords at least eight characters long is one way to make passwords difficult for hackers to crack. You can set these password-restriction options:

    - Maximum and minimum password age

    - Minimum password length

    - Password uniqueness

✔ **Automatic account lockout:** Hacking into someone's workstation is harder when the hacker can't keep trying password after password. The account lockout option limits the number of wrong passwords that a user can enter before being locked out of the workstation. You can set these account-lockout options:

- • Number of attempts allowed
- • Amount of time after the lockout before another attempt is allowed

✔ **Password changes allowed only when logged on:** You can set this option to require that users log on if they want to change their passwords.

Make sure that you know how to configure the password settings for your account policies, such as expiration, account lockout, and each of their features. You'll almost definitely see some questions on the exam.

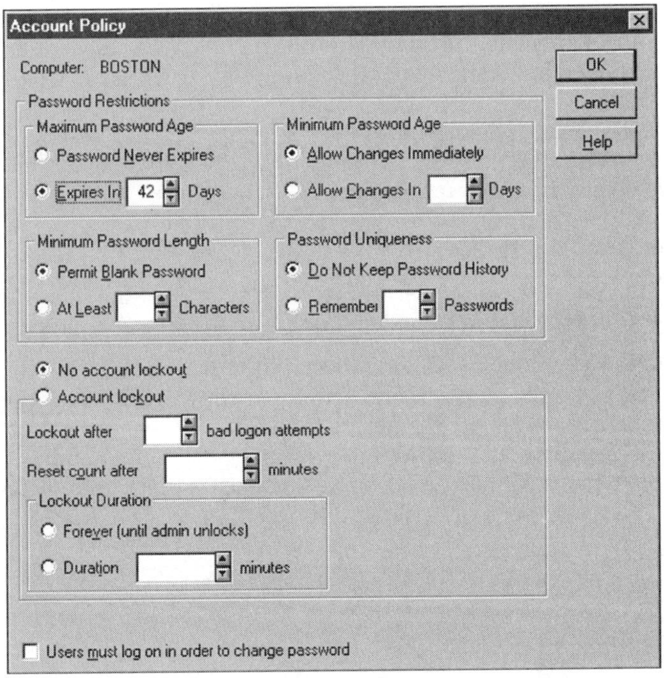

Figure 8-1:
Enforcing password security in the Account Policy dialog box.

Account Policy	✕

Computer: BOSTON [OK] [Cancel] [Help]

Password Restrictions

Maximum Password Age
- ○ Password Never Expires
- ● Expires In [42] Days

Minimum Password Age
- ● Allow Changes Immediately
- ○ Allow Changes In [   ] Days

Minimum Password Length
- ● Permit Blank Password
- ○ At Least [   ] Characters

Password Uniqueness
- ● Do Not Keep Password History
- ○ Remember [   ] Passwords

- ● No account lockout
- ○ Account lockout

Lockout after [   ] bad logon attempts

Reset count after [   ] minutes

Lockout Duration
- ○ Forever (until admin unlocks)
- ○ Duration [   ] minutes

☐ Users must log on in order to change password

User rights

A *user right* is the authorization for a user to perform certain actions on the system. When a user tries to do something that he or she doesn't have the appropriate rights for, the system blocks the attempt to perform the action. As the administrator of your workstation or "master of your domain," you have to make sure that every user right is locked down and secure, or you may have problems with users who are — how should I put it — curious?

User rights apply to the system as a whole and are different from permissions, which apply to specific objects. See Chapter 9 for more about permissions.

User rights allow for different privileges for certain users and groups on the workstation. Every member of a group has all the rights granted to that group. Adding a user to the appropriate group is much easier than having to add each individual user right to that user.

Be careful that you don't accidentally grant a user right that will come back to haunt you later. User rights can be dangerous if you don't know what you're doing! Especially be careful about the Log on locally, Manage auditing and security log, and Take ownership of files.

To administer user rights, choose User Manager⇨Policies⇨User Rights, which brings up the User Rights Policy dialog box that Figure 8-2 shows. You have two sets of user rights to manage:

- **Basic user rights:** See Table 8-1.

- **Advanced user rights:** See Table 8-2. Note that if the Show Advanced User Rights box is not checked, only the basic user rights appear.

  Generally, the only advanced user rights that you need to deal with are Log on as a service and Bypass traverse checking. All the other advanced user rights are for programmers to use in writing applications; these rights usually aren't granted to groups or users. Remember that, and you may be able to eliminate some incorrect answer options on the exam.

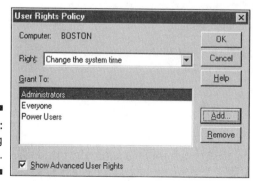

Figure 8-2:
Managing
user rights.

Table 8-1	Basic User Rights
Right	*Description*
Access this computer from network	Connect over the network to a computer.
Add workstations to domain	Add a workstation to the domain, allowing the workstation to recognize the domain's user and global group accounts and the user accounts in trusted domains.
Back up files and directories	Back up files and directories, allowing the user to read all files. This right supersedes file and directory permissions and also applies to the Registry.
Change the system time	Set the time for the computer's internal clock.
Force shutdown from a remote system	This right is not currently implemented. It is reserved for future use.
Load and unload device drivers	Install and remove device drivers.
Log on locally	Log on at the computer itself, from the computer's keyboard.
Manage auditing and security log	Specify what types of resource access (such as file access) are to be audited. View and clear the security log. ***Note:*** This right does not allow a user to set system auditing with the Policy⇨Audit command of User Manager for Domains; only the Administrators group holds this ability.
Restore files and directories	Restore files and directories, allowing the user to write to all files. This right supersedes file and directory permissions and also applies to the Registry.
Shut down the system	Shut down Windows NT Workstation.
Take ownership of files or other objects	Take ownership of files, folders, and other objects on a computer.

Table 8-2	Advanced User Rights
Right	*Description*
Bypass traverse checking	Allows a user to change folder and travel through a directory tree, even if the user has no permissions for those folders.
Log on as a service	Allows a process to register with the system as a service; used to administer the Directory Replicator service.
Act as part of the operating system	Allows a user to perform as a secure, trusted part of the operating system. Some subsystems are granted this right.
Create a page file	Allows a user to create a page file.
Create a token object	Allows a user or a program to create access tokens. Only the Local Security Authority can perform this task.
Create permanent shared objects	Allows a user to create special permanent objects, such as \Device, which are used within the Windows NT platform.
Debug programs	Allows a user to debug various low-level objects, such as threads.
Generate security audits	Allows a user or a program to generate security audit log entries.
Increase scheduling priority	Allows a user to boost the priority of a process.
Lock pages in memory	Allows a user to lock pages in memory so that they can't be paged out to a backing store, such as Pagefile.sys.
Log on as a batch job	Allows a user to log on by using a batch queue facility for delayed logons.
Modify firmware environment variables	Allows a user to modify system environment variables. (Users can always modify their own user environment variables.)
Profile single process	Allows the use of Windows NT platform profiling (performance sampling) capabilities on a process.
Profile system performance	Allows the use of Windows NT platform profiling capabilities on the system. (This option can slow the system down.)
Replace a process-level token	Allows a user to modify a process's security access token. This option is a powerful privilege used only by the system.

Audit policy

If you're getting suspicious (or paranoid!) about your security level, you can implement auditing on the workstation to track security breaches. When you configure your audit policy options, you have a great deal of power to discover whether a potential hacker is trying repeatedly to access your system. Auditing is like Big Brother, keeping track of all types of access to the system. This option is handy for such security issues as system shutdowns, the use of user rights, and user and group management in general.

To set up auditing, choose User Manager⇨Policies⇨Auditing, which brings up the Audit Policy dialog box that Figure 8-3 shows. Table 8-3 describes the types of auditing that you can enable on your workstation.

Table 8-3	Auditing Options
Option	*Description*
Logon and Logoff	Monitors who is logging on and off the workstation.
File and Object Access	When used specifically with NTFS partitions, tracks what is being done to files and folders on your workstation — creating and deleting files and folders or modifying printers. (Remember that *everything* in Windows NT is an object.) This option is only available when you're using NTFS, not FAT.
Use of User Rights	Monitors any attempts to use a user right that a user does not have.
User and Group Management	Details any security conflicts that may arise.
Security Policy Changes	Monitors changes made to the security policies.
Restart, Shutdown, and System	Monitors who restarts and shuts down the system.
Process Tracking	Monitors process activation, indirect access of an object, and process exit.

With the auditing settings enabled, you can find out what's causing problems by turning to the security log in the Event Viewer. Only members of the Administrators group can view the security log, which records all security events on your workstation.

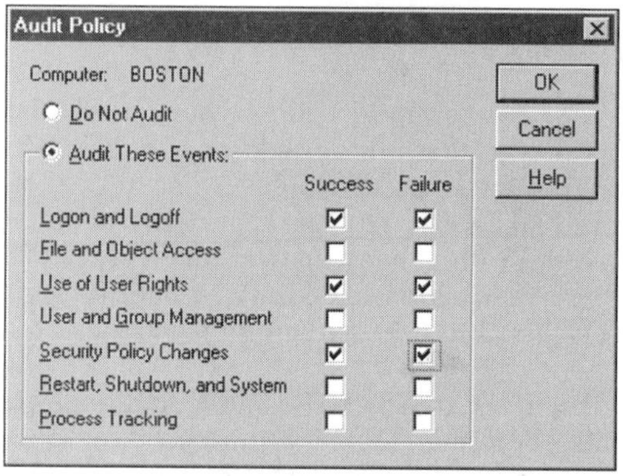

Figure 8-3:
Auditing NT
Workstation.

Here are a few things to keep in mind for the exam:

✔ NTFS is the only file system that offers the File and Object Access auditing option. In any question that asks about enabling object or file auditing, you can immediately rule out answer options dealing with FAT. To audit File and Object Access, you need to have NTFS on your partitions, and then you have to enable auditing by checking File and Object Access box in the Audit These Events section of the Audit Policy dialog box.

✔ Files, folders, *and printers* are considered objects under Windows NT. If a question asks about auditing modifications to a printer, look for the answer that involves the File and Object Access option.

✔ To enable auditing on your workstation, you have to click on the "Audit These Events" button *first* and then select what events you would like to audit on your workstation.

✔ Only a member of the Administrators group can access the security log in the Event Viewer.

Applying Security Functions to Objects

With Windows NT Workstation and its applications, everything (and I mean *everything*) is considered an object: groups, files, folders, users, printers, and so forth. Workstation security capitalizes on this object-based structure by assigning every object an Access Control List, which in turn contains a set of permissions called Access Control Entries (ACEs). Just in case you haven't noticed, get ready for a lot of three-letter acronyms!

Using these ACEs, Windows NT Workstation security starts with the logon process and extends through every aspect of the user's interaction with network resources. The standard logon authentication procedures are a strong form of security, and you can change the procedures to fit your security needs.

Access Control Lists (ACLs)

Access Control Lists (ACLs) are the basis of NT security. An ACL consists of Access Control Entries (ACEs), which list all the pertinent permissions. At the top of the ACL are the ACEs that the user does *not* have permission to access. The rest of the ACEs detail exactly which permissions the user *does* have access to.

Whenever a user tries to access a resource, NT checks the pertinent ACE on the user's ACL against the resource. If the two ACEs do not conflict, the user is granted access to the resource. In the case of a conflict, the most restrictive permission is adhered to (depending on what type of permission was required).

Logon authentication and access tokens

The Windows NT logon authentication process starts as soon as your workstation boots up and attempts to find a server that processes logons (in a domain environment, of course). In a workgroup environment, each logon is processed by the Security Accounts Module (SAM) on the local workstation. For a workgroup, this is where all authentication takes place. Window NT logon authentication involves comparing the user name and password from the logon with the user name and password stored in the SAM. If the passwords match, the user is allowed to log on to the workstation or domain and is issued an access token, which is the key to accessing different resources that are part of the local workstation or domain.

For example, if you want to access a printer located on the network, Windows NT attempts to validate your token. If the permissions on your token match the printer's permission requirements, you're granted access to that printer. You can think of an access token as a kind of ATM card or card key. When you want to make a transaction in your bank account, you use the ATM card; whenever you try to access an object under Windows NT, you use your access token.

Each access token is unique and based on three types of data stored in the SAM database:

- ✓ **Security ID (SID):** Issued to every user when the user account is created. SIDs are calculated with a special algorithm and are nearly mathematically impossible to duplicate. Figure 8-4 shows how you can find an SID in the Registry.

  NT checks a user's SID every time the user attempts to access a different resource. (Of course, SIDs are too complicated for mere humans — even network administrators! — to remember, so NT lets you substitute user names for SIDs when you're communicating with the system to administer the workstation.)

- ✓ **Group ID:** Issued to every group that's created, just as each user account receives an SID. When a member of a group tries to access a resource, his or her Group ID is checked along with the appropriate SID to determine whether access to the resource should be granted.

- ✓ **Permissions:** Can be shared permissions for network shares or NTFS permissions for files, folders, user rights, and system policies; see Chapter 9 for more details. A user's access token identifies the types of permissions that the user has been granted.

Only when a user logs off is he or she issued a new, updated access token. Here's where access tokens can get tricky: What if someone changes the user's permissions when that user is currently logged on to the network or the workstation? Those new permissions can't take effect until the user logs off and then logs on again.

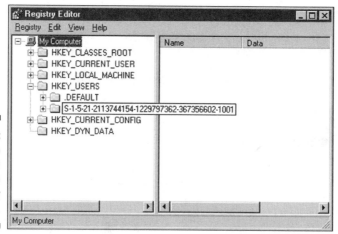

Figure 8-4:
Looking up
an SID
in the
Registry
Editor.

Customized logons and the Registry

A lesser-known (but still likely to show up on the exam) way of securing your Windows NT Workstation is customizing user logons by editing the Registry. You customize the logon process by following the steps in Lab 8-1.

One small mistake in editing the Registry can crash your computer. Be careful!

Lab 8-1	Customizing Logon with the Registry Editor

1. **Open Regedit.exe to view the Registry Editor.**

2. **Navigate to HKEY_LOCAL_MACHINE⇨Software⇨Microsoft⇨WindowsNT⇨ CurrentVersion⇨Winlogon.**

   Figure 8-5 shows the default settings for these Registry keys.

3. **Adjust one or more of the following settings:**

   - **DontDisplayLastUserName:** By default, the last user name that logged on to the workstation appears at logon. Some people view this default setting as a possible security hole. To prevent the last user name from appearing, change the DontDisplayLastUserName setting to 0.

   - **ShutdownWithoutLogon:** You can prohibit a user from shutting down the machine before he or she logs on to the workstation by changing the ShutdownWithoutLogon setting to 1. With this Registry key turned off, the Shutdown button is grayed out during logon.

   - **LegalNoticeCaption and LegalNoticeText:** For security and legal purposes, you can change your logon notice to warn potential hackers and ordinary users that they're about to log on to a secure LAN and that unauthorized logon attempts are prohibited.

     Double-click the LegalNoticeCaption key and enter the logon notice in the Value data text box. Then double-click the LegalNoticeText key and enter your company name in the Value data text box. Your changes appear the next time you log on to the workstation.

     Figure 8-6 shows an example of an edited notice in the Registry.

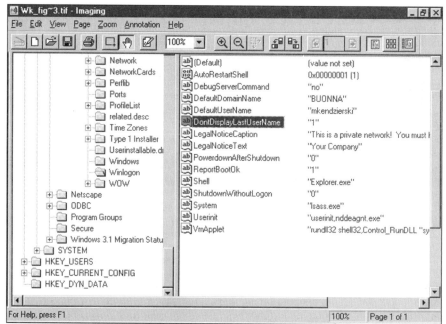

Figure 8-5:
Customizing
logon with
the Registry
Editor.

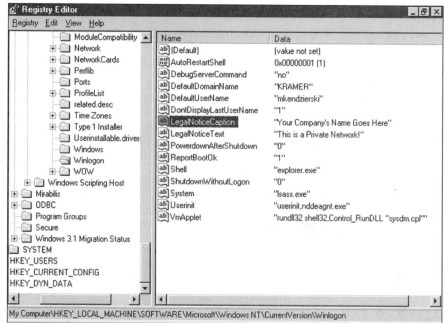

Figure 8-6:
Changing
the logon
notice in
the
Registry.

Securing Your Data with NT Backup

Although most computer professionals use a third-party backup application to create backup sets of their NT data, you need to know only about the Windows NT Workstation Backup software for the exam. Be sure that you're comfortable with the user interface (which you can see in Figure 8-7) before you take the exam. They love to test you on this subject!

Here's what you need to know about NT Backup:

✔ **User right to back up and restore files and folders:** Give out this user right (as outlined in Lab 8-2) sparingly — just imagine the security mess if any user on your NT Workstation could get hold of your valuable data and restore it from tape. Chapter 7 on users and groups discusses the Backup Operators group, which by default has the user right to back up and restore files and folders. (The Administrators group also has this right by default.)

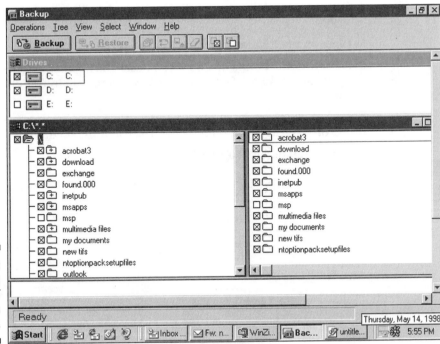

Figure 8-7:
Using Windows NT Workstation Backup.

✔ **Backup strategy:** Each time you run a backup of your NT Workstation, you have two options:

- Running a full backup of all your data

- Running a backup of just the changed files

✔ **Backup medium (tape drive):** With the version of NT Backup included with Windows NT 4.0 Workstation, your only option for backing up files is a tape drive. You can connect the tape drive to NT and back up your data continually, if you want.

Be sure to configure your tape device before trying to use NT Backup. Click the Tape Devices icon in the Control Panel to configure the tape drive and load all the necessary drivers. (See Chapter 6 for more about the Control Panel.) To connect your tape drive to your NT Workstation, you probably need to configure your SCSI device as well, which you also do in the Control Panel.

Lab 8-2   Granting the Backup and Files and Directories User Right

1. **Open up User Manager located in Administrative Tools program group.**

2. **Click on the Policies menu and click on User Rights.**

3. **A User Rights Policy box appears, describing specific rights on the workstation. In the Drop down list box, navigate to Backup files and directories.**

4. **Now click on the Add button to add either users or groups, depending on your needs and then click OK when finished.**

5. **Congratulations! You're all done!**

An essential part of Windows NT backup (and something you need to know how to do for the exam) is making sure that you have a valid copy of the Registry in case anything goes wrong. You can back up the registry with an ERD or a Full Backup.

Prep Test

1 To enforce password security on the workstation, what type of policies must you implement?

A ○ System policies

B ○ Account policies

C ○ Network policies

D ○ Auditing

2 Where do you make the appropriate configuration to lock users out of their accounts after three bad logon attempts?

A ○ Account Policy

B ○ Control Panel

C ○ Windows NT Security

D ○ Device Manager

3 Laura enabled auditing for file and object access on her workstation, but nothing is appearing in the security log. What could be the problem?

A ○ She doesn't have Admin rights.

B ○ The system isn't using NTFS partitions.

C ○ She's not a member of the Power Users group.

D ○ The Service Pack isn't installed.

4 Rich just installed new backup software and needs to log on as a service. Where can Rich enable this privilege, if he has the necessary privileges?

A ○ Advanced User Rights

B ○ Control Panel

C ○ Auditing

D ○ Event Viewer

5 Where can you configure advanced user rights in NT 4.0 Workstation?

A ○ Control Panel

B ○ WINMSD

C ○ User Manager

D ○ Administrative Tools

6 Where do you go to set up a configuration in which users who have made three bad logon attempts are locked out for 25 minutes?

A ○ Auditing

B ○ Policy Editor

C ○ Administrative Tools

D ○ Account Policy

7 You have a group of users who need permission to back up and restore files on their workstations. However, you don't want to add them to the Backup Operators group. What can you do to allow them to back up and restore files?

A ○ Set up a Default Profile.

B ○ Edit the Registry.

C ○ Specify this user right for their group.

D ○ Enable auditing.

8 How do you keep track of such security issues as file and object access and use of user rights on a workstation that you're not on?

A ○ System Policy

B ○ Auditing

C ○ Registry Dump

D ○ User Policy

9 You're having trouble with a printer that's connected directly to your NT Workstation. What form of auditing should you enable to track its progress?

A ○ Process Tracking

B ○ Logon and Logoff

C ○ File and Object Access

D ○ Security Policy Changes

10 Which Registry key do you change to make sure that when users log off the workstation, they can't see the last user who logged on?

A ○ HKEY_LOCAL_MACHINE

B ○ HKEY_CURRENT_USER

C ○ HKEY_SECURITY

D ○ HKEY_DYNAMIC_DATA

11 What's the name of the list of entries that detail a user's exact permissions?

A ○ Access Control List

B ○ Access Security List

C ○ Access Control Entries

D ○ Access Entries Controls

12 If you want to prohibit users from shutting down the machine, where in the Registry can you make this change?

A ○ HKEY_LOCAL_MACHINE\Software\Microsoft\ ProhibitShutdown\Winlogon

B ○ HKEY_LOCAL_MACHINE\Security\Windows\Winlogon

C ○ HKEY_CURRENT_USERS\Securiy\ProhibitShutdown\1

D ○ HKEY_LOCAL_MACHINE\Software\Microsoft\WindowsNT\ CurrentVersion\Winlogon

13 What is generated every time you log on to your Windows NT Workstation?

A ○ Password security

B ○ Access Control List

C ○ Access token

D ○ Access privilege

14 You configure automatic account lockout through which administrative tool?

A ○ Windows NT Diagnostics

B ○ Server Manager

C ○ User Manager

D ○ Performance Monitor

15 Colleen has been logged on to her NT Workstation all day. She has Full Control on the \Accounting and \Compensation shares on her network. Meanwhile, her network administrator has removed her access permissions from her account on the \Accounting share. What access permissions does she have when she tries to access the \Accounting share?

A ○ Read Only

B ○ Full Control

C ○ No Access

D ○ List

16 Daniel is logged on to his NT Workstation and calls the help desk so that he can get to the \HumanResources share on his network. The network administrator grants him access to the share, but when Daniel tries to access the share, he still can't do it. What must he do to get access to the share?

A ○ Configure User Manager.

B ○ Log off and log back on to his workstation.

C ○ Give himself access to the share.

D ○ Call the help desk again.

17 Where can you change such workstation parameters as the logon notice, display of the last user name that logged on, and the ability to shut down the workstation?

A ○ Control Panel⇨Security

B ○ Control Panel⇨Network

C ○ Registry

D ○ Windows NT Diagnostics

18 What is the common factor among all Windows NT printers, permissions, hardware devices, files, folders, and policies?

A ○ They all run in Kernel mode.

B ○ All are considered objects.

C ○ All are security devices.

D ○ All are configurable within the Control Panel.

Answers

1 *B.* In the Account Policy dialog box, you can set up guidelines, such as account lockout, minimum password length, maximum password age, and password uniqueness. *See "Account policy: Passwords and automatic account lockout."*

2 *A.* In the Account Policy dialog box, you can enforce account lockout after *x* number of bad logon attempts. *See "Account policy: Passwords and automatic account lockout."*

3 *A.* Laura must be a member of the Administrators group in order to view the security log. *See "Audit policy."*

4 *A.* Logon as a service is an advanced user right. *See Table 8-2.*

5 *C.* You configure advanced user rights in User Manager. *See "User rights."*

6 *D.* You set up password policies in the Account Policy dialog box. *See "Account policy: Passwords and automatic account lockout."*

7 *C.* Choose User Manager⇨Policies⇨User Rights to add user rights to individual users or groups. *See "User rights."*

8 *B.* If you want to keep track of security on the workstation while you're away, enable auditing to track a variety of changes to the workstation. *See "Audit policy."*

9 *C.* Remember that everything in NT is considered an object, including printers. You audit objects with the File and Object Access setting. *See "Audit policy."*

10 *A.* Use HKEY-LOCAL-MACHINE for this change. *See "Customized logons and the Registry."*

11 *C.* Each Access Control Entry specifies a permission; Access Control Lists are made up of Access Control Entries. *See "Access Control Lists (ACLs)."*

12 *D.* You edit this Registry key to prohibit users from shutting down the workstation. *See "Customized logons and the Registry."*

13 *C.* Your access token details your security privileges at the time that you logged on to your workstation. *See "Logon authentication and access tokens."*

14 *C.* Use User Manager to configure automatic account lockout. *See "Account policy: Passwords and automatic account lockout."*

15 *B.* Until Colleen logs off her workstation, she retains the security access privileges that she had when she logged on. *See "Logon authentication and access tokens."*

16 *B.* The new access token doesn't take effect until the user logs off and logs back on. *See "Logon authentication and access tokens."*

17 *C.* You need to edit the Registry to make these changes. *See "Customized logons and the Registry."*

18 *B.* In the world of Windows NT, everything is considered an object — file permissions, hardware devices, files, folders, policies, and so on. *See "Applying Security Functions to Objects."*

Chapter 9

File and Folder Permissions: Saying Please

Exam Objectives

▶ Setting up shared folders and permissions

▶ Setting permissions on NTFS pertitions, folders, and files

▶ Using various methods to access network resources

*N*ow what good would a network be if you couldn't give others access to your files and folders? But you still want to control exactly who can access what, and with what level of access. Windows NT offers a standard set of share permissions so that when you share a file or folder, you can assign it a particular level of access for different individual users and groups. Share permissions are available regardless of which file system you use. However, if you really want to protect your workstation, you need to use NTFS permissions. With NTFS, you get much greater security, as well as more flexibility. (See Chapter 3 for more details about the various file systems.)

Remember that when you share a file or folder, you're using share permissions, which offer just a few security options. When you apply real security to a shared file or folder, you're using NTFS permissions — assuming, of course, that your file system is NTFS. Share permissions don't offer as much flexibility as NTFS permissions, but for the basics — full control, simple read and write, no access at all — you can achieve the same results with share permissions as you do with NTFS security.

Quick Assessment

Set permissions on NTFS partitions, folders, and files

1 When you copy a file from one NTFS partition to another, the file permissions are _____.

2 True/False: When you move a file from one folder to another on the same NTFS partition, the file permissions are retained.

Set up shared folders and permissions

3 Name the default shares on your workstation.

4 Name the syntax for connecting to a network share over the Internet.

5 _____ permissions are least restrictive for remote users.

6 Name the four permissions for sharing folders.

Use various methods to access network resources

7 _____ allows you to set up permissions on files and folders on your workstation.

8 The _____ file system allows you to setup secure permissions on both files and folders on your Windows NT Workstation.

Answers

1 *Inherited.* See "Copying and moving files and folders."

2 *True.* See "Copying and moving files and folders."

3 *Local hard disks, IPC$, Admin$.* See "Using the default shares."

4 *//ServerName./ShareName.* See "Accessing a share by mapping to it."

5 *Share.* See "When Permissions Collide: How Different Permission Levels Interact."

6 *Full Control; No Access; Change; Read.* See "Share Permissions."

7 *NTFS.* See "NTFS Permissions."

8 *NTFS.* See "NTFS Permissions."

Share Permissions

When you initially share a folder or file — and later, if you go back and adjust the original settings — you can choose from the following types of permissions to use on the shared folder or file. (You have more flexibility with NTFS permissions, as you see later in this chapter.)

- ✔ Full Control: This one is pretty self-explanatory. With this permission, you have total control over the files and folders that are contained in this share.

- ✔ Change: Read, Change, and Delete.

- ✔ Read: Read-Only. The only permission that you have on this file or folder is to view the contents of a directory or data inside the file.

- ✔ No Access: This permission prevents any access to the shared directory or any of it's subfolders or files.

With share permissions, you're assigning access permissions on the network share point. Remember to be careful when assigning network shares; you may think you chose a high enough level of share security, but someone can still get access to sensitive data.

Share permissions enable you to set permissions only on the network share. NTFS permissions enable you to set security on both individual files and folders on your workstation.

Sharing a folder and viewing permissions

Lab 9-1 shows how to share a folder and set the permissions for it.

Lab 9-1	Sharing a Folder and Setting Share Permissions

1. **In Windows NT Explorer, right-click the folder that you want to share, and click Sharing.**

2. **Click the Shared As radio button to initiate the share.**

3. **Type the share name and any comments.**

4. **To assign permissions for the share, click the Permissions button.**

   You see the Access Through Share Permissions dialog box, which Figure 9-1 shows.

5. **Click the Add button to specify the individual users and/or groups and their types of access in the Add Users and Groups dialog box.**

   Figure 9-2 shows this dialog box. After you're finished with this step, press the Apply button to confirm your changes.

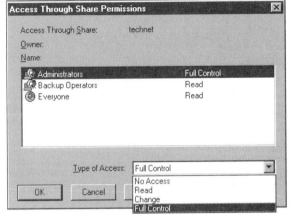

Figure 9-1:
Assigning
permissions
to a share.

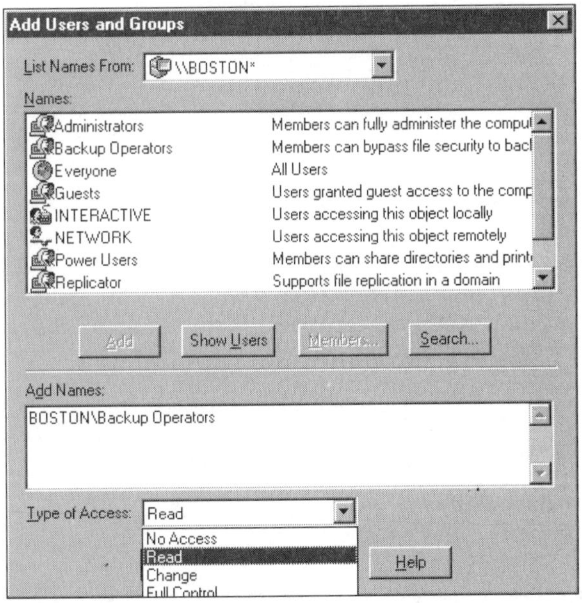

Figure 9-2:
Specifying
who can do
what with
a share.

To see whether a folder or file is shared and what its permissions are, simply
right-click the folder or file and click Properties. Figure 9-3 shows the
Properties dialog box of a share called technet.

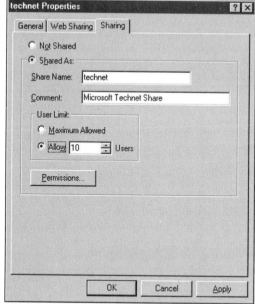

Figure 9-3:
Viewing
share
information
in the
Properties
dialog box.

Using the default shares

When you log on, NT creates a set of shares by default. These shares are normally hidden from view, but if you know what they are, you can access them in case you need to administer the workstation remotely. Here are the default shares for NT Workstation:

- C$, D$, and so on (Local hard disks)
- IPC$ (Admin Share and remote-control purposes)
- Admin$ (\Winnt folder)

Accessing a share by mapping to it

The easiest method of access is to map to the desired network share. If you have permissions on the share, you can use its files and folders. If you don't have permissions, you're denied access.

Remember that your share-level privileges are the same or more restrictive on a network share as opposed to accessing the resources from your local workstation. See "When Permissions Collide: How Different Permission Levels Interact," later in this chapter, for more details.

To map to a network share, you use the Universal Naming Convention (UNC), which allows you to simulate the network drive as part of your workstation. The newly mapped drive appears as the logical drive letter that you gave it when you initiated the share. Here's the syntax for using UNC:

```
\\ServerName\SharePoint
```

You have two methods to choose from when mapping to a network share over a LAN:

- ✔ **Windows NT Explorer:** In Explorer, open the Tools menu to map the drive and have Explorer automatically assign you a drive letter.

- ✔ **Command line:** At the command line, use the net use command as follows, substituting your chosen drive letter for G:

```
net use G: \\ServerName\SharePoint
```

You can also map a network drive to an Internet path, using basically the same UNC syntax, with the addition of a period at the end of the server name. When using DNS names, you separate each part of the name with a period; the period appended to the end of the DNS server name is optional. For example:

```
\\SyngressMedia.Com.\WindowsNT
```

Removing a share

To stop sharing your files, you can just eliminate your network share. Here are two methods to stop sharing a particular folder:

- ✔ **Windows NT Explorer:** In Explorer, right-click the network share, click Properties, and click the Not Shared radio button.

- ✔ **Command line:** At the command line, use the net command as follows:

```
Net share SharePoint /delete
```

NTFS Permissions

When you share a folder or file, the share-permission access options that you can choose from are limited. But if you're using NTFS as your file system, you have a flexible array of security options to apply to those shared folders and files.

Only NTFS permissions enable you to set security on both individual files and folders on your workstation. Share permissions let you set permissions just on the network share.

Setting, gaining, and viewing permissions

Here are the basic NTFS permissions options and their abbreviations:

- ✔ Read (R)
- ✔ Write (W)
- ✔ Execute (X)
- ✔ Delete (D)
- ✔ Change Permissions (P)
- ✔ Take Ownership (O)

NTFS offers a standard set of access types that you can choose from, with the most popular combinations of the preceding permissions. Tables 9-1 and 9-2 show the standard permissions sets for files and folders, respectively. (Note that in Table 9-2 the second column shows the permissions set for the folder and then for files within that folder.)

Table 9-1	Standard NTFS Permissions Sets for Files	
Type of Access	*Permissions*	*Description*
No Access	None	User cannot access the file in any way, even if the user is a member of a group that has been granted access to the file.
Read	RX	User can read the contents of the file and run it if it's an application.
Change	RWXD	User can read, modify, and delete the file.
Full Control	All	User can read, modify, delete, set permissions for, and take ownership of the file.

Table 9-2	NTFS Levels of Folder Access	
Type of Access	*Folder/File Permissions*	*Description*
No Access	None/None	User can't access the folder in any way, even if the user is a member of a group that's been granted access to the folder.

Type of Access	Folder/File Permissions	Description
List	RX/Not Specified	Users can view filenames and directories and make changes to subdirectories in the folder, but they cannot access files unless granted by another set of permissions.
Read	RX/RX	User can read the contents of files in this folder and run applications in this folder.
Add	WX/Not Specified	User can add files to the folder but can't view the contents of the folder.
Add & Read	RWX/RX	User can add files to the folder and read current files but can't change files.
Change	RWXD/RWXD	User can read and add files and change the contents of current files.
Full Control	All/All	User can read and change files, add new files, change permissions for the folder and its files, and take ownership of the folder and its files.

You can also choose to customize the permissions for a file or folder your-self, rather than use one of the standard sets.

To set or change the permissions on a file or folder, either using a standard permissions set or customizing the permissions, follow the steps in Lab 9-2.

To change the NTFS permissions on a file or folder, you must have necessary rights on the specific resource. If a file within a folder has different permis-sions than the parent folder, the NTFS permissions are followed for that specific file. For example, if you have set Read-Only permission to the Compensation directory for the Everyone Group, but the file Accounting is set at Full Control for the Everyone Group, the Accounting file will be open to the Everyone Group. The NTFS permission is followed by the individual file rather than the NTFS permissions of the parent folder.

Lab 9-2   Setting or Changing NTFS Permissions

1. In Windows NT Explorer, right-click the file or folder that you want to set permissions for; click Permissions on the shortcut menu.

You see the File Permissions dialog box or the Directory Permissions dialog box.

If you want to modify the permissions for all the files and/or subfolders under a chosen folder, simply mark the Replace Permissions on Subdirectories and/or Replace Permissions on Existing Files check boxes.

2. **To specify permissions for more individual users or groups than listed, click the Add button and make your selections.**

   The Add Users and Groups dialog box appears. After you make your selections, you return to the File Permissions or Directory Permissions dialog box.

3. **Highlight the user(s) and/or group(s) for which you want to assign permissions.**

4. **Choose the permission type by clicking the Type of Access drop-down list box.**

   You can click one of the standard permissions sets, or click Special Access to configure a customized permissions set.

   If you choose Special Access, you see either the Special File Access or the Special Directory Access dialog box, where you make your choices.

Viewing a file or folder's permissions is no problem for users who have at least Read permissions on the file or folder. They can view the permissions on the resource, but they can't change the permissions unless they have the necessary rights to do so.

By default, files and folders on an NTFS partition are accessible to anyone; no security is set by default. The user who has control of a folder is responsible for setting up permissions to prevent unwanted access.

The creator of the file or folder has ownership rights to that particular object, meaning that he or she has total control and can set permissions at will — similar to what an administrator can do on a local workstation.

So what happens if that owner is fired or leaves the company? Any user who holds Administrator rights to the local workstation can take ownership of the folders and files on that workstation, following the steps in Lab 9-3.

Note: Ownership rights apply only to NTFS partitions, not FAT partitions.

Lab 9-3   Taking Ownership of a Folder or File

1. **In Windows NT Explorer, right-click the folder or file and click Properties.**

2. **On the Security tab, click the Ownership button.**

   NT asks whether you want to try overwriting the current owner. When you respond yes, you see the Owner dialog box that Figure 9-4 shows.

3. **Click the Take Ownership button.**

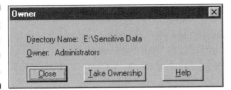

Figure 9-4:
Taking
ownership
of a folder.

You must be a member of the Administrators group to take ownership of files or folders on the workstation.

Copying and moving files and folders

One heavily covered section on the Windows NT Workstation exam is the effects of moving and copying (see Table 9-3). With file permissions on an NTFS partition, if you move a file from one folder to another on the same partition, the file "attribute" or permission is retained. This permission is retained no matter what the state of the destination folder. If you move a file to a compressed folder, the file will remain uncompressed after the move. However, if you decide to copy a file from one folder to another, the permission is changed so that the copied file will inherit the attributes of the destination directory. Files moved from a FAT partition to an NTFS partition always inherit the permission of the destination folder. Any files moved from an NTFS partition to a FAT partition lose their NTFS permissions on the FAT partition.

Table 9-3	Moving and Copying Files on NTFS Partitions	
Function	*Partition*	*Permission*
Copy	Same Partition	Inherited
	Different Partition	Inherited
Move	Same Partition	Retained
	Different Partition	Inherited

When Permissions Collide: How Different Permission Levels Interact

What happens when a resource has two different access levels, in the case of either an NTFS permission versus a network share permission, or a user who's a member of two groups with different permissions?

✔ **NTFS versus network shares:** When connecting to a network share, the permissions are the same or *more* restrictive as opposed to sitting at the local workstation where the permissions are the same or *least* restrictive. So, if a user has Read Only permission on a network share but Full Control on the NTFS permission, the user has Read-Only. *Remember:* More restrictive on network shares!

✔ **Local versus remote access:** When logging on to your local workstation, a user's level of access for a file or folder is determined by their least restrictive level of access. When accessing a network share, the user's level of access for a file or folder is determined by their most restrictive level of access. The next Time Shaver Icon gives you the specifications.

✔ **No Access versus other permissions:** In *all* cases, users who are members of any group that has No Access permission on any form of share are given No Access. No Access is always the result when combined with any type of share or permissions. You can think of No Access permission as the Terminator.

When you go into the exam, here is a little hint that will hopefully give you a head start when trying to remember how to separate the user's level of access depending on where they are accessing the files or folders (either local or remote). Here is a table to help you sort this out.

✔ When accessing files and folders from the local workstation, think least restrictive. Try to remember **L=least** and **L=local.**

✔ When accessing files and folders from over-the-network, think more restrictive. Try to remember **R=Remote** and **R=Restrictive.**

✔ Always remember that any permission combined with No Access is determined to be No Access.

Memorize the following bulleted list on exam day, and you'll be ready for the permissions-versus-share question that pops up on the exam:

✔ When using share permissions, remote users are given the same or least restrictive permissions on the share. For example, if you are a member of two groups, one with Read access and the other with Full Control permissions, your effective remote permissions are Full Control.

✔ The most restrictive level of access, whether share or NTFS, determines a user's level of access to a shared NTFS folder from a remote computer. Thus, the user's effective level of access to a folder from a remote location must be either the same or more restrictive than his or her level of access to the folder had the user been logged on locally.

Prep Test

1 To set up permissions on your network share, which type(s) of permissions can you use? (Choose all that apply.)

- A ❑ Full Control
- B ❑ No Access
- C ❑ Read
- D ❑ Special

2 Bryant has Full Control on the NTFS permissions of a folder that he's trying to access over the network. On the network share permissions, he only has Read. What are his permissions for the folder that he needs access to?

- A ○ Read
- B ○ Full Control
- C ○ Special
- D ○ No Access

3 Laura just formatted her workstation's hard disk with NTFS. She then decides to share a folder off her workstation. What are the default permissions on her shared folder?

- A ○ Full Control
- B ○ Read
- C ○ List
- D ○ Read/Execute

4 You just copied a file from a FAT partition to an NTFS partition on the same folder. The file on the FAT partition did not have any security, but the NTFS partition was marked Read. What is the new permission on the file?

- A ○ Read
- B ○ Full Control
- C ○ List
- D ○ No Access

5 What is the syntax required to map a drive under Windows NT?

- A ○ \\SharePoint\ServerName
- B ○ \\Domain\SharePoint
- C ○ \\ServerName\SharePoint
- D ○ \\IPAddress\ServerName

6 If you move a file on an NTFS partition from one folder to another on the same partition, the permission attributes are

A ○ Inherited

B ○ Retained

C ○ Full Control

D ○ No Access

7 You want to map a network drive across the Internet to a share named Iceberg on the YourCompany.com network. What syntax should you use to accomplish this?

A ○ \\YourCompany\Iceberg.com

B ○ \\YourCompany.com\Iceberg

C ○ \\Iceberg\YourCompany.com

D ○ YourCompany.com\\Iceberg

8 Jane belongs to the Accounting group and the Marketing group on the \Compensation share on her NT Workstation. The Accounting group has Full Control on the share, and the Marketing group has No Access. What access level does Jane have on the share?

A ○ Full Control

B ○ Special Directory Access

C ○ Special Folder Access

D ○ No Access

9 Which type of permissions allows you to set security on files and folders on your workstation?

A ○ Share

B ○ User Rights

C ○ System Rights

D ○ NTFS

10 You have just set up NTFS permissions on a shared folder on your workstation. The NTFS permissions are as follows: No Access for Guests and Read access for Accounting. The share permissions are Full Control for Everyone. What are the effective permissions on the workstation if you try to access the network share as a member of the Accounting group?

A ○ Full Control

B ○ Read

C ○ List

D ○ No Access

Answers

1 *A, B, C.* For share permissions, you can use Full Control, Change, Read, or No Access. NTFS permissions give you more flexibility on configuring permissions. *See "Share Permissions."*

2 *A.* For remote users, if Bryant has Full Control over a folder on an NTFS partition and Read on the network share, he has the same or more restrictive permissions on the folder. *See "When Permissions Collide: How Different Permission Levels Interact."*

3 *A.* Although NTFS enables you to create secured files and folders, the default access is Full Control — you have to implement the NTFS permissions. *See "Setting, gaining, and viewing permissions."*

4 *A.* Whenever you copy a file from a FAT partition to an NTFS partition, the file attributes are always inherited. *See "Copying and moving files and folders."*

5 *C.* You map to a drive by using the Universal Naming Convention. *See "Accessing a share by mapping to it."*

6 *B.* Whenever you move a file on an NTFS partition to another folder on the same partition, the NTFS permission attributes are retained. *See "Copying and moving files and folders."*

7 *B.* Once you get the correct syntax, you can connect to any valid share point. *See "Accessing a share by mapping to it."*

8 *D.* Although Jane is a member of a group that has Full Control of the \Compensation share, she is also a member of a group that has No Access permissions, which overrides any other permission. *See "When Permissions Collide: How Different Permission Levels Interact."*

9 *D.* Only NTFS permissions enable you to set security on both individual files and folders on your workstation. Share permissions let you set permissions on the network share only. *See "Share Permissions" and "NTFS Permissions."*

10 *B.* NTFS permissions are the same or most restrictive on a network share; share permissions are the same or least restrictive on a network share. A member of the Accounting group has Read access because it's more restrictive than the Full Control given for share permissions. *See "When Permissions Collide: How Different Permission Levels Interact."*

Part IV
Connecting Networks

The 5th Wave   By Rich Tennant

AT 11:18 ON APRIL 25th IN THE YEAR 2018, SERVER
SOFTWARE AND HARDWARE REACHED A PERFECT
APPLICATION-TO-MEMORY SYNCHRONICITY.

What the heck...?

In this part . . .

What good is a network or NT Workstation if your computer can't communicate with any other computers on the network? Part of connecting your NT Workstation to a network is configuring the networking components of Windows NT Workstation to begin with. After mastering NT Workstation components, you can move on to other networks, such as configuring your NT Workstation as a client for Novell NetWare. Watch out for all the NetWare questions on the exam! Although Microsoft and Novell aren't buddies, you'd better know how to integrate your NT Workstation in a NetWare environment.

Last but not least is Windows NT Remote Access Service (RAS) for dial-up networking. RAS enables you to dial in to a server and become a remote node on the network, which is a great way to keep in touch with your files and folders from any geographic location. You can also take advantage of the RAS multi-link to achieve greater bandwidth on your workstation. All the stuff about RAS may sound like marketing information, but you need to know it for the exam — Microsoft wants you to know the power of RAS!

Chapter 10

Adding and Configuring Network Components

▶ Install, configure, and remove hardware components for a given situation

▶ Adding and configuring the network components of Windows NT Workstation

*W*indows NT consists of many network components that allow for communication on your network. Your job is to decide which components to install and how to configure them.

Especially important for the exam are

✔ Understanding the different protocols, particularly TCP/IP (which Chapter 13 covers in more detail)

✔ Understanding the essential NT network services

✔ Understanding how to configure your Network Adapters and binding for your network card

The exam tests you on which components to install in a given situation and how to configure those components. Get comfortable with the Control Panel, which is where you go to access the Network dialog box that enables you to control all these aspects of networking. You should also be prepared to answer any questions regarding any of the network services that you can install. So it would be a good idea to go over some of the labs that will prepare you for what you have to know for the exam.

Quick Assessment

Adding and configuring the network components

1 NetBEUI's main limitation is that it is not _____.

2 Your network _____ determine(s) which protocol is used first for a specified network service.

3 The NWLink protocol is mainly used to connect to _____ networks.

4 The DLC protocol connects to HP-series network-interface print devices and _____ computers by using 3270 emulation.

5 The _____ service controls accessing resources on other computers.

Using the bindings settings to order the initialization priority of your network components

6 The _____ service allows you to share your files, folders, and printers.

7 Some characteristics of the _____ protocol are its routing capability, widespread use, and use on the Internet.

8 True/False: The first protocol in the bindings order has priority over all the other protocols in the order.

Choosing network components

9 To add, remove, or change any network services, click the _____ icon in _____.

Answers

1 *Routable.* See "NetBEUI."

2 *Bindings.* See "Network Bindings."

3 *NetWare.* See "NWLink IPX/SPX Compatible Transport."

4 *Mainframe.* See "DLC (Data Link Control)."

5 *Workstation.* See "Network Services."

6 *Server.* See "Network Services."

7 *TCP/IP.* See "TCP/IP."

8 *True.* See "Network Bindings."

9 *Network; Control Panel.* See "Working with NT Workstation Components."

Working with NT Workstation Components

To allow your computer to communicate properly with other computers on the network, you must correctly configure the three default components of your NT Workstation:

- ✔ Network protocols
- ✔ Network services
- ✔ Network adapters

You also need to set the bindings on your computer to connect the network services, protocols, and adapters and control the order of operation. The rest of this chapter goes into detail about each network component and about bindings. (Keep 'em tight. There's 4–6 inches of fresh powder on the expert trail.)

Which components you install on your NT Workstation depends on how you want to use the workstation. When planning your NT installation (see Chapter 4), decide how you want to install and configure your default components to make your NT Workstation meet your specific demands.

You can install default components as part of the Windows NT setup. At any time after setup, you follow basically the same procedure for installing, configuring, and removing default components; see Lab 10-1 for this procedure. You also follow the steps in Lab 10-1 to adjust the bindings settings.

If you see an exam question that asks where you configure a specific default networking component, focus on the answer or answers that relate to the Control Panel. Ignore any answers that relate to the NT Setup utility.

Lab 10-1	Installing, Configuring, or Removing a Network Component and Modifying the Bindings Settings

1. Open the Control Panel.

2. Double-click the Network icon to view the Network dialog box.

Figure 10-1 shows the Network dialog box.

3. Click the appropriate tab: Services, Protocols, Adapters, or Bindings.

4. Make your changes and then reboot your workstation for the changes to take effect.

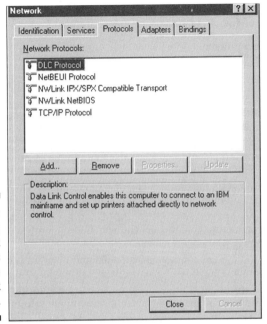

Figure 10-1:
Configuring
network
components
through the
Network
dialog box.

Remember that you always have to reboot your NT Workstation after configuring network settings to allow NT to make the changes.

For the exam, keep the following in mind:

✔ The more components you install, the more resources NT has to account for, thus slowing down performance. Remember that if other computers on your network use just TCP/IP for communication, then you may have to install only TCP/IP. If you have any other protocols installed on your NT Workstation that are not used on your network, you are just wasting resources. NT will try to access your Network resources with ALL of the protocols that are bound to your network adapter even if your network uses only TCP/IP. Unbind them and set them free.

✔ Make sure that you have the correct drivers for the components that you plan to install. Not having the right drivers can make for a long, tough installation process. You can find this information located in the Hardware Compatibility List. And if you're too tired or plan on having a beer or two while you configure the network, make sure that you plan for a designated driver.

Network Protocols Are NT's Alphabet Soup

Networked computers need to use a transport, in the form of network protocols, to communicate with one another. Sounds simple enough, but deciding which protocol or protocols best fit your network is anything but simple: You have so many different network protocols to choose from (each protocol with its advantages and disadvantages) and so many configuration options that the decision-making process can really get confusing.

For this exam, you can focus on TCP/IP, NetBEUI, NWLink IPX/SPX Compatible Transport, and DLC (Data Link Control). Any other protocols that the exam offers as potential answers are there just to confuse you, as if the live ones don't confuse you enough — ignore them.

Which network protocol or protocols you should use depends on the goals for your LAN or WAN (see Chapter 11 for more about network models). Table 10-1 gives you a quick summary of when to use which protocol, and Table 10-2 gives you some tips about how to answer certain scenarios on the exam. See the upcoming subsections for more details about each protocol.

Table 10-1	Summary of Network Protocols
Protocol	*Characteristics*
DLC	Connects to HP printers
	Connects to mainframes for 3270 emulation
NetBEUI	Small, quick protocol
	Not routable
	For small networks
NWLink IPX/SPX Compatible Transport	Normally used in NetWare networks
	Routable
TCP/IP	Connects to the Internet
	Routable
	Peer Web Services uses TCP/IP to run the FTP, Telnet, and HTTP applications

Table 10-2	Instant Answers to Questions of Protocol
For This Scenario . . .	*The Best Answer Is . . .*
Connection to a NetWare server	NWLink IPX/SPX Compatible Transport
Best network protocol for a small LAN	NetBEUI
Protocol with excellent routing capabilities	TCP/IP
Direct connection to the Internet	TCP/IP

Whatever your choice of protocols, remember that installing any extra protocols causes unnecessary traffic on your network. For example, if you have NWLink, TCP/IP, and NetBEUI installed on your workstation and you're connecting to a server that uses only TCP/IP, you're making NT Workstation try to contact the server with all three protocols, leading to extra traffic. Accidents will happen.

DLC (Data Link Control)

The two principal functions of the DLC protocol are

✔ Connecting to Hewlett-Packard printers

✔ Connecting to mainframe computers via 3270 Terminal Emulation

Unlike other protocols, DLC is not mainly used for direct communication between computers.

To let your network clients communicate with the HP printer, you install the DLC protocol on the server — you don't need to install the protocol on the network clients. However, you don't necessarily need DLC to connect to HP printers; you can give your HP printer a TCP/IP address and connect to the printer via TCP/IP printing in Windows NT 4.0.

NetBEUI

The NetBEUI protocol is used for communicating through small Windows computer networks. The protocol is very fast on a LAN but has one serious limitation in that it is not a routable protocol — it can't talk to other computers or networks on the other side of a router. This limitation restricts NetBEUI use to LANs of 20 to 200 workstations.

If a question sets up a situation requiring a routable protocol, you can safely eliminate any answer based on using NetBEUI.

Instead of communicating via a network address, NetBEUI communicates with other computers on the network with valid NetBIOS names.

NWLink IPX/SPX Compatible Transport

When someone mentions the NWLink protocol, he or she is usually talking about a NetWare-compatible network. NetWare networks usually use the NWLink IPX/SPX Compatible Transport. NWLink can

- Be routed to other networks
- Connect to NetWare client/server applications, such as SQL Server
- Browse NetBIOS networks where NWLink is run on top of NetBIOS

Choose the NWLink protocol as your answer if the question is about using NT Workstation to access a NetWare network or a NetWare client/server application on a NetWare network. Check out Chapter 12 for more information.

Be sure to know all about installing NT Workstation as a NetWare client for the exam; see Chapter 12 for details about NWLink and NetBIOS.

Make sure that you correctly configure the Frame-Type for NWLink. Windows NT sometimes has trouble with the auto-detect feature for NWLink, so you should specify what frame-type you are using on your network. This is a famous exam question that often appears when the question is focusing on NWLink and connectivity.

TCP/IP

TCP/IP, an industry-standard suite of protocols designed for LANs and WANs, has gained most of its popularity through its wide use for Internet communication. Connecting computers together throughout the world, TCP/IP is known for being both reliable and routable and for being able to talk to foreign networks.

Windows NT TCP/IP enables users to connect to either of the following:

- The Internet
- Any machine running TCP/IP and providing TCP/IP services, including some applications that require TCP/IP to function

Routing

The exam has several questions about TCP/IP and NT Workstation; check out Chapter 13 for all the details you need to know.

Network Services

Part of making sure that your Windows NT 4.0 Workstation can communicate with other computers is making sure that all of your network services are performing as planned. What you will see on the exam is how to install and configure network services as well as how to troubleshoot them.

For more information on monitoring your network resources, check out Chapter 7.

Here are the two network services that you're most likely to deal with. By default, these services are initialized at startup. To adjust the initialization, see Lab 10-2, following this list.

- ✔ **Workstation service:** Controls your ability to access different types of resources on the network. This service is what allows your NT Workstation to connect automatically (almost) to other resources on your network. Whenever you try to access a network share or printer on the network, the Workstation service is doing its job.

- ✔ **Server service:** Allows you to share files and printers with other computers on the network.

  Without this service starting, you can't share any resources on your computer. You can purposely disable this service if you want to prohibit people from accessing your NT Workstation from the network.

Lab 10-2   Installing, Configuring, or Removing a Network Service

1. **Follow the steps in Lab 10-1 (see "Installing, Configuring, or Removing a Network Component and Modifying the Bindings Settings"), with the following steps added.**

2. **In the Services tab of the Network dialog box, click the Add button.**

   You see the Select Network Service dialog box that Figure 10-2 shows.

3. **Click Simple TCP/IP Services.**

4. **Specify the location of the Windows NT source files for the network service that you want to install.**

5. **Reboot NT Workstation for the changes to take effect.**

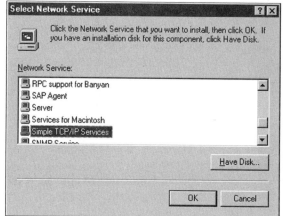

Figure 10-2:
Choosing
the network
service to
configure.

Network Bindings

The bindings settings for your computer connect the network services, protocols, and adapters on your workstation by controlling which component is handled in which specific binding order. Figure 10-3 shows the Bindings tab of the Network dialog box, where you set the binding order. (Lab 10-1, earlier in this chapter, gives you a couple more details about the Network dialog box.)

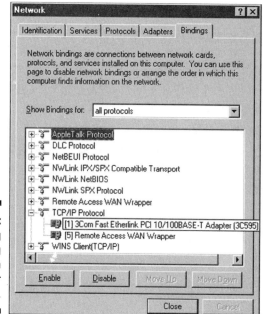

Figure 10-3:
Configuring
the binding
options on
your
workstation.

For maximum performance, place your required service at the top of the binding order. For example, if you have TCP/IP, NWLink, and NetBEUI bound to the Workstation service on your workstation, make sure that the most-often-used protocol is at the top of the bindings so that it's used first. On the exam, put the protocol that's used the most, first in the binding order. The other protocols can be removed or placed at the bottom of the binding order.

The protocol you use the most should be bound first to the network service. Each protocol down the binding ladder is used in order if the initial protocol doesn't work.

Prep Test

1 Your network is running the TCP/IP protocol to connect to a file and print
server. On your personal NT Workstation, you have TCP/IP, NetBEUI, and
NWLink installed. How can you configure your bindings to get good network
performance when accessing the print server?

A ○ On the Workstation service, make sure that TCP/IP is bound last.

B ○ On the Server service, make sure that NetBEUI is bound first.

C ○ On the Workstation service, make sure that TCP/IP is bound first.

D ○ On the Server service, make sure that TCP/IP is bound last.

2 Where can you configure your network protocols on your NT Workstation?

A ○ User Manager

B ○ Administrative Tools

C ○ Network icon in the Control Panel

D ○ Windows NT Diagnostics

3 What does the Workstation service control on your NT Workstation?

A ○ Share files and printers

B ○ Printing spooler

C ○ Access to resources on the network

D ○ Network bindings

4 What are some benefits of using the DLC protocol on your network? (Choose
all that apply.)

A ❏ Connects to mainframes via 3270 terminal emulation

B ❏ Used on NetWare networks

C ❏ Backbone of the Internet

D ❏ Connects to HP printers jet-direct cards

5 You just installed the NWLink protocol on your NT Workstation but still can't
connect to any of the network servers. You know that the servers that have
NWLink installed on them are running fine. What could be the problem?

A ○ Incorrect frame type

B ○ IPX routing is not installed

C ○ Corrupt routing table

D ○ NetBIOS over NWLink is not configured correctly

6 Your Server service on your NT Workstation is not starting correctly. What will you *not* be able to do?

A ○ Share files, folders, and printers

B ○ Connect to the Internet

C ○ Access files, folders, and printers

D ○ Route to different networks

7 What network components can you configure from the Network icon in the Control Panel? (Choose all that apply.)

A ❑ Network adapter

B ❑ Bindings

C ❑ Network Diagnostics

D ❑ Ping

E ❑ Services

F ❑ Protocols

G ❑ Cables

H ❑ Network monitoring

8 Which protocol(s) can be configured for routing to other networks? (Choose all that apply.)

A ❑ NetBEUI

B ❑ NWLink

C ❑ TCP/IP

D ❑ DLC

E ❑ Streams

Answers

1 *C.* To increase performance, make sure that the protocol to be used the most is first in the binding order. *See "Network Bindings."*

2 *C.* From the Network icon within the Control Panel, you can configure protocols, network adapters, network services, identification, and bindings. *See "Working with NT Workstation Components."*

3 *C.* The Workstation service on your computer controls access to different network resources on the network, including files, folders, share points, and printers. *See "Network Services."*

4 *A, D.* The DLC protocol is not normally used to share files and folders over a network but is mainly used to connect to mainframes and HP printers. *See "DLC (Data Link Control)."*

5 *A.* A common problem when installing and configuring NWLink is that sometimes NT does not detect the correct frame type. When you install the NWLink protocol, make sure that you specify the frame type on your network. *See "NWLink IPX/SPX Compatible Transport."*

6 *A.* The Server service on your computer controls the sharing of network resources. *See "Network Services."*

7 *A, B, E,* and *F.* You can configure identification, protocols, network adapters, services, and bindings from the Network icon in the Control Panel. *See "Working with NT Workstation Components."*

8 *B, C.* Only the NWLink and TCP/IP protocols can be configured to route to other networks. *See Table 10-1.*

Chapter 11

Creating Domains and Workgroups

Exam Objectives

▶ Understanding how NT Workstation integrates with workgroups and domains

▶ Creating and managing local user accounts and local group accounts to meet given requirements

*W*indows NT 4.0 Workstation can integrate into many different network environments. Whether you have a really large network with multiple domains or a workgroup with as few as ten computers, Windows NT can make it work.

Your job as the administrator of your NT Workstation is to make sure that you can integrate effectively within both domains and workgroups. This means creating both users and groups on your workstation and making sure that the correct permissions are in place for sharing resources. Domains and workgroups are covered significantly on the Windows NT 4.0 Workstation exam. Make sure that you understand all the concepts behind them.

A major part of creating every Windows NT network is setting up and configuring network browsing. If you configure NT browsing correctly, you have an efficient and up-to-date network. If you don't keep track of how browsing is being controlled, you could end up with a nightmare of incorrect browse lists and broadcast storms generated by workstations trying to browse the network.

This chapter covers the domain and workgroup network models and the way network browsing works.

Quick Assessment

1 Workgroups are usually made up of _____ or fewer computers networked together.

2 True/False: The workgroup networking model relies on centralized security for the sharing of resources.

3 When adding a computer to a domain, you need at least _____ privileges.

4 The _____ Domain Controller and the _____ Domain Controller replicate copies of the user-accounts database between each other.

5 Name three criteria in configuring browsing on the network.

6 True/False: The Master Browser hands off the most recent browse list to client requests.

7 True/False: Windows NT member servers can process domain logons if they have the necessary privileges.

8 The _____ always wins a browser election on a Windows NT domain.

9 You can specify whether your NT computer will or will not become a browser on your Windows NT network by editing the _____.

Answers

1 *Ten.* See "Workgroups."

2 *False.* See "Workgroups."

3 *Account Operator.* See "Joining a domain."

4 *Primary; Backup.* See "Servers and domain controllers."

5 *Operating system; operating system version; browse role on the network.* See "Browsing the Network."

6 *False.* See "Backup Browsers."

7 *False.* See "Servers and domain controllers."

8 *PDC.* See "Configuring a Preferred Master Browser."

9 *Registry.* See "Setting browser roles."

Choosing Workgroup or Domain

The Windows NT network model comprises many different configurations of workgroups and domains.

- A workgroup generally consists of ten or fewer computers using share-level security and decentralized administration.

- A domain consists of a combination of NT Servers and NT Workstations in a centralized network environment. All administration on the network is centralized from the NT Server.

Both network models have certain advantages and disadvantages. The type of network you're using determines what type of network model you use.

- Generally, workgroups are for smaller, peer-to-peer networks. The workgroup model targets smaller networks of usually ten or fewer users who don't require centralized security and want to manage their own resources. All members of a workgroup are their own network administrators, so essentially they manage their own resources.

- Domains comprise many users — hundreds or even thousands of computers in one network. Normally, if you decide to go ahead with a domain model, you are looking for a network that can handle a large number of user accounts, utilizes centralized user accounts, and has a centralized security model. All your security and user accounts can be managed from one central location, which gives you the ability to administer many different types of domain models from any given location.

All user accounts on a workgroup are considered local whereas all user accounts for a domain are held on a Domain Controller. This determines what type of security you will have on your network.

Whether you decide on the domain or workgroup network model, you have to add up all the advantages and disadvantages of each. Otherwise, you may end up with a network that's falling apart all over the place because you didn't prepare for the security and functionality issues that each network model brings with it.

Workgroups

When you decide to use a workgroup, you have to keep in mind what your goals are.

- If your network consists of fewer than ten computers, a workgroup model is for you.

✔ If resource allocation across computers isn't a problem, consider using a workgroup model. Workgroups allow for individualized security sessions — every user in the workgroup is in charge of his or her own workstation. If someone needs to access a resource on someone else's computer, the person who owns the resource has to give that person access.

This feature of no centralized security can make for a lot of work if you have more than ten users in the workgroup; you have to keep updating security settings because no centralized user-accounts database exists. For example, if you want to access a resource that's part of your workgroup, the person who owns that specific resource needs to give you permission.

Every resource in the workgroup is controlled by the owner of that resource.

Here are some common features of workgroups:

✔ Fewer than ten computers

✔ No centralized security

✔ Decentralized resources

As you can see in Figure 11-1, this is the general topology for a workgroup.

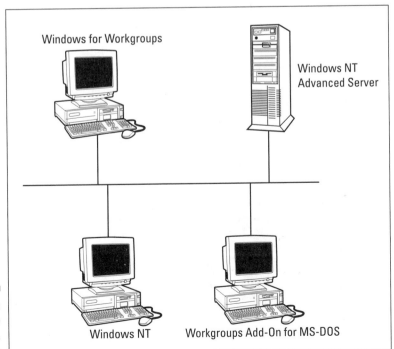

Figure 11-1:
Workgroup
overview.

Joining a workgroup is a simple matter of providing the name of the workgroup that you want to join. You don't need special permission to join a workgroup, you just need administrative rights on a local machine to change a workgroup name to the workgroup name of your choice. If you do not have the necessary rights, you're out of luck and can't become a member of the workgroup.

When you join the workgroup, be aware of these rules:

- Your workgroup cannot have the same name as your computer. Windows NT doesn't allow it because it would cause problems with browsing.

- The workgroup name can be up to 15 characters but cannot contain any of the following characters:

  ; : " < > * + = \ | ?

  Essentially, you can name your workgroup anything that conforms to the NetBIOS naming standard. Take a look at Figure 11-2 and you can see where you have to be (the Network icon in Control Panel) in order to change your workgroup. Also, review Lab 11-1, just to make sure that you understand how this process works.

Lab 11-1   Joining a Workgroup

1. Open the Network icon in the Control Panel window.

2. Under the Identification tab, click the Change button.

3. You're now at the Identification Changes box. Where you see Member of in the Workgroup text box, type the name of the workgroup that you want to join.

4. Click OK to exit.

5. Reboot your system for the changes to take effect.

Domains

In a Windows NT environment, a domain is a logical collection of computers that share a common user-accounts database and security policy. Each domain provides logon validation to make sure that each user account is valid and that all security policies are enforced.

Your NT Workstation is designed to participate in a domain and take advantage of all the benefits of centralized security. When you log on to your NT domain, you're automatically given an access token that identifies all your security privileges. (See Chapter 8 for more about security and access tokens.)

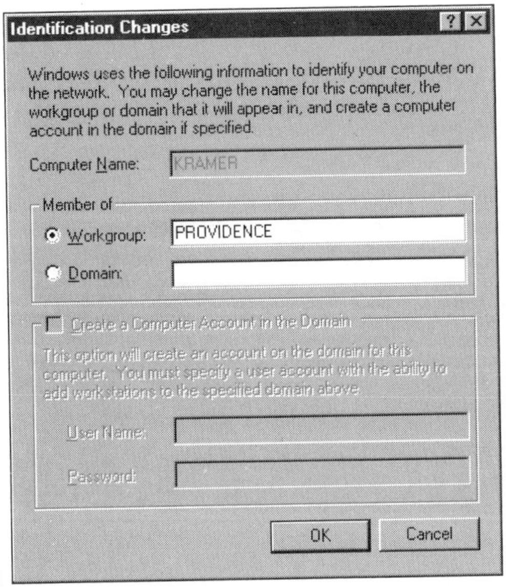

Figure 11-2:
Joining a
workgroup.

A domain has its own user-accounts database that is maintained by a Primary Domain Controller and possibly one or several Backup Domain Controllers. The user-account database is then replicated periodically to other Domain Controllers to reflect any updates.

Because domains use a central account database, you can do all your administration right from a central location, which eliminates having to track hundreds or thousands of user permissions and user rights. You can just make one simple change, and the security changes are implemented.

Here are some features that are specific to domains:

✔ Centralized security

✔ Centralized administration

✔ Supports large numbers of workstations

✔ Centralized network logons

Joining a domain

To join a domain, a user needs the appropriate rights to add his or her computer to the domain accounts database. You must have at least Account Operator privileges to add computers to a domain. If you have the necessary privileges, you can add computers to the domain whenever they're needed. See Lab 11-2.

If your administrator has not yet added your workstation's computer name to the domain, you use the Create a Computer Account in the Domain option for the name of the workstation that you're working on. This option saves you the hassle of trying to add a computer that's not part of the domain. See Lab 11-2.

You add computers to the domain through the Network icon in the Control Panel, as you can see in Figure 11-3.

Lab 11-2   Joining a Domain

1. **Open the Network icon in the Control Panel window.**

2. **Under the Identification tab, click the Change button.**

3. **You're now at the Identification Changes box. Where you see Member of in the Domain text box, type the name of the domain that you want to join.**

4. **If you're not already part of the domain, you need to create a computer account in the domain.**

5. **Enter a User Name and Password with at least Account Operator privileges in order to become part of the domain.**

6. **Click OK to exit.**

7. **Reboot your system for the changes to take effect.**

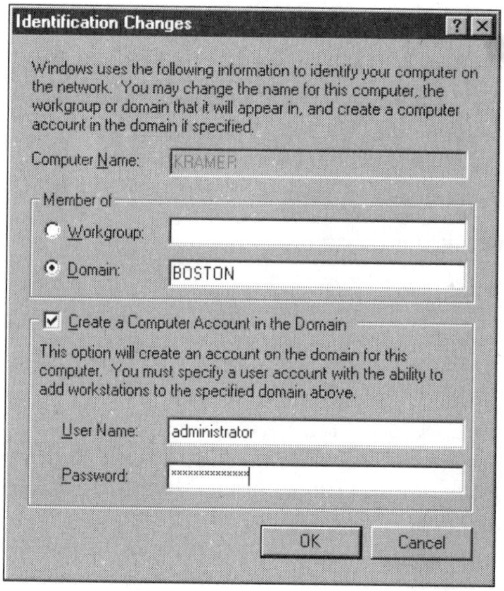

Figure 11-3:
Adding computer accounts to your domain.

> **Identification Changes**   ? X
>
> Windows uses the following information to identify your computer on the network. You may change the name for this computer, the workgroup or domain that it will appear in, and create a computer account in the domain if specified.
>
> Computer Name: KRAMER
>
> Member of
>   ○ Workgroup: [   ]
>   ● Domain: [BOSTON   ]
>
> ☑ Create a Computer Account in the Domain
> This option will create an account on the domain for this computer. You must specify a user account with the ability to add workstations to the specified domain above.
>
>   User Name: [administrator   ]
>   Password: [xxxxxxxxxxxxx   ]
>
>   [OK] [Cancel]

Servers and domain controllers

A Windows NT network has two types of servers:

- ✔ **Domain controllers** control the central user-accounts database where all the user accounts are located. They're also responsible for replicating the user-accounts database and processing user-account logons to the network.

  The network has two types of domain controllers:

  - • The **Primary Domain Controller (PDC)** is the one computer running Windows NT Server in a Windows NT Server domain. This NT Server keeps track of the user-accounts database and authenticates domain logons as its first duty; it also tracks changes made to accounts of all computers on a domain. The PDC is the only computer to receive these changes directly.

  - • The **Backup Domain Controller (BDC)** complements the Primary Domain Controller on a Windows NT domain; the BDC also has a copy of the user-accounts database and processes network logons.

  A Windows NT domain can have only one PDC, but you can have as many BDCs on your network as you choose. However, the BDC is not responsible for keeping the master copy of the user-accounts database. Whenever any changes are made to the account database, replication occurs on the PDC and the BDCs to ensure an up-to-date copy of the user-accounts database.

- ✔ **Member servers** are ordinary servers on the network that are used for data storage, for printing, or even as application servers. These servers don't process logon requests or have a copy of the user-accounts database on their systems. They can be considered the blue-collar computers on your network that do most of the data transfer.

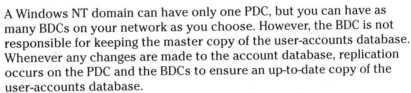

Browsing on your NT network is more than just opening up the Network Neighborhood icon on your desktop and double-clicking various computers. A detailed process is at work behind the scenes to make sure that the browse list for your network is always up-to-date. This complex process is maintained in a tiered system of NT Servers and NT Workstations that make up various types of browser roles on your network.

Configuring browsers and browser elections is a complicated process. However, if you remember a few key points, it doesn't have to be.

This topic is just background information that you won't see on the Workstation exam.

Setting browser roles

An NT network has many different browser roles. These various roles are mixed together to form a hierarchical layout of "who's in charge" of your network browse list. The job of providing a browse list of network resources to various clients is distributed among multiple computers on your NT network. The following list gives you the names by which the browser service knows the browsing roles of these computers. All these types of browsers work together to ensure that your Network Neighborhood browse list is always up-to-date.

- ✔ **Master Browser:** Maintains the master copy of the network resource list. That's the only job of the Master Browser. It sends updates to all the Backup Browsers.

  Which computer is the Master Browser is determined by a set of criteria; see "Browser elections."

- ✔ **Backup Browser:** Receives a copy of the network resource list from the Master Browser. The Backup Browser's job is to distribute the list to the browser clients whenever a client asks for an updated browse list.

- ✔ **Preferred Master Browser:** If you want, you can specify a certain computer on your network to be the Preferred Master Browser. When this computer is started, it designates itself as the Master Browser for the domain or workgroup, which may force an election (see "Browser elections").

- ✔ **Potential Browser:** A computer is marked as a Potential Browser when it's capable of maintaining a network browse list but won't receive the list until instructed to do so by the Master Browser.

- ✔ **Non-Browser:** When a computer is marked a Non-Browser, the computer never maintains a network browse list. You set this configuration as No in the Registry MaintainBrowseList. Most client computers are configured as Non-Browsers to reduce network traffic and conserve bandwidth.

To specify the computer's role on the network, you edit the computer's Registry parameters.

If you want to edit the Registry to specify your browser role, navigate to

```
\HKEY_LOCAL_MACHINE\SYSTEM\CurrentControlSet\Services\Browser\
            Parameters\MaintainServerList
```

The MaintainServerList parameter can have the values listed in Table 11-1.

Table 11-1	MaintainServerList Parameter Values
Parameter	*Value*
No	This computer will *never* participate as a browser server.
Yes	This computer will become a browser server. Upon startup, this computer attempts to contact the Master Browser to get a current browse list. If the Master Browser cannot be found, the computer forces the election of a Master Browser. This computer will either be elected as the Master Browser or become a Backup Browser. Yes is the default value for Windows NT Server domain controller computers.
Auto	This computer may or may not become a browser server, depending on the number of currently active browsers, and is referred to as a Potential Browser. This computer will be notified by the Master Browser as to whether or not it should become a Backup Browser. Auto is the default value for Windows NT Workstation and Windows NT Server (non-domain controller) computers.

Browser elections

Certain criteria must be followed when determining what browsing role your computer will have on the network. Each browser computer has certain criteria, depending on the type of system. The criteria include

- ✔ Operating system
- ✔ Operating system version
- ✔ Browser role on the network

These criteria are used to rank computers during a browse election. This browse election is a way to determine which computer should be the Master Browser in the event that the current Master Browser is determined unavailable. You can think of it as a technical game of King of the Hill.

Configuring a Preferred Master Browser

The many types of browsers on your network are all fighting to become the Preferred Master Browser. Whenever a computer thinks it has the right privileges, it tries to force an election to become Master Browser.

A Windows NT Workstation or Windows NT Server can be configured as a Preferred Master Browser. When the Browser service is started on a computer configured as a Preferred Master Browser, the browser service forces a browser election to occur. Also, if a Master Browser already exists and other computers are up and running in the workgroup before this one was turned on, the Preferred Master Browser forces an election.

Preferred Master Browsers are given an advantage in elections, such that if all other things are equal, a Preferred Master Browser will always win an election and become the Master Browser.

To configure a computer as a Preferred Master Browser, set the following Registry parameter value to True or Yes:

```
\HKEY_LOCAL_MACHINE\SYSTEM\CurrentControlSet\Services\Browser\
        Parameters\IsDomainMaster
```

Unless the computer has already been configured as the Preferred Master Browser, this value is False or No. That's true even if the computer is currently the Master Browser.

Prep Test

1 What types of Windows NT Servers authenticate user logons? (Choose all that apply.)

A ❑ Member servers

B ❑ Logon servers

C ❑ Primary Domain Controllers

D ❑ Secondary Domain Controllers

E ❑ Backup Domain Controllers

2 Bryant has just installed his NT Workstation and then logs on to his workstation as Administrator. When he tries to access resources in his domain, he is getting Access Denied errors. What is the problem?

A ○ Not enough permissions

B ○ Not part of the network

C ○ Logged onto the local workstation, not the domain

D ○ User right not specified

3 Lorna is going to set up a Windows NT domain that will require 18 member servers and 7 backup domain controllers. How many Primary Domain Controllers should she implement for her domain?

A ○ One

B ○ Two

C ○ Three

D ○ Four

4 What are some characteristics of the Windows NT domain model? (Choose all that apply.)

A ❑ Fewer than ten users

B ❑ Centralized security

C ❑ Centralized administration

D ❑ Personal administration

E ❑ Decentralized resources

F ❑ Central user-accounts database

5 A computer on the network forces a browse election. Four computers are configured to be browsers on the network. Which one will win the election?

A ○ NT 4.0 Server - BDC

B ○ NT 3.51 Workstation

C ○ NT 3.51 Server - PDC

D ○ Windows 95

6 What group do you have to be a member of to add user account to the domain? (Choose two.)

A ❑ Power User

B ❑ Account Operator

C ❑ Guest

D ❑ Administrator

E ❑ Backup Operator

7 Susan wants to move her workstation from the "Marketing" workgroup that she is currently a member of to the "Communications" workgroup. She is currently a local administrator on her Windows NT Workstation. What does she have to do to make the necessary change? (Choose four.)

A ❑ Open up Windows NT Diagnostics.

B ❑ Open up the Network Icon in Control Panel.

C ❑ Click on the Workgroup tab.

D ❑ Enter the name of the "Communications" Domain.

E ❑ Click the Change button on the Identification tab.

F ❑ Enter the name of the "Communications" workgroup.

G ❑ Restart the computer.

Answers

1 *C, E.* Only Primary and Backup Domain Controllers can authenticate user logons on a domain. Members servers are used for work-based tasks, such as file and print or applications. *See "Servers and domain controllers."*

2 *C.* Workstation accounts have privileges only on the local workstation; domain accounts have rights throughout the domain. *See "Choosing a Workgroup or Domain."*

3 *A.* No matter how big your network ever gets, a domain can have just one PDC , though you can have multiple BDCs and member servers. *See "Servers and domain controllers."*

4 *B, C, F.* These factors separate the domain model from the workgroup model. *See "Domains."*

5 *C.* Although the BDC (NT 4.0 Server) is the latest version of Windows NT, a PDC will always win the election, no matter what. *See "Browser elections."*

6 *B, D.* If you want to add a user account to the domain, you need to have at least Account Operator privileges or Administrative rights on the domain.

7 *B, E, F, G.* If Susan wants to change the name of her workgroup, she has to open up the Network icon in Control Panel, click the Change tab, enter in her desired workgroup, and restart her computer.

Chapter 12

NetWare and Connectivity: The True Story

Exam Objectives

▶Implement Windows NT Workstation as a client in a NetWare environment

*W*hen you install Client Service for NetWare (CSNW), your NT 4.0 Workstation can integrate seamlessly into a NetWare environment — after all, NetWare networks still make up a large part of the corporate marketplace.

One of the Microsoft goals for the NT Workstation MCSE exam is that you be able to "Implement Windows NT Workstation as a client in a NetWare environment." The exam tests you on the CSNW features that enable NT Workstation to act as a NetWare client. You need to be able to configure the NWLink protocol, print and configure printing options on NetWare printers, use NetWare-compatible logon scripts, connect to an NDS tree, run NetWare-compatible command-line utilities, connect to a preferred server, and change your password on a NetWare 3.x and 4.x Server. This chapter covers those very topics.

Quick Assessment

Implement
Windows
NT
Worksta-
tion as a
client in a
NetWare
environ-
ment

1   You can use the _____ utility from the command line to change your password while using Client Service for NetWare on a NetWare 3.*x* Server.

2   Some _____-bit MS-DOS utilities cannot be run from the command line, even when Client Service for NetWare is installed.

3   The four frame types for NWLink are _____, _____, _____, and _____.

4   The three printing options in configuring Client Service for NetWare are _____, _____, and _____.

5   The _____ command-line utility is used to bring up the server console for a NetWare server.

6   You can set the Notify When Printed option in _____.

7   Your _____ _____ is the server that you connect to by default and validates your user credentials.

8   When you are connecting to a NetWare _____.*x* Server, changing your password is similar to NT because you press Ctrl+Alt+Delete to bring up the Change Password tab.

9   When installing the _____ protocol, the default frame type is set to Auto Detect.

10 A NetWare 4.*x* Server uses a(n) _____ hierarchical tree to store information, such as network resources and network hardware.

Answers

1 *Setpass.* See Lab 12-2.

2 *16.* See "Running command-line utilities in CSNW."

3 *802.2, 802.3, Ethernet II, and Ethernet SNAP.* See "Frame type."

4 *Add Form Feed, Notify When Printed, and Print Banner.* See Table 12-1.

5 *Syscon.* See "Running command-line utilities in CSNW."

6 *Client Service for NetWare print options.* See "Installing and configuring CSNW."

7 *Preferred Server.* See "Installing and configuring CSNW."

8 *4.* See "Changing your password in CSNW."

9 *NWLink.* See "Frame type."

10 *NDS.* See "Integrating with Client Service for NetWare (CSNW)."

Linking Up to NetWare

The NWLink protocol is Microsoft's version of the NetWare IPX/SPX. (The terms *NetWare Link, NWLink,* and *IPX/SPX* all refer to the same protocol.) Many NetWare networks use this network protocol. NWLink can

- ✔ Be routed to other networks
- ✔ Connect to NetWare client-server applications (SQL)
- ✔ Browse NetBIOS Networks where NWLink is run on top of NetBIOS

You choose this protocol if your NT Workstation is going to access a NetWare network (like the example in Figure 12-1) or a NetWare client/ server application on a NetWare network. The exam includes one to three questions regarding how to configure and manage NWLink.

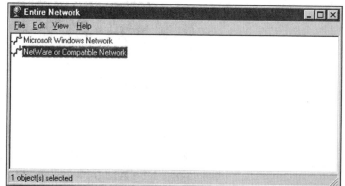

Figure 12-1:
A NetWare-
compatible
network.

The NWLink over NetBIOS is the Microsoft version of Novell NetBIOS; it sends Novell NetBIOS packets between a NetWare Server running Novell NetBIOS and a Windows NT computer, or between two Windows NT computers.

One of Microsoft's favorite exam questions relates to using NWLink outside of NetWare. Here's what you need to know:

- ✔ With NWLink installed, an NT Workstation can connect to a NetWare client-server database even if Client Service for NetWare isn't installed. Only the NWLink protocol is required for accessing client-server applications that run on a NetWare server. CSNW is designed for NT Workstations that require a direct link to NetWare servers and access to files or printers on NetWare servers. See "Integrating with Client Service for NetWare (CSNW)" later in this chapter.

✔ Different clients can connect to a NetWare Server with NWLink without being part of a domain. Pay particular attention to NWLink's capability to connect a client-server application, such as an SQL Server.

Installing NWLink

The exam covers the process of installing the NWLink protocol, which you can review in Lab 12-1. (You don't need to have a NetWare Server handy to follow along; just keep the general steps in mind.)

Lab 12-1   Installing the NWLink Protocol

1. **In the Control Panel, go to the Network Protocols settings (as Figure 12-2 shows), where you see the various protocols that are already installed.**

2. **Add the NWLink IPX/SPX Compatible Transport and enter the source files when prompted.**

3. **Restart your NT Workstation so that the changes can take effect.**

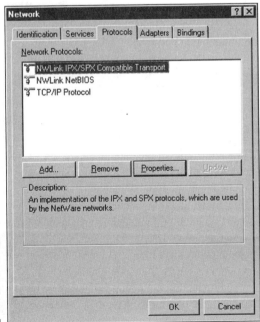

Figure 12-2:
Installing
the NWLink
protocol.

Configuring NWLink

After installing the NWLink protocol, you need to configure a couple of options specific to NWLink to route it correctly: the frame type and the network number. To set the configurations, go back to the Network Protocols and click the Properties button for NWLink IPX/SPX Compatible Transport.

Frame type

Although Windows NT 4.0 Server offers the option of automatically detecting the correct frame type, NT sometimes experiences problems auto-detecting the frame type for NWLink. To be on the safe side, manually pick a frame type to use on your network so that you're sure you can communicate with other computers that use IPX/SPX.

Figure 12-3 shows your four frame-type options:

- 802.2
- 802.3
- Ethernet II
- Ethernet SNAP

You can see in Figure 12-3 what options you have when configuring the options for the NWLink protocol.

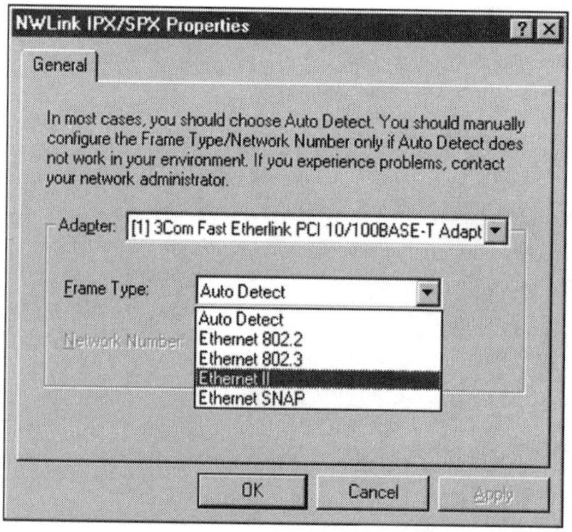

Figure 12-3:
Configuring
the NWLink
protocol.

Here's a troubleshooting question that you're likely to see: "Why can't you connect to the NetWare Server?" The answer has to do with correct frame type. The default setting when installing NWLink is Auto Detect, which doesn't always result in the correct frame type. Remember that you must set the NWLink frame type manually to one of the four options available.

Integrating with Client Service for NetWare (CSNW)

Client Service for NetWare (CSNW) is designed for Windows NT Workstations that require a direct link to NetWare Servers and access to files or printers on NetWare Servers. The exam asks several questions about configuring CSNW, so be sure that you understand how each configurable option works together with a NetWare Server.

One thing you need to be aware of is which version of NetWare you're working with:

- ✔ NetWare 3.*x* Servers use the Bindery, a flat database that requires the use of multiple passwords to access network resources because one NetWare Server can't share security information with another NetWare Server.

- ✔ NetWare 4.*x* Servers run NetWare Directory Services (NDS), a hierarchical-tree structure that allows single-password access to resources throughout the tree.

- ✔ NT Workstation 4.0 supports NDS, the benefits of which relate to the ease of changing your password (see "Changing your password in CSNW," later in this chapter).

A great resource to help understand each of the configurable resources in CSNW is the Help button, which brings up the Help Topics page.

Installing and configuring CSNW

You install Client Service for NetWare in the Network Services dialog box (accessed from the Control Panel).

Before installing CSNW, prepare a list of the properties that you're going to configure. Memorize each of these configurable properties, which you set by double-clicking the CSNW icon in the Control Panel (see Figure 12-4):

- **Preferred Server:** Know your NetWare preferred server. This NetWare Server validates your presence on the network (kind of like a domain controller in Windows NT).

- **Default Tree and Context:** If you are using NetWare 4.*x* and running NDS, know your default tree and context. (This is your Novell Domain Service.)

- **Print Options:** Table 12-1 goes over your options for configuring a printer. (The exam tests you on these options.) Know which printing options you can configure.

- **Login Script Options:** Are you going to be processing login scripts when your users log on to your workstation? This is used to set up parameters, such as network drives and printers.

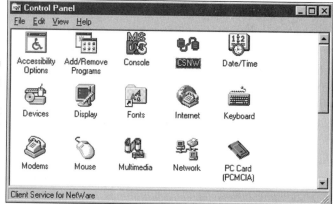

Figure 12-4:
Configuring
Client
Service for
NetWare
from the
Control
Panel.

Table 12-1	NetWare Printer Options
Option	**What It Does**
Add Form Feed	Ejects a blank page at the end of every print job
Notify When Printed	Notifies you when your document is finished printing
Print Banner	Prints a banner page after each print job that you send to the printer

Changing your password in CSNW

If you're running Client Service for NetWare, the first question you have to ask yourself when changing your password from your NT Workstation is what version of NetWare Server you're working with.

Table 12-2 gives you the quick answer to the question of how to change your password. Check out Labs 12-2 and 12-3 for a review of the entire processes.

Table 12-2   Changing Your NetWare Password Options

Type of NetWare Server	Option
NetWare 3.x Bindery Server	Setpass utility
NetWare 4.x NDS tree	Ctrl+Alt+Delete keys and change domain to NetWare or Compatible Network

Lab 12-2   Changing Your Password on a 3.x NetWare Bindery Server

1. **Go to the command prompt and type** cd\public **to change to the drive for the NetWare server.**

2. **Type** setpass **and then the name of the NetWare server on which you want to change your password.**

3. **Change your password and confirm it.**

   If prompted, press Y and then press Enter to change your password on other NetWare servers that also use your old password.

To change your password on a 3.x NetWare Server that is not running in Bindery Emulation, you can use the Setpass utility that is run from a command line.

Lab 12-3   Changing Your Password on a 4.x NetWare NDS Tree

1. **Press Ctrl+Alt+Delete to get to the Change Password dialog box (shown in Figure 12-5).**

2. **In the Domain box, click NetWare or Compatible Network.**

3. **Change your password and confirm it.**

   You've changed your password for all NDS trees to which you are currently connected.

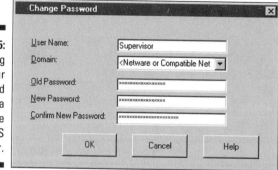

Figure 12-5:
Changing
your
password
on a
NetWare
4.*x* NDS
Server.

When you're connected to a NetWare 3.*x* Bindery, you can change your password with the NetWare Servers that you are currently connected to only. For NDS, you can change your password on that NetWare Server and not worry about any further passwords until you access resources on another tree entirely.

Running command-line utilities in CSNW

Client Service for NetWare supports many utilities and doesn't support a few others. You can use these MS-DOS 16-bit-compatible NetWare utilities:

Colorpal	pstat
Dspace	remove
Fconsole	revoke
Filer	rights
Flag	security
Flagdir	send
Grant	setpass
Help	settts
Listdir	slist
Map	syscon*

Ncopy   tlist

Ndir   userlist

pconsole   Whoami

psc

*Enables bringing up the System Console of a NetWare Server.

Memorizing just the MS-DOS 16-bit NetWare utilities that don't work may be faster for you:

Attach   Rconsole

Capture   Session

Login   Volinfo

Logout

Prep Test

1 What are some of the configurable options for Client Service for NetWare? (Choose all that apply.)

A ❑ Logon Script Processing

B ❑ Preferred Server

C ❑ Auto-Reconnect Feature

D ❑ Banner Page

2 What do you need to have set in order to make sure that your logon scripts run when you have Client Service for NetWare installed? (Choose all that apply.)

A ❑ Correct Preferred Server

B ❑ SAP Advertising

C ❑ TCP/IP protocol installed

D ❑ Enable Logon Script Processing

3 You have to connect a SQL Server database that is running on a NetWare server from your NT Workstation. What must be installed on your workstation to connect to the SQL Server?

A ○ Microsoft's Client for NetWare Networks

B ○ File and Print Services for NetWare

C ○ NWLink Protocol Compatible Transport

D ○ TCP/IP Protocol

4 What does the Preferred Server option in Client Service for NetWare signify?

A ○ Load Balancing for NetWare's application server

B ○ Logon Server that validates your user account when you try to access resources

C ○ Your default NetWare print server

D ○ IntraNetWare Web server

5 Which command-line utilities can be run from your NT Workstation if you have Client Service for NetWare installed? (Choose all that apply.)

A ❑ Syscon

B ❑ Logon

C ❑ QOTD

D ❑ Attach

E ❑ Logout

F ❑ Setpass

6 What steps must you perform if you want to change your password from your NT Workstation on your NetWare NDS tree? (Choose all that apply.)

A ❑ Press Ctrl+Alt+Delete.

B ❑ Click Change Password.

C ❑ Click Syscon.

D ❑ In Domain, click NetWare or Compatible Network.

E ❑ Click SAP Advertising.

F ❑ Execute HTML 3.0 Password Changer.

7 Amy is a graphics design artist and wants to allow for a separator page between her print jobs that she sends to her NetWare print server from her NT Workstation. What does she have to configure?

A ◯ Allow Banner Page.

B ◯ Configure the Printer Manually.

C ◯ Install New Printer Drivers.

D ◯ Reboot the Print Server.

8 You have installed NWLink and Client Service for NetWare on your NT Workstation, but you still cannot connect to your NetWare Server. What could be the problem for not connecting to your NetWare Server? (Choose all that apply.)

A ❑ Incorrect frame type.

B ❑ Client Service for NetWare is not installed properly.

C ❑ Did not install File and Print Services for NetWare.

D ❑ Incorrect preferred server.

9 Sean wants to change his password on his NetWare 3.x Server that's running Bindery Emulation. How can he change his password if he has Client Service for NetWare installed on his NT Workstation?

A ◯ Sequential Access Protocol.

B ◯ Service Advertising Protocol.

C ◯ Ctrl+Alt+Delete.

D ◯ Setpass utility.

E ◯ Advertise his existence on his network.

Answers

1 *A, B, C, D.* Using Client Services for NetWare has many advantages: a high-performance 32-bit client, an auto-reconnect feature, Plug and Play awareness, full integration with the Windows NT 4.0 interface, the ability to run NetWare command-line utilities, user-level security, NetWare logon command processor, and Point and Print Support. *See "Integrating with Client Service for NetWare (CSNW)."*

2 *A, D.* To make sure that your NetWare server will process your logon scripts, you need to make sure that you have the correct Preferred Server indicated and the Enable Logon Scripts check box checked in the Client for NetWare Networks applet. See *"Integrating with Client Service for NetWare (CSNW)."*

3 *C.* If you need to connect to a NetWare server that is running a client/server application such as SQL Server, all you need is NWLink to access the server. *See "Linking Up to NetWare."*

4 *B.* The Preferred Server is the Logon Server for your NetWare networks. This server authenticates you on the network. You need to log on to this server to become part of the NetWare environment. *See "Installing and configuring CSNW."*

5 *A, F.* You can't run Attach, Logon, Logout, QOTD, or Map. *See "Running command-line utilities in CSNW."*

6 *A, B, D.* Changing your password on a NetWare 4.*x* Server is very similar to changing your password in a Windows NT domain. *See "Changing your password in CSNW."*

7 *A.* You can configure all your printing options from the Client Service for NetWare icon located in the Control Panel. *See "Table 12-1."*

8 *A, D.* By default, NWLink automatically detects the frame type used by the network adapter card to which it is bound. If NWLink detects no network traffic or any frames of type 802.2, it sets the frame type to 802.2. Otherwise, it sets the frame type to match the frames it detects. *See "Frame type."*

9 *D.* If you're connected to a NetWare 3.*x* Server running Bindery Emulation, you can connect to that server and change your password by using the setpass utility from the cd\public directory. *See "Changing your password in CSNW."*

Part V
Connecting to the Internet

"Sales on the Web site are down. I figure the server's chi is blocked, so we're fudgin' around the feng shui in the computer room, and if that doesn't work, Ronnie's got a chant that should do it."

In this part . . .

With the Internet taking off, everyone is talking about TCP/IP, which is the network transport you need for communicating with other computers on networks far and wide. Part of connecting to the Internet is knowing how to configure all the options of the TCP/IP client for your NT Workstation: your IP address, Subnet Mask, and Default Gateway, for starters. Knowing how to configure your NT Workstation as a TCP/IP client is essential for the exam and is covered by some of the labs in the upcoming chapters.

While on the subject of TCP/IP, you should be familiar with Peer Web Services (PWS), included with NT Workstation. PWS is a diluted version of Internet Information Server, which comes as part of Windows NT 4.0 Server. For the most part, PWS gives you just what Internet Information Server does, but with some minor adjustments to limit the number of concurrent connections and fewer performance-monitoring tools. Be sure to know how to configure PWS for the exam — features, options, and Web services.

Chapter 13

Do You See What I TCP/IP?

Exam Objectives

▶ Using various configurations to install Windows NT Workstation as a TCP/IP client

*T*his chapter deals with the main protocol that Windows NT 4.0 Workstation uses. You get an overview of the TCP/IP protocol and some of the features and options that you should know how to configure for the exam.

The TCP/IP protocol suite is made up of many different individual protocols and services. Some of these protocols and services are integrated into a Windows NT network and are used as part of your NT Workstation to dynamically assign network protocols and name resolution or test out TCP/IP connectivity.

To fully understand how TCP/IP works, you must know how TCP/IP integrates into the OSI model, which represents how networking actually works and communicates with various protocols. You also need to know the various NT Workstation tools available that help you work with TCP/IP.

Quick Assessment

Use various configurations to install Windows NT Workstation as a TCP/IP client

1   A _____ mask separates the network ID from the host ID.

2   _____ takes care of name resolution for Windows computers to IP addresses.

3   True/False: With DHCP, you have to specify your IP address for your workstation.

4   _____ is used to map host names to IP addresses.

5   Name three TCP/IP protocols located in the Internet layer.

6   Your _____ identifies your computer on the network.

7   If you are going to connect to other networks, you have to configure your _____.

8   True/False: You can still use TCP/IP to communicate with other computers if you don't have your subnet mask configured.

9   True/False: The TCP/IP protocol is made up of a suite of protocols.

10   You configure all your TCP/IP properties from the _____ icon in the Control Panel.

11   The _____ protocol maps Mac addresses to remote IP addresses.

12   TCP/IP stands for _____ Protocol/_____ Protocol.

13   TCP/IP is the backbone for the _____.

Answers

1   *Subnet.* See "Subnet Mask."

2   *Windows Internet Naming Service.* See "Name resolution."

3   *False.* See "Configuring via DHCP."

4   *Domain Name Server.* See "Name resolution."

5   *ARP; IP; ICMP.* See "Internet layer."

6   *IP address.* See "IP address."

7   *Default gateway.* See "Default Gateway."

8   *False.* See "Subnet Mask."

9   *True.* See "TCP/IP Overview."

10   *Network.* See "TCP/IP Configuration."

11   *ARP.* See "Internet layer."

12   *Transmission Control; Internet.* See "TCP/IP Overview."

13   *Internet.* See "TCP/IP Overview."

TCP/IP Overview

TCP/IP (Transmission Control Protocol/Internet Protocol) has gained most of its acceptance (popularity would be too strong a sentiment) through its wide use for Internet communication; this protocol is *the* Internet protocol.

The following list summarizes the advantages of the TCP/IP protocol:

- Provides connectivity across operating systems and hardware platforms
- Serves as the Internet backbone; you connect to the Internet using TCP/IP
- Is a routable protocol, meaning that you use it to talk to other networks through routers
- Is very popular — think of all the computers on the Internet
- Is a required protocol for some applications
- Provides connectivity across operating systems and hardware platforms; for example, Windows NT can FTP to a UNIX workstation via TCP/IP
- Supports Simple Network Management Protocol (SNMP), which is used to troubleshoot problems on the network
- Supports Dynamic Host Configuration Protocol (DHCP), which is used for Dynamic IP addressing
- Supports Windows Internet Name Service (WINS), which resolves Windows NetBIOS names on the network

TCP/IP and the OSI Layers

Just when you thought it was safe to come back to your computer, the OSI model shows up again. But don't worry; the OSI Model is being supplied for background purposes only and to give you an idea of how the OSI model is integrated throughout the TCP/IP protocol suite. Several different protocols are connected to one another throughout the OSI model. This connectivity lets the TCP/IP protocol suite communicate with other protocols that are tied in throughout the various layers of the OSI model.

Although you don't have to know all seven layers of the OSI model for this exam, you should at least be familiar with the four layers of the TCP/IP model and how they are all connected. Check out Figure 13-1 for a visual of the OSI model and the TCP/IP protocol.

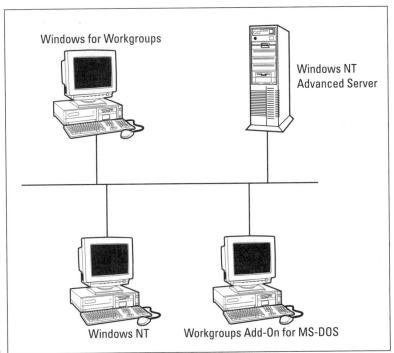

Windows NT
Advanced Server

Windows NT   Workgroups Add-On for MS-DOS

Figure 13-1:
How TCP/IP
integrates
with the OSI
Model.

The layers of the TCP/IP model are as follows. To remember these layers, think *ATIN:*

✔ *A*pplication layer

✔ *T*ransport layer

✔ *I*nternet layer

✔ *N*etwork layer

Network layer

This layer is where everything starts for TCP/IP. The Network layer is responsible for grabbing frames off the network card from the network and vice versa. These network transports can be a variety of different types, such as Ethernet or Token Ring. All the Network layer information is proprietary to how the TCP/IP protocol operates.

Internet layer

The Internet layer of the OSI model is made up of three protocols:

- **Address Resolution Protocol (ARP)** is the protocol used when you try to locate another computer on your network. ARP first looks in its ARP cache and compares IP address to MAC address in the attempt to locate the remote computer. ARP's job is to determine the MAC address for the remote computer. You can think of this protocol as the first line in the TCP/IP protocol suite.

- **Internet Protocol (IP)** is the protocol that has been described as the mailroom of the TCP/IP stack because here is where packet sorting and delivery take place. At this layer, each incoming or outgoing packet is in charge of routing to different networks.

- **Internet Control Message Protocol (ICMP)** is the error-checking protocol on the Internet layer. ICMP also reports messages and errors regarding network packet delivery.

Transport layer

The Transport layer is made up of both the TCP and UDP protocols. These two protocols are a foundation as to how the TCP/IP protocol applications will work on the Application layer.

- **TCP** is a connection-oriented protocol, which means that when you send a packet using TCP, the packet is guaranteed to get to its destination and return confirmation of receipt. Before TCP sends packet information with a remote system, it begins a session to ensure delivery. Some applications that use TCP are FTP, HTTP, and GOPHER.

- **UDP** is a connectionless-oriented protocol, which means that once a packet is sent, you have no guarantee that the packet delivery will reach its destination in one piece and no confirmation of receipt is sent back to the sender. UDP is essentially a "fire and forget" protocol; it's an unreliable, best-effort protocol. Some applications that use UDP are TFTP and SNMP and, yes Vanna, I would like a vowel.

Application layer

The Application layer is part of a set of Application Programming Interfaces (APIs) that are provided with TCP/IP. These APIs give programmers a set of guidelines to use when programming for the TCP/IP protocol. Think of this layer as being where all your applications are run.

Three APIs make up the Application layer:

- ✓ **Windows Sockets** provide a standard interface between socket-based applications and various TCP/IP protocols.
- ✓ **NetBT** provides a programming interface for NetBIOS naming and session standards.
- ✓ **NetBIOS API set** provides a standard interface for NetBIOS-based applications and TCP/IP protocol.

The Application layer is also joined by various TCP/IP utilities, such as FTP, Ping, Tracert, and NBTSTAT.

TCP/IP Configuration

When you install the TCP/IP protocol, you still need to configure all the different options before your workstation can talk to other computers on the network. These options make up all the features that you have to become comfortable with. The NT Workstation exam specifically asks how to configure certain settings for the TCP/IP protocol.

Your NT Workstation becomes configured for TCP/IP in one of two ways: either as the benefactor of a DHCP configuration, or through a manual configuration of the TCP/IP settings.

Configuring via DHCP

Dynamic Host Configuration Protocol (DHCP) is a service provided by a Windows NT Server to allocate IP addresses. A DHCP server on your network maintains and dynamically allocates IP configuration information to computers requesting IP addresses.

When you are assigned a DHCP address, you receive all the TCP/IP information that was configured on the DHCP server, including subnet masks, DNS, WINS, default gateway, or any other IP information that you configure. DHCP is a great way to administer your IP address information from a central location.

If you're using DHCP, you don't have to manually enter any IP information on your computer.

If you're using DHCP, any manually entered IP options have priority over the DHCP settings.

Manually configuring TCP/IP

If you're not going to be using DHCP to get your TCP/IP configuration information, you're going to need to manually configure your TCP/IP settings. This includes setting your TCP/IP address, Subnet Mask, Default Gateway, and any type of name resolution that you need on your network. Get very familiar with Lab 13-1, which explains how to manually configure the TCP/IP protocol; you need to know this information for the exam.

Lab 13-1   Installing and Manually Configuring the TCP/IP Protocol

1. **In Control Panel⇨Network, click the Protocols tab and click the Add button.**

2. **Navigate to the TCP/IP protocol and configure these four options:**

   • **IP address information**

   • **Subnet Mask**

   • **Default Gateway**

   • **WINS and/or DNS for name resolution**

3. **Reboot for the changes to take effect.**

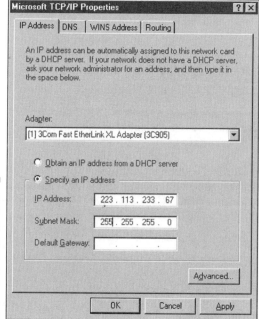

Figure 13-2:
An IP
Address
and the
Subnet
Mask for
your
computer.

IP address

The IP address can be described as your personal house number; it distinguishes you from other computers on the network. Each TPC/IP host is identified on your network by an IP address. Figure 13-2 shows an example of an IP address.

Each IP address is unique on your network. Here are the characteristics of an IP address:

- Made up of 32 bits and broken up into four individual 8-bit octets. Each octet is divided from the others by a period and represents a number between 1 and 255. The leftmost octet is numbered between 1 and 223.

- Has two parts:

  - **Network ID:** All computers on the same physical network have the same network ID.

  - **Host ID:** The host ID is what identifies the computer on the network.

Subnet Mask

Because an IP address consists of 32 individual bits in four quadrants, you need something to mask the host ID from the network ID. That's what the Subnet Mask does. In other words, the Subnet Mask separates the ones and zeroes that make up your IP address into a logical number that identifies the IP address for the workstation.

Therefore, a large corporation with many computers on the network can divide one large network into many different subnets, and thus divide and expand the network. A Subnet Mask is most useful when you're configuring computers using the TCP/IP protocol on a routed network.

Figure 13-2 also shows what a subnet mask is good for.

Default Gateway

To communicate with other computers on remote networks, you must have a Default Gateway configured in your TCP/IP settings. A Default Gateway is essentially a router whose job is to receive packets from one subnet and route them to their destination. A Default Gateway acts as a type of traffic light and sends packets in the right direction to other networks.

If you want to communicate with other computers on the Internet, you must have a Default Gateway configured, to ensure that your protocols are routed to the correct remote network.

You can think of the default gateway on your computer as a door to other networks. Figure 13-3 gives a look at a configured Default Gateway.

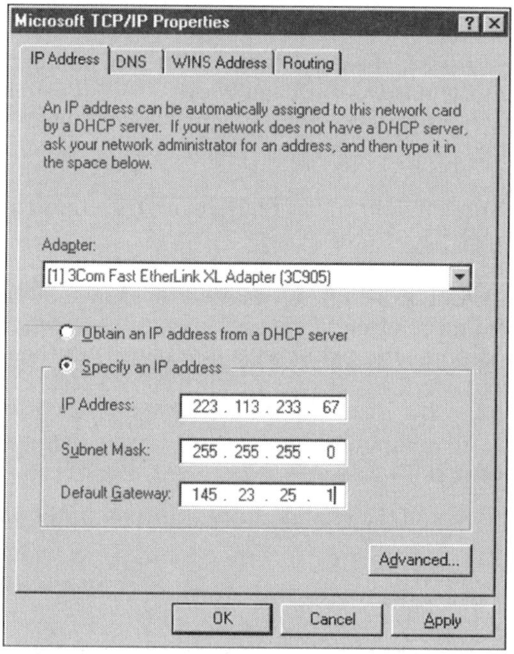

Figure 13-3:
The Default
Gateway
for your
computer.

Name resolution

Name resolution is used to resolve IP addresses to computers on your network. Name resolution is taken care of by either a Windows Internet Naming Service or a Domain Name Server. You can implement either server depending on what type of network you are going to be participating in.

✔ **Domain Name Server (DNS)** performs name resolution for IP addresses to host names. Although computers communicate with one another via their IP addresses, remembering a "computer name" is much easier. A DNS has a database full of these friendly computer names, and when contacted, the DNS resolves the IP address of the host name. You need to have a DNS configured if you're going to be connected directly to the Internet. You can see in Figure 13-4 how to configure your DNS server for your NT Workstation.

✔ **Windows Internet Name Service (WINS)** maintains a database of IP addresses to NetBIOS computer names. It is also used to register NetBIOS names on the network so that they can be resolved later. The main function of a WINS server is to eliminate broadcast traffic on a Windows network. Just as a DNS resolves IP addresses to host names, WINS resolves IP addresses to NetBIOS names. When a computer is configured to use a WINS server, the client computer contacts the WINS whenever it cannot resolve the name on its own. Every time a WINS client boots up, it registers itself with the WINS server so that the WINS server has an up-to-date database of registered IP address information. Figure 13-5 demonstrates how to configure your WINS server for your NT Workstation.

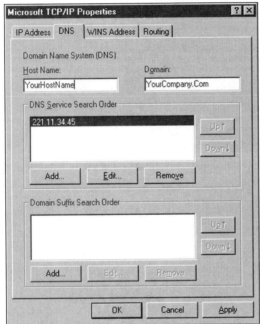

Figure 13-4:
DNS con-
figuration
for your
computer.

Reconfiguring TCP/IP

At some point while having the TCP/IP protocol installed on your computer, you will have to reconfigure some options, due to unforeseen circumstances on your network or a change in IP configuration. It's no problem, however. You can just make your changes and then reboot your system, and the changes are in effect. Whatever the case, you shouldn't feel uncomfortable changing some TCP/IP settings. You change TCP/IP options from the Network icon in the Control Panel.

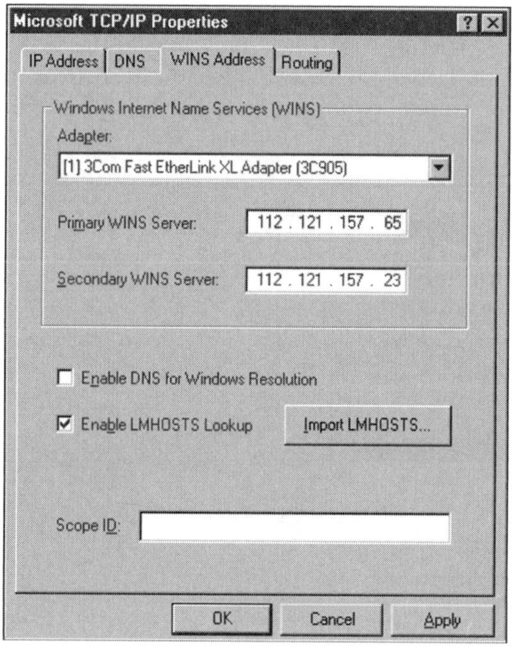

Microsoft TCP/IP Properties

IP Address | DNS | WINS Address | Routing

Windows Internet Name Services (WINS)

Adapter:

[1] 3Com Fast EtherLink XL Adapter (3C905)

Primary WINS Server: 112 . 121 . 157 . 65

Secondary WINS Server: 112 . 121 . 157 . 23

☐ Enable DNS for Windows Resolution

☑ Enable LMHOSTS Lookup   Import LMHOSTS...

Scope ID:

OK   Cancel   Apply

Figure 13-5:
Setting up
your WINS
server for
name
resolution.

TCP/IP Tools

Various TCP/IP tools are available to help solve some of your configuration and connectivity problems. These tools help resolve connectivity, check your IP routes, verify correct IP configuration, and display IP protocol statistics. You should become familiar with these tools because they come in handy when you have to troubleshoot a configuration issue.

Ping

The Packet Internet Groper Utility (ping) is used to verify connectivity with other computers running the TCP/IP protocol. You can also use this utility on *any* computer running the TCP/IP protocol. Ping works on both UNIX and Windows computers.

If you want to check connectivity with other computers, you can ping the other computer's IP address or computer name directly. In other situations, you can ping the Default Gateway if you can't connect to other networks, or the computer name of the destination computer to check for name-resolution problems.

This utility has many useful functions to ensure connectivity in all types of situations.

Tracert

When you use the tracert utility, you can see the route that the network packets travel from your workstation. You can also use this utility to verify the route that each network packet is taking if you're having problems with packets timing out before they reach their destination.

Ipconfig

To get a quick peek at your IP address information, you can use the command-line utility ipconfig. This utility gives you a detailed summary of all your IP info for your host name, IP address, Subnet Mask, and Default Gateway. All you have to do is bring up a command window and type ipconfig at the command-line.

Prep Test

1 What are some characteristics of the TCP/IP protocol? (Choose all that apply.)

A ❑ Not routable.

B ❑ Connects to the Internet.

C ❑ Supports WINS for name resolution.

D ❑ Only used in very small LANs.

2 Holly has just installed and configured the TCP/IP protocol onto her NT Workstation. She has rebooted her computer and can connect to computers on her local subnet, but she is having problems accessing remote computers. What could be her problem?

A ○ WINS

B ○ DNS

C ○ Incorrect Default Gateway

D ○ Bad network packets

3 Gary has just installed the TCP/IP protocol onto his NT Workstation. He is having trouble connecting to other computers via their computer names but is not having any trouble accessing with their IP addresses. What could be wrong? (Choose all that apply.)

A ❑ Incorrect Subnet Mask

B ❑ Incorrect Default Gateway

C ❑ Wrong DNS

D ❑ Wrong WINS

4 Domain Name Server performs name resolution from IP addresses to which type of computer name?

A ○ Windows computer name

B ○ Friendly name

C ○ Host name

D ○ UNIX name

5 Which TCP/IP utility commands can you use to make sure that you have connectivity with other computers using TCP/IP?

A ○ nbtstat

B ○ tracert

C ○ ping

D ○ ipconfig

6 Which TCP/IP utility can you use to view all of your TCP/IP configured information?

A ○ nbtstat

B ○ tracert

C ○ ping

D ○ ipconfig

7 Lorna installs TCP/IP on her NT Workstation and is not using DHCP. Which TCP/IP parameters must she configure to allow connectivity with both local and remote computers? (Choose all that apply.)

A ❑ Subnet Mask

B ❑ Default Gateway

C ❑ WINS proxy

D ❑ LMHOSTS file

E ❑ RFC

F ❑ Internet Explorer

G ❑ IP address

8 Domain Name Server maps _____ to _____.

A ❑ Host name

B ❑ Windows name

C ❑ Mac address

D ❑ WINS address

E ❑ IP address

F ❑ WINS proxy

9 Which service does a DHCP server provide on a TCP/IP network?

A ○ Name resolution

B ○ Routing

C ○ Automatic assignment and maintenance of TCP/IP address information

D ○ Server installation

10 Which three TCP/IP protocols make up the Internet layer of the OSI model?

A ○ ICMP

B ○ FTP

C ○ ping

D ○ ip

E ○ ARP

F ○ tracert

G ○ gopher

H ○ TFTP

Prep Test

1 *B, C.* TCP/IP is the protocol of the Internet. This protocol has many features, including routing and support for WINS, DNS, FTP, and DHCP. *See "TCP/IP Overview."*

2 *C.* In order to communicate with computers on remote networks, you have to successfully configure the default gateway. The default gateway routes the network packets to their destination network. *See "Default Gateway."*

3 *C, D.* The problem is with name resolution because Gary can connect with the IP address, just not with the friendly computer name. The IP addresses cannot be resolved, so connectivity has failed. *See "Name resolution."*

4 *C.* A DNS maps IP addresses to host names on a network. When you want to resolve a host name to an IP address, a DNS must be present. *See "Name resolution."*

5 *C.* To test connectivity with other computers using the TCP/IP protocol, you can ping each workstation with its host name, IP address, or NetBIOS name. *See "Ping."*

6 *D.* To gain quick access to your TCP/IP configuration, you can use the command-line utility ipconfig, which is great for checking whether you've configured all your settings when troubleshooting a TCP/IP installation. *See "IPConfig."*

7 *A, B, G.* If you're not using DHCP, you have to manually enter your IP address information, including your IP address, subnet mask, and default gateway for remote connectivity. *See "Manually configuring TCP/IP."*

8 *E, A.* A DNS's job is to map IP addresses to host names for name resolution. A WINS server maps IP addresses to NetBIOS computer names. *See "Name resolution."*

9 *C.* A DHCP server's function is to dynamically allocate and maintain IP address information to client computers on the network. When a client computer requests a DHCP address, the DHCP server sends the IP information that was configured on the server. *See "Configuring via DHCP."*

10 *A, D, E.* The Internet layer is made up of ARP for address resolution, ICMP for error checking, and IP for addressing and routing information. *See "Internet layer."*

Chapter 14

The Internet and Intranets: Walking the Wire

Exam Objectives

▶ Configuring Microsoft Peer Web Services in a given situation

*T*his chapter details the relationship between Windows NT 4.0 Workstation and the publishing and sharing of documents with other computers on personal intranets and on the Internet. Windows NT 4.0 Workstation has many different uses on the Internet as both a modified Web server and as a client.

Windows NT 4.0 Workstation includes Peer Web Services (PWS), a modified version of Internet Information Server (IIS) as a configurable network service. This modified version of IIS controls the WWW, FTP, and Gopher services on your NT Workstation, services that are necessary for sharing, publishing, and transferring your files over your intranet or the Internet. PWS is a great tool as an introductory Web server or a development platform. For the exam, make sure that you know the differences between Internet Information Server, which is included with NT 4.0 Server, and Peer Web Services, which is included with NT 4.0 Workstation.

You need to know how to configure Microsoft Peer Web Services in a given situation for the NT Workstation exam, so you should make sure that you know PWS inside and out. The rest of the information provided in this chapter is mainly background. This background information helps to give you a feel for how NT Workstation fits into the role of Web provider.

Quick Assessment

Configure
Microsoft
Peer Web
Services

1 Name the three Web services that are part of Peer Web Services.

2 You cannot create _____ servers with Peer Web Services.

3 True/False: HTTP allows you to transfer files over the Internet.

4 Name three differences between PWS and IIS.

5 A _____ server performs name resolution from IP addresses to host names.

6 The _____ application lets you log on to a remote computer using the TCP/IP protocol.

7 True/False: When using Peer Web Services, you can log your data to a SQL Server/ODBC database.

8 Peer Web Services runs on _____ and _____ computers.

9 If you're connecting directly to the Internet, you need a(n) _____ IP address.

Answers

1 *WWW; FTP; Gopher.* See "Using Peer Web Services (PWS)."

2 *Virtual.* See "Limitations of Peer Web Services."

3 *False.* See "Using Peer Web Services (PWS)."

4 *Lack of virtual servers; logging to ODBC; access control via IP address.* See Table 14-1.

5 *DNS.* See "Name resolution."

6 *Telnet.* See "Using Peer Web Services (PWS)."

7 *False.* See "Limitations of Peer Web Services."

8 *NT Workstation; Windows 95.* See "Using Peer Web Services (PWS)."

9 *Unique (or valid).* See "Accessing the Internet with NT Workstation."

Accessing the Internet with NT Workstation

The stability of Windows NT and the security features built in make NT a popular choice for connecting to the Internet as either a client or as a server platform. Not only can you use your NT Workstation to run TCP/IP applications on a network, but more importantly, you can publish or share your documents as well. Windows NT Workstation is an extremely attractive choice for a client to support a secure TCP/IP network.

Windows NT Workstation supports either a direct LAN connection to the Internet or a Remote Access Service connection.

All these elements are required to connect to the Internet:

- ✔ Unique TCP/IP address
- ✔ Remote Access Service connection (modem or ISDN) or direct LAN connection (network card)
- ✔ Correctly configured default gateway
- ✔ Name resolution (DNS, WINS, LMHOST file, or HOST file)

Direct LAN Internet connection

With your direct connection to the Internet, the Internet is just a double-click away in any application. Having a direct connection to the Internet has a price, though: You *must* be using a valid TCP/IP address, which is unique to your workstation and identifies your computer on the network.

If you have a direct Internet connection, you are probably part of a LAN and have a default gateway configured so that you can communicate with other computers on remote networks. Your default gateway routes any network packets that are destined to other remote networks. All you have to do is make sure that your default gateway is configured, and off you go!

Remote-Access Service Internet connection

With Remote-Access Service (RAS), whenever you need to reach the Internet, you use RAS to connect to your dial-up server, which is connected to the Internet. Such a temporary connection to the Internet is usually described as a *dial-up* or *dial-up on demand.* This option is more relevant if you do not need continuous Internet access or you cannot afford a dedicated line. Most times when you use a temporary Internet connection, your dial-up server provides your TCP/IP information, such as IP address, Default Gateway, and either WINS or DNS servers.

Using Peer Web Services (PWS)

Peer Web Services (PWS) is required knowledge for the NT 4.0 Workstation exam. The PWS included with your Windows NT Workstation is a modified version of the Internet Information Server (IIS) included with NT Server. With PWS, you have all the benefits of the WWW, FTP, and Gopher services.

The two most common (and thus most testable) Peer Web Services used on an NT Workstation are

✓ **World Wide Web (WWW) Service** controls all access to your Web site; just as the Server service in Windows NT must be running for clients to connect to the server, the WWW service must be running for clients to access your Web site. If this service isn't running, you can't publish any documents from your NT Workstation.

Clients that are connected to the Internet and have Web browsers, such as Internet Explorer 4.0, send HTTP (HyperText Transfer Protocol) requests to the Web server they're trying to contact. The Web browser sends a simple GET command asking to download every file — every background image or graphic — on the Web page being contacted.

HTTP is very similar to the Gopher and FTP protocols in that it acts as a communications link to the Web server. The Gopher and FTP protocols can connect to Gopher; FTP and Web servers can connect to Web browsers; and HTTP can connect only from the Web server to Web browsers or vice versa.

Figure 14-1 shows an example of the screen you see when configuring the WWW for Peer Web Services.

✓ **File Transfer Protocol (FTP) Service:** FTP allows you to transfer files from one Internet machine to another. In order to transfer files by using the FTP protocol, you need several things:

• One major prerequisite is a client computer running TCP/IP. On this computer, you also need a client FTP application, along with an FTP server on the other end that you can connect to.

• If you're using the character-driven FTP application, you need to know where the files are that you want to transfer. If you're using a Graphical User Interface FTP application to transfer files, you can monitor your way until you decide on the file of your choice.

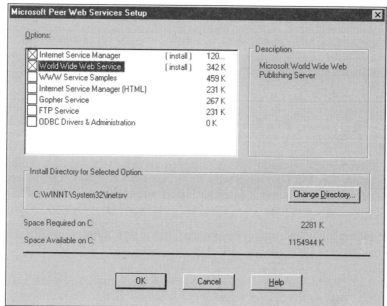

Figure 14-1:
Configuring
the WWW
Service
for PWS.

You won't see any information regarding the Gopher service on this exam.

Installation

Internet Service Manager is used to configure Peer Web Services that publish on the Internet, such as WWW, FTP, and Gopher services. When installing NT Workstation for the first time, you have the option of installing PWS from the Windows NT 4.0 Workstation setup or installing PWS after your workstation has finished building.

Neither choice offers a performance gain; you may want to choose the second option — installing PWS after you've already installed your NT Workstation — just to give yourself time to plan the structure for your WWW, FTP, and Gopher folders and plan your security strategy as well. You can see in Figure 14-2 that you add PWS through the Network Control Panel.

The PWS installation is a simple process of following the steps of the Installation wizard. After you begin installation, you can specify which services you want to install and where you want to place each root folder. Study Lab 14-1 — that information is on the exam.

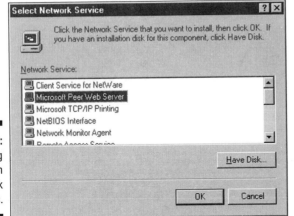

Figure 14-2:
Adding
PWS in
Network
Services.

Lab 14-1   Installing Peer Web Services

1. From Control Panel⇨Network, click the Services tab and click the Add button.

The Select Network Service dialog box appears.

2. Choose Microsoft Peer Web Server.

The Microsoft Peer Web Services Setup dialog box appears.

3. Verify that the correct source-file location is displayed and then check the options that you want installed.

Normally, the source file is in the I386 folder on the NT Workstation CD.

See Figure 14-3 for an example of where you decide which Network Services you need to install (WWW, FTP, or Gopher).

4. When prompted to start creating the appropriate installation folder, click Yes.

You may accept the default folder names for the services or modify them. You can see in Figure 14-4 where you setup your Internet publishing directories.

If you installed the Gopher service and haven't assigned an Internet domain name to the computer, you're prompted to assign a domain name to your computer.

If you installed ODBC drivers and administration, you're prompted to close the Control Panel and select the drivers that you want to install.

PWS will not recognize any 16-bit ODBC drivers. If PWS detects any 16-bit drivers on your computer, it asks whether to convert them to 32-bit.

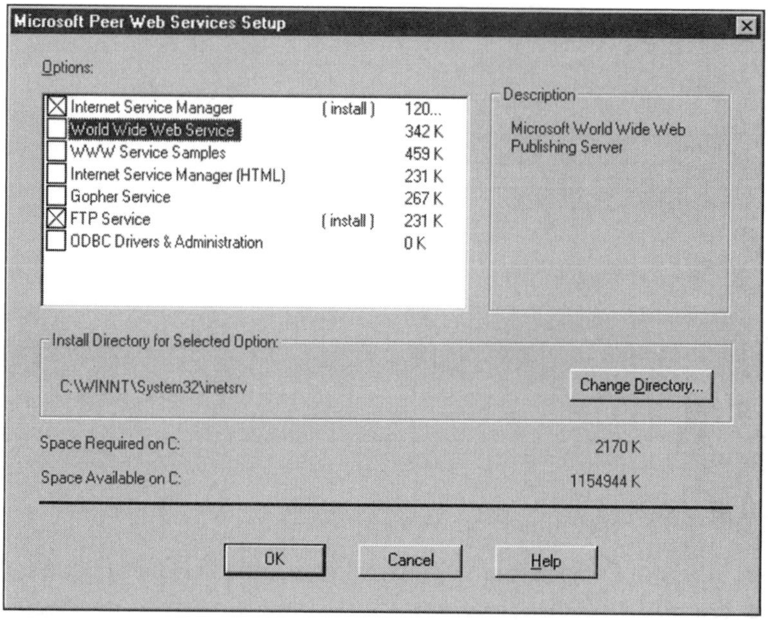

Figure 14-3:
Selecting
the services
you want
to install.

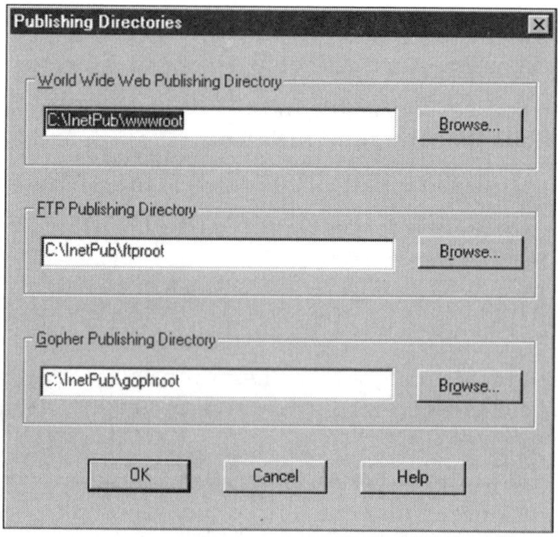

Figure 14-4:
Setting up
Internet
publishing
directories
in NT.

5. Click OK to confirm that the Peer Web Services have been installed; then click the Close button in the Network dialog box, and you're done.

After PWS finishes loading, you can install any Service Packs that you may require. Whenever you install a network service, you're supposed to re-install any Service Packs that you've installed on your workstation so that your newer files can be copied over your new network services. The files found on Service Packs (such as SP3) are new updates and need to be re-installed in case a network service accidentally replaced an updated file.

Limitations of Peer Web Services

Peer Web Services suffers under some of the limitations that make up your NT Workstation, such as concurrent connections, although you have the ability to publish, transfer, and share your documents through your intranet or the Internet.

Peer Web Services may be okay for a development environment or a small network, but it has significant limitations:

- ✔ Can't create virtual servers
- ✔ Can't control IP address access
- ✔ Can't log on to ODBC database
- ✔ Limited network bandwidth

Make sure that you know the difference between Peer Web Services and the less limited Internet Information Server that is provided with NT Server. See Table 14-1.

Table 14-1	Comparing IIS and PWS
IIS Feature	*PWS Limitation*
Access control via IP addresses	Restricts access via the IP address of the client
Virtual servers (multiple home folders for different domain names)	Creates virtual folders, either local or remote, that are located on the logical server
Bandwidth throttling	Sets a level of bandwidth for Peer Web Services
Logging to SQL/ODBC database	Detailed logging for Peer Web Services

Advantages of Peer Web Services

Peer Web Services is an integral part of your Windows NT Workstation operating system, which gives PWS a significant advantage over other Web applications that need to be customized in order to run well under Windows NT 4.0 Workstation.

Another example of the integration between Peer Web Services and NT 4.0 is the creation of the IUSR_ComputerName account. This account is installed automatically when PWS is set up and is the default anonymous account for your FTP and WWW services. This account is visible within the User Manager and should be paid attention to.

Data protection

When you provide access to your data over the Internet, you're leaving yourself open to all types of security trouble. Here are some ways to protect your data and your server:

- Carefully plan the outline for your Web access on your NT Workstation. This plan includes file security, authentication, and accessibility for your Web server. Because you'll be publishing your files for everyone to see, you want to make sure that only people with the necessary privileges can edit the Web pages.

- Use NTFS partitions for all your Web data. With NTFS, you can make sure that you lock down your file system and prevent any accidental changes.

- The security considerations for this account are the same as the Guest account that is created during Windows NT 4.0 Workstation setup. If you are using PWS for a secured Web site, you may want to consider disabling the default user account (IUSR_ComputerName) and using Microsoft Challenge Authentication Protocol (MS CHAP).

- MS CHAP is a security option that's part of PWS.

Switching to MS CHAP security will have your Web site authenticate any user who tries to access the Web page (by using Windows NT Security). Look for this option in an exam question!

You're lacking some of the privileges that are used with IIS. Peer Web Services is suitable for a small intranet or development environment but shouldn't be used for heavy access.

Name resolution

You have so many computers on your local intranet and on the Internet that remembering the right IP address for each one would be impossible. That's why you usually use a friendly computer name instead of a TCP/IP address when accessing a remote computer. To allow this name substitution, different types of servers perform name resolution — they keep track of each TCP/IP address and the friendly computer name associated with it. So when you try to access a remote computer, your name-resolution server resolves the required name to the IP address. If you're connecting directly to the Internet, you need DNS for name resolution. If you're using PWS on an intranet, you can use either DNS (resolves Host names) or WINS (resolves Windows NetBIOS names) for name resolution.

WINS

The Windows Internet Name Service (WINS) provides a dynamic database of NetBIOS names with their IP addresses. (The friendly computer name is just one of many NetBIOS names.) So instead of broadcasting for name resolution, a network client contacts the WINS server, and WINS searches its database and informs the client of the correct address.

DNS

Normally, computers communicate via their MAC (Media Access Control) addresses on a network. To communicate by name, some form of name resolution from TCP/IP address to computer name is necessary. Domain Name Server (DNS) maps TCP/IP addresses to computer host names on the network. DNS uses a distributed database over hundreds of different computers resolving computer host names, which helps locate computers all over the Internet.

Prep Test

1 Olive is having trouble deciding whether to install NT Server with IIS or NT Workstation using Peer Web Services. What are the limitations she faces if she chooses PWS? (Choose all that apply.)

A ❑ No logging to SQL/ODBC.

B ❑ Ten concurrent users.

C ❑ Can't create virtual servers.

D ❑ Can't restrict access via TCP/IP.

2 Gary has just installed his PWS server so that his clients can access his Web site on his company's intranet. For some reason, his clients cannot connect to his Web server by its host name. What can he install to solve this problem?

A ○ DNS

B ○ DHCP

C ○ WINS

D ○ SQL Server

3 Which user account is automatically created when you install Peer Web Services?

A ○ Guest

B ○ SMS_Installer

C ○ IUSR_ComputerName

D ○ Administrator

4 Your boss wants you to load PWS onto your brand-new Pentium II workstation to do some developmental testing. Where do you install Peer Web Services? (Choose all that apply.)

A ❑ Windows NT Setup

B ❑ Control Panel⇨System

C ❑ Control Panel⇨Network

D ❑ Control Panel⇨Internet

5 Which ODBC driver is incompatible with Peer Web Services?

A ○ 16-bit

B ○ 32-bit

C ○ Oracle

D ○ SQL

6 What functionality does the Windows Internet Name Service provide for your local intranet?

A ○ Remote connectivity

B ○ Logging to an SQL Server database

C ○ Network management

D ○ Name resolution

7 Which security feature do you use if you want to restrict users on your network from accessing a secured part of your Web site?

A ○ Microsoft Challenge Authentication Protocol

B ○ Clear text

C ○ Encryption

D ○ Nothing

E ○ Share permissions

8 Which protocol do the applications FTP, HTTP, and Telnet use to establish a remote connection?

A ○ NetBIOS

B ○ IPX

C ○ RIP for TCP/IP

D ○ TCP/IP

E ○ SPX

F ○ DLC

G ○ Streams

9 What must you have configured if your NT Workstation is directly connected to the Internet? (Choose all that apply.)

A ❑ Valid IP address

B ❑ Default gateway

C ❑ Routing protocol

D ❑ WINS

E ❑ DLC protocol

10 Which three Web services are included with Peer Web Services? (Choose all that apply.)

A ❑ Gopher

B ❑ TCP/IP

C ❑ WWW

D ❑ FTP

E ❑ Routing

Answers

1 *A, B, C,* and *D.* If you install PWS instead of IIS, you lose functionality of creating virtual servers, ten concurrent connections, logging to an ODBC data source, and IP address restrictions. *See "Limitations of Peer Web Services."*

2 *A.* If your clients cannot connect to your Web server, you may be having a name-resolution problem. You can install DNS to map TCP/IP addresses to host names on your network. *See "DNS."*

3 *C.* When you install IIS on your server, the IUSR_ComputerName account is automatically generated. Remember that if you install IIS on a domain controller, you're giving the IUSR_ComputerName account domain user rights. *See "Advantages of Peer Web Services."*

4 *A, C.* You can install IIS from Windows NT 4.0 Setup or from the Network applet in the Control Panel. *See "Installation."*

5 *A.* 16-bit drivers are not compatible with Peer Web Services. You can use only 32-bit drivers. *See "Installation."*

6 *D.* WINS provides name resolution for NetBIOS names. *See "WINS."*

7 *A.* If you want to protect your data, you can use MS CHAP on your folders. MS CHAP requires passwords from the users to ensure authentication. *See "Data protection."*

8 *D.* The TCP/IP protocol is used for all types of Internet applications, such as FTP, HTTP, Telnet, and Gopher. *See "Accessing the Internet with NT Workstation."*

9 *A, B.* If your NT Workstation is directly connected to the Internet, you must have a unique and valid TCP/IP address to identify your NT Workstation on the network and a default gateway configured to route any network packets to remote networks. *See "Accessing the Internet with NT Workstation."*

10 *A, C, D.* The WWW, FTP, and Gopher Services are installed by default. However, you decide which Web services you want to install. *See "Using Peer Web Services (PWS)."*

Chapter 15

Remote-Access Service: Commanding from Beyond

Exam Objectives

▶ Configuring and installing dial-up networking in a given situation

● ●

*R*emote-Access Service (or Dial Up Networking) is a big part of your NT Workstation. Like any meaningful relationship, it's important to stay in touch even though you're apart. RAS not only allows you to stay in touch with your network when you're away, but you can also use RAS to connect to other networks from other geographic locations. Sounds great to me. You never have to leave the house to do your work! Remote-Access Service allows you to become a remote node on your Local Area Network from any geographic location as long as long as you have a phone line or an ISDN connection to do so.

Many different features of Remote-Access Service are unique to Windows NT Workstation. A tremendous benefit to using Remote-Access Service with Windows NT is that you can take advantage of the Windows NT Security model. By using the Windows NT Security model, you won't have to worry about any unauthorized users accessing parts of your network that they shouldn't be. When users are authenticated with Remote-Access Service, they are authenticated as if they are part of the Local Area Network.

Windows NT provides a few troubleshooting tools in case you have any difficulties with RAS. For example, these tools supply a way to add counters with Performance Monitor and a logging feature for RAS. For this exam, you need to make sure that you understand how to use these tools to optimize your Remote-Access Service and troubleshoot any problems that might occur.

To do well on the exam, you need to understand all the configurable features and options for Remote-Access Service. Be sure to review the labs in this chapter, and you won't have too much trouble with RAS questions on the exam.

Quick Assessment

Configuring
and
installing
Dial Up
Networking

1   If you are going to connect to the Internet with RAS, you need to have the _____ protocol installed.

2   Quick. . . Name the three requirements before installing Remote-Access Service.

3   When you install RAS, you are automatically given new counters to monitor through _____ _____.

4   True/False: Multi-link allows you to cut your network bandwidth in half by splicing your network cable.

5   Quick. . . Name three different forms of Remote-Access Security.

6   True/False: Remote-Access Service allows you to take control over another workstation.

7   True/False: The Device.log file to help troubleshoot your RAS connection is located in your \Winnt\System32\Rep\Import\Scripts directory.

8   If you don't have a modem installed already, you can install one from the _____ icon in Control Panel.

9   True/False: You can enable Remote-Access Service logging on your NT Workstation.

10 True/False: You can use either TCP/IP, IPX/SPX, or NetBEUI to setup Virtual Private Networks.

11 You can specify dial-in permission for Remote-Access Service through the _____ _____ _____ _____.

Answers

1   TCP/IP. Check out "RAS and the Internet."

2   Network protocol (TCP/IP, IPX, NetBEUI), Modem Compatible device, Privileges. See "Remote Access Service (RAS) Requirements."

3   Performance Monitor. Check out "RAS Port and RAS Total Counters."

4   False. Take a look at "Using multi-link with communication devices."

5   Dial-back, Challenge/Response, Windows NT Security. See "RAS Security."

6   False. Look over "Remote Access versus Remote Control."

7   False. Go over "Dial-Up Networking Monitor and Device Log."

8   Modem. See "Installing RAS."

9   True. See "Dial-Up Networking Monitor and Device Log."

10   True. Check out the "Remote access via "Point-to-Point Tunneling."

11   Remote Access Service Admin. See the section on "Remote Access Service (RAS) Requirements."

Remote-Access Service (RAS) Requirements

Remote-Access Service enables you to be close to your network even when you are away from your office. By dialing in to your LAN, you can simulate that your workstation is on the LAN and part of the logical network even if you are in a distant geographic location. This is a great way to check on e-mail, grab a few extra files that you left at work, or check on your system from home.

Before you can install RAS on your workstation, you need to make sure that your workstation meets some requirements, or RAS will never work.

- ✔ The first requirement is a communication device that can use RAS. This device can be an analog modem, ISDN device, or any other type of modem that is configured and installed to use RAS. The exam specifically focuses on using devices with the multi-link feature in NT Workstation.

- ✔ The next requirement is properly configured network protocols and dial-up connections.

  - Ask your network administrator what protocol is used on the network's Remote-Access Servers so that your workstation can communicate with the server. This step is very important. Configuring network protocols for RAS can be a memorable experience — and I don't mean a pleasant memory — if you're not careful. The type of server and the type of access that your dial-up server allows is what determines the type of protocols you need to install.

  - Your dial-up connections can be to an NT Server or to any other operating system for which you can configure a dial-up account. You just need a common protocol on both the client and server, and a user account to use when dialing up. If those criteria are met, you should have no problem using Remote-Access Service.

- ✔ After you have Remote-Access Service and the necessary protocols installed on your NT Workstation, you need access permissions. These permissions guarantee that when you establish a connection with your dial-up server, you can be granted access. Your network administrator can take care of this for you on the server end. This chapter doesn't deal with permissions; check Chapters 8 and 9 for more details.

The following sections deal with the specific information that the exam tests you on.

Remember that you need to configure your modem through the Control Panel if you want to enable Remote-Access Service. You'll be prompted to install a modem as soon as you begin installing RAS. Remember the Control Panel!

Using multi-link with communication devices

A great new feature that is included with Remote-Access Service for Windows NT 4.0 Workstation is multi-link. You can achieve higher communications throughput with multi-link because it combines the bandwidth of two or more physical communications links, thus increasing your remote access bandwidth and throughput. Beam me up, Scotty!

With multi-link, you can combine your analog modems, ISDN paths, and even mixed analog and digital communications links on both a client and a server PC. This speeds up access to the Internet or to your intranet and cuts down on the amount of time you have to be remotely connected so that your multi-link costs for remote access are lower.

For example, say you have three 33.6 modems and three physical communication links hooked up to your NT Workstation. Windows NT Workstation with three modems can achieve a transfer rate of 100Kbps, which is a major performance improvement over conventional phone lines. Imagine — you could play two interactive video games while you download the Mona Lisa from the Louvre. What would Alexander Graham Bell say to that?

Multi-link is almost certain to be covered on your exam, so make sure that you understand the practices for setting up multi-link and the concepts for using more than one modem to generate extra bandwidth.

Remote access via Point-to-Point Tunneling

In the most common remote-access scenario, you connect your workstation to a remote network by making a Dial Up Networking connection to an Internet Service Provider (ISP) and then tunnel through the Internet to a Point-to-Point Tunneling Protocol (PPTP) server that is attached both to the Internet and to the remote network. After you are connected to the PPTP server, you can transparently access any public or private network that is connected to the PPTP server.

PPTP works with RAS that supports multi-protocol, virtual private networks (VPNs). Say this three times quickly and you pass the exam (just kidding, folks). PPTP uses a VPN device to establish and maintain private, secure communication between computers. It does this by using Remote-Access Service (RAS) and Dial Up Networking to communicate over dial-up lines and public and private networks. See Lab 15-1 for installing and configuring instructions.

A virtual private network (VPN) is an on-demand connection between two computers in different locations. The VPN consists of two computers (one computer at each end of the connection) and a route, or *tunnel,* over the public or private network. To ensure privacy and secure communication, data transmitted between the two computers is encrypted by the remote-access Point-to-Point Protocol (PPP) and then routed over a previously established dial-up or LAN connection by a PPTP device — which, in Windows NT and Windows 95 terminology, is referred to as a virtual private network or VPN.

PPTP offers the following advantages:

- ✔ Allows the creation of secure VPNs via the Internet
- ✔ Provides secure remote access because all data is encrypted
- ✔ Encapsulates network protocols allowing use of IPX or NetBEUI over the Internet

Above all, just remember that the PPTP connection over the Internet is encrypted and secure, and it works with any protocol (including, IP, IPX, and NetBEUI).

Lab 15-1   Installing and Configuring PPTP on a Windows NT-Based Client Workstation

1. **Navigate to the Control Panel and double-click the Network icon.**

2. **Click the Protocols tab and then click Add.**

3. **Now, select Point-To-Point Tunneling Protocol and click OK.**

   The PPTP files are copied from the installation directory, and the PPTP Configuration dialog box appears, as shown in Figure 15-1.

4. **Click the Number of Virtual Private Networks drop-down arrow and select the number of VPN devices you want the client to support. You can select a number between 1 and 256 for computers running Windows NT Workstation Version 4.0 or Windows NT Server Version 4.0. Typically, only one VPN is installed on a PPTP client.**

   Note: If the PPTP client is an ISP server running Windows NT Server Version 4.0, you can select multiple VNP devices as needed to simultaneously support the PPP clients using the ISP server to connect to a

PPTP server. Windows NT Server Version 4.0 supports a maximum number of 256 VPN devices.

5. Click OK, and then click OK in the Setup Message dialog box.

6. In the Remote Access Setup dialog box, you can do either of the following:

a) Temporarily stop installation of PPTP by clicking Cancel, closing Network, and then shutting down and restarting the computer. Note that you must perform the procedure described in the following section "Installing RAS" (Lab 15-2) to complete installation of PPTP.

b) Click Add to continue installation, adding the VPN device installed with PPTP to RAS. (See Step 5 of the procedure described in the following section.)

Figure 15-1:
Selecting
the PPTP
network
protocol on
the PPTP
client.

Installing RAS

With a little setup time, you can use Remote-Access Service to connect to your dial-up server and become a remote node on your network. All that is required is that you have a modem-compatible device, a network protocol installed, and a user account on your dial-up server. After these necessities are installed and configured, you can begin accessing your network from almost any location.

Be sure that you understand the following sections because they are covered on the MCSE exam.

Like any other network service that you have to install on your NT workstation, you can install Remote-Access Service from the Network icon in the Control Panel. From there, you can install, remove, or change any of your Remote-Access Settings that you have configured.

After you've opened the Control Panel and accessed the Network icon, the installation process can begin. When you install RAS for the first time, you will be prompted to install a modem-compatible device. If you already have one installed, you are all set. When you get past the modem setup phase, you still have to configure your workstation to dial out, receive, or both. Because you are using NT Workstation, you will probably be configuring Remote-Access Service for dial-out only. This is where you configure your NT Workstation to connect to a dial-up server.

To connect to a dial-up server, you have to make sure that you have a compatible network protocol installed on your computer. If your dial-up server is using NetBEUI, then you should install NetBEUI for Remote Access Service as well. It's a simple matter of making sure that you have the same protocol(s) on both the client and server.

Lab 15-2   Installing Remote-Access Service on Your NT Workstation

1. **Go into Control Panel and double-click the Network icon.**

2. **Click the Services tab and select Remote-Access Service.**

3. **If you don't already have a modem-compatible device installed, you are prompted to do so.**

4. **After you have installed and configured your modem, you can proceed to set up remote access.**

5. **When you get to the Remote-Access Setup window, click Configure to configure your port usage.**

6. **The Configure Port Usage applet opens. Depending on how you want RAS setup, you can choose either**

   a) Dial out only

   b) Receive calls only

   c) Dial out and Receive calls

7. **Click OK when you are done.**

8. **Now click the Network button. This is where you specify the network protocols that you are going to install.**

9. **When you are finished specifying protocols, click the Continue button.**

10. **You now have to specify the location of the source files so that Windows NT can add the necessary drivers and system files.**

11. **Reboot your NT Workstation so that the Remote-Access Service can start and changes to the system can be initialized.**

Troubleshooting RAS

Testing RAS is a complicated process because sometimes it's not always easy to figure out what is going wrong. If you are having problems with Remote-Access Service, you want to narrow down the problem to a few specific areas. Places to troubleshoot first include the following:

- Hardware (modem or cable)
- Network protocols
- User account (passwords and so on)
- Default configuration

Included with Remote-Access Service are some tools, as outlined in the following sections, that help make the troubleshooting process a little easier.

RAS Port and RAS Total counters

When you install RAS, you are also installing the Remote Access Service RAS Port and RAS Total counters that are now available in Performance Monitor. To open Performance Monitor, go to Start Menu⇨Programs⇨Administrative Tools⇨Performance Monitor.

- The RAS Port counters monitor performance of a single RAS port.
- The RAS Total counters monitor all the ports as a single unit.

Many counters, such as Bytes Received and Frames Received, are familiar to anyone who monitors network servers, and most RAS performance monitoring involves such counters.

Remember that the only way to add these counters on your workstation is to add Remote-Access Service. These counters are installed by default whenever you install RAS!

Dial Up Networking Monitor and Device.log

Two ways to troubleshoot connection problems with RAS are the Device.log file and Dial Up Networking Monitor.

✔ Dial Up Networking Monitor provides generic information about RAS connections and is a good place to start checking when you're troubleshooting a connection problem. Dial Up Networking Monitor provides information regarding the speed at which you are connected, the duration of the connection, the names of the users connected to an RAS server, the protocols used during the connection, and which devices are part of the connection.

✔ If Dial Up Networking Monitor doesn't help you to determine the source of a problem, then activate the Device.log file for a more detailed analysis of what is occurring when you are connecting. The Device.log file records all the dialog between the RAS server and the modem.

You'll almost certainly have an exam question about troubleshooting a bad RAS connection. To enable logging, you have to go into the registry at HKEY_LOCAL_MACHINE⇨Current Control Set⇨Services⇨RasMan⇨ Parameters⇨Logging. After you're at this key, you need to set the logging value from 0 to 1.

A popular Remote-Access Service troubleshooting question that you are likely to see covers the Device.log. Make sure that you remember that you can troubleshoot your RAS connection by looking at the Device.log file and making sure that its location is C:\WINNT\system32\ras.

RAS Security

Just like Windows NT, Remote-Access Service has built-in security to make sure that the bad guys don't access places that they aren't supposed to. If you're dialing up to a Windows NT Server, you are bound by the same access controls as if you were physically logging on to the Local Area Network. This means that when you try to log on to the LAN, you have to be authenticated with your Windows NT user account. If this doesn't exist, then you are out of luck. Chapters 8 and 9 discuss security and permissions issues in more detail.

Besides having Windows NT Security behind Remote-Access Service, other types of RAS built-in security features include Dial-back security, Encryption and Challenge/Response, and specifying whether to access only one computer or the whole network. These security features help eliminate anyone (figuratively speaking, of course) from hacking into your NT network.

When you try to access a secured site, you can be challenged into entering your password so that you can be authenticated over the network. When this happens, you will see a dialog box asking you for your password. If you want to protect your passwords during transmission from your client workstation to your dial-up server, you can use encryption authentication. This type of authentication uses a special hashing algorithm that securely transmits your password over a public or private network. If this type of encrypted authentication is enabled on your dial-up server, your password and username are relatively safe.

If you are using multi-link, you must disable the Call-back security feature on your RAS Server because Call-back security can be configured to call-back only one number, not two. Therefore, when your RAS server tries to call back your number, it connects with only one of your modems, not both.

RAS and the Internet

With Remote-Access Service installed, you have a convenient way of getting to the Internet. Every time that you dial-up to a RAS server that is using the TCP/IP protocol and is connected directly to the Internet, so are you. Remember that when you use RAS, you are simulating that you are part of the physical network.

When using RAS for connecting to the Internet, you must keep these items in mind:

- The first prerequisite that you must follow is that you *must* have the TCP/IP protocol installed on your NT Workstation. This is absolutely necessary because the language of the Internet is TCP/IP.

- After you have TCP/IP installed on your NT Workstation, all that you need is a modem or compatible device and privileges on your dial-up server that is connected to the Internet.

- If your dial-up server is giving you a dynamic IP address, then after you are connected and authenticated, you have nothing to worry about. You will be given all of the necessary TCP/IP address information, such as DNS servers for name resolution and a default gateway to access other computers all over the world.

- If you have a static IP address that you are using, make sure that you have all of your TCP/IP address information correct. Otherwise, you will be stuck without Internet access and won't understand why.

Remote Access versus Remote Control

Remote Access and Remote Control are two totally different subjects. No, Remote Control isn't something you lost under the couch a year ago. They might sound similar, but their concepts are nothing alike. Remote-Access

Service is used to dial up and connect to the remote network. When connected to this remote network, you are your own computer. This is great for checking your e-mail or grabbing a file off your network. Using Remote Access over a normal phone line is possible because you're not using up too much bandwidth to connect to the network.

Much more than simply connecting to a remote network is involved when you want to use Remote Control. With Remote Control, you are actually taking control of the computer as if you were "physically" at the server.

For remote control possibilities, you need to have a third-party application installed on both the host and destination computers. After you have both sets of software installed, you need to make sure that you have enough bandwidth for this to be successful. It's almost impossible to take complete control of a remote system over a normal 28.8 baud modem. There's just too much information that must be relayed back between the phone lines. Remote control is much more effective over a LAN where network bandwidth has fewer restraints.

Compression

Windows NT RAS offers software compression, with an average 2:1 compression ratio. Files that can be easily compressed may achieve greater compression ratios. However, if you're doing any heavy-duty computing, I wouldn't recommend sending large files over your phone line, no matter what type of compression ratio you can achieve. If not, you might be waiting a long time for your file to finally reach you.

Prep Test

1 What file will help you troubleshoot your dial-up problems with Remote-Access Service?

A ○ Install.log

B ○ Modem.inf

C ○ RAS.log

D ○ Device.log

2 Colleen wants to install Remote-Access Service on her NT Workstation. What does she need to install? (Choose all that apply.)

A ❑ Network protocol

B ❑ Internet Explorer

C ❑ Modem-compatible device

D ❑ User account

3 What counters are installed on Performance Monitor when you install Remote-Access Service? (Choose all that apply.)

A ❑ RAS Port

B ❑ RAS Multi-Link

C ❑ PPTP

D ❑ RAS Total

4 Jeff wants to connect up to his dial-up server that is running TCP/IP, NetBEUI, and IPX. What protocol does he have to install in order to connect to the Internet with Remote-Access Service?

A ○ NetBEUI

B ○ PPTP

C ○ IPX

D ○ TCP/IP

5 What is required for Point-to-Point Tunneling protocol to work successfully? (Choose all that apply.)

A ❑ PPTP Client

B ❑ Network Protocol

C ❑ PPTP Server

D ❑ Internet Explorer

E ❑ Network Card

F ❑ Administrative privileges

6 What allows you to combine the bandwidth of two or more physical communication links to increase your network bandwidth?

A ○ PPTP

B ○ Multi-Link

C ○ ISDN

D ○ FTP

7 What type of Remote Access Security is used to secure password authentication over a network?

A ○ Challenge/Response

B ○ Clear Text

C ○ Encrypted Authentication

D ○ MIME

8 Where can you enable logging for Remote-Access Service on your NT Workstation?

A ○ Remote-Access Service Admin

B ○ Network icon in Control Panel

C ○ Modems icon in Control Panel

D ○ Windows NT Diagnostics

9 What Remote-Access Service security option requires a phone number?

A ○ Encryption

B ○ Call-back

C ○ Dial-out

D ○ MS CHAP

10 What protocol allows you to set up a virtual private network?

A ○ TCP/IP

B ○ NetBEUI

C ○ IPX/SPX

D ○ Point-to-Point Tunneling Protocol

Answers

1 *D.* If you have to troubleshoot any of your Remote-Access problems, you can check out the Device.log that is located in \Winnt\System32\Ras. *See "Dial Up Networking Monitor and Device.log."*

2 *A, C,* and *D.* If you are going to install Remote-Access Service, you need to have a few options installed. These would be a network protocol, a modem-compatible device, and a user account on the dial-up server so that you can be authenticated. *See "Installing RAS" for more information.*

3 *A, D.* When you install Remote-Access Service on your NT Workstation, the RAS Total and RAS Port counters are installed on your workstation. *See "Installing RAS" and Lab 15-2 for more information.*

4 *D.* No matter what protocols are installed on your dial up server, you still need the TCP/IP protocol installed on your NT Workstation if you want to connect to the Internet with Remote-Access Service. *Review "RAS and the Internet."*

5 *A, B,* and *C.* If you are going to use PPTP to create a Virtual Private Network, you need to have the PPTP client and PPTP server installed. Either TCP/IP, IPX, or NetBEUI will work as well for network protocols. *See "Remote access via Point-to-Point Tunneling."*

6 *B.* Multi-link provides the ability to use two or more modems to combine physical links and increase your network bandwidth. *See "Using multi-link with communication devices."*

7 *A.* The only way to make sure that you can be authenticated over the network is to challenge the dial-up users for their User Name and Password. This will ensure that they are logging on with their account and access privileges. *See "RAS Security."*

8 *C.* Although you configure Remote-Access Service through the Network icon in the Control Panel, you have to enable logging through the Modem icon in the Control Panel. Just click Properties/Advanced to "Record a Log File" and enable logging. *See "Installing RAS."*

9 *B.* If you grant dial-out permission to a specific user, you can set up "Call-back" security so that your computer will call back the specific computer at the preset phone number. *Again, see "Installing RAS."*

10 *D.* To setup Virtual Private Networks, you first need to have Point-to-Point Tunneling Protocol installed. However, you can use either TCP/IP, NetBEUI, or IPX/SPX along with PPTP to create VPNs. *Review "Remote access via Point-to-Point Tunneling" for more information.*

Part VI
Running Applications

The 5th Wave   By Rich Tennant

Fault-Tolerant Rickshaw

In this part . . .

Over the course of time, you run a variety of very different applications on your NT Workstation, all needing to access different workstation resources. That's why Windows NT provides different subsystems across your NT Workstation to emulate different environments. These different subsystems are fundamental to how your NT Workstation operates.

Part of the problem of running various applications on your NT Workstation is that not all applications are created equal. Some applications, made for the 32-bit world, usually run fine under Windows NT. But some legacy applications are still on the 16-bit level and usually cause Windows NT some problems because they can't run in the same memory space as other 32-bit applications. In an effort to protect itself from harm, NT runs these 16-bit apps in their own memory space in case they run out of control and try to crash your workstation.

One of the greatest features of Windows NT is the ability to take control of your workstation and determine when to eliminate an application (by using Task Manager to your advantage) or start applications at various priorities on either Intel or RISC platforms. The exam expects you to know how to do these things.

Knowing how to install and configure printers in a given situation is essential to creating a working environment that keeps both you and your users happy for a long time to come. If users can't print, they can't work. If they can't work, someone is not going to be very happy!

Chapter 16

Working with Legacy and 32-Bit Applications

Exam Objectives

▶ Start applications on Intel and RISC platforms in various operating system environments

▶ Start applications at various priorities

▶ Choose the appropriate course of action when an application fails

*E*very time you fire up an application on your NT Workstation, a number of threads are launched that control which processes are running at which priority for the processor. Every running application has to share the processor with Windows NT. No application can hog the processor and cause poor performance for any other applications that may be running on your workstation, because Windows NT supports symmetric multiprocessing (SMP).

For the exam, you should know how Windows NT handles threads, processes, and priorities. You won't be tested on Windows NT application subsystems or the way in which Windows NT handles different types of memory, but this information is great background and useful information to know.

Quick Assessment

Start applications on Intel and RISC platforms in various operating system environments

1 Name three Windows NT subsystems.

2 VDM stands for _____ and is used to emulate a 286 running MS-DOS.

3 You can run a 16-bit application in its own _____.

4 Running each 16-bit application in its own memory space prevents Windows NT from _____.

5 You can change the priority of a process through _____.

6 Under Windows NT, WOW stands for _____.

7 You can specify that a 16-bit application run in its own memory space from the _____ or from Start⇨_____.

Choose the appropriate course of action to take when an application fails

8 True/False: For each MS-DOS application, Windows NT creates an individual VDM.

9 True/False: If a thread is running at Realtime, the thread's priority is running in the kernel.

Start applications at various priorities

10 Name the four levels of thread priorities.

11 Multiple threads make up a _____ in Windows NT.

Answers

1   *WIN32; POSIX; MS-DOS.* See "NT Application Subsystems."

2   *Virtual DOS Machine.* See "Virtual DOS Machines (VDM)."

3   *Memory space.* See "Memory protection."

4   *Process.* See "Processes Prioritization."

5   *The Task Manager or the command line.* See "Threads and scheduling."

6   *Windows On Windows.* See "Working with WIN16 legacy applications."

7   *Command line; Run.* See "Running 16-bit applications."

8   *True.* See "Working with DOS legacy applications."

9   *True.* See "Threads and scheduling."

10 *Real-time; High; Normal; Low.* See "Threads and scheduling."

11 *Crashing.* See "Memory protection."

Legacy Applications

Legacy applications are those apps that people just can't seem to get rid of because they don't want to upgrade to a nice, quick, robust 32-bit application. Most of these legacy applications are 16-bit and require special attention under Windows NT because 16-bit apps have a tendency to crash when they try to access certain memory spaces. Windows NT doesn't allow direct access to these memory spaces because they have a tendency to crash when that happens. As any good operating system would!

To protect your 16-bit applications, run each one in its own memory space. If you don't, when one 16-bit app crashes, all the 16-bit apps crash.

Virtual DOS Machines (VDMs)

To work with legacy applications, Windows NT utilizes Virtual DOS Machines (VDMs).

✔ Standard VDMs emulate the MS-DOS environment and make sure that Windows NT protects itself from a bad 16-bit MS-DOS application. Each 16-bit MS-DOS application that's activated in NT Workstation starts in its own VDM; if you have five MS-DOS applications active on an NT machine, you'll have five different VDMs.

✔ Windows On Windows (WOW) VDMs are part of a user-mode application (the WOW environment) that essentially emulates a Windows 3.1 operating environment. Every 16-bit Windows 3.1 (WIN16) legacy application shares a single WOW VDM — so if you have six WIN16 applications active in Windows NT, they all run in the same WOW VDM.

Working with DOS legacy applications

To make sure that Windows NT is compatible with other environments, Windows NT has to be compatible with MS-DOS applications. Windows NT still has trouble running some MS-DOS applications because when these applications were written, sharing memory and accessing the hardware directly weren't problems. However, with Windows NT this is a no-no. Windows NT does not allow MS-DOS applications to affect other applications or access the hardware directly. That's one reason why NT is so hard to crash. Whenever you try to run an MS-DOS or 16-bit application, Windows NT tries to protect itself from crashing by running these applications separately. That's a common reason why legacy applications and MS-DOS games do not run well under Windows NT.

A Virtual DOS Machine for MS-DOS applications is designed to emulate an Intel 80286 PC running the MS-DOS operating system.

✔ Every time an MS-DOS 16-bit application is executed, Windows NT creates a VDM to protect itself against the MS-DOS application crashing Windows NT and to keep those 16-bit applications from harming other applications.

✔ If an MS-DOS application running in a VDM crashes, the worst it can do is crash its own VDM; it harms only other 16-bit applications that aren't running in their own memory spaces.

✔ Because each MS-DOS application has a single thread, these applications can be preemptively scheduled for execution just like any other processes in the system.

VDMs are challenging for NT for several reasons. The biggest problem is that MS-DOS is completely unsecured and will try to access hardware and memory directly. NT doesn't allow free access to the computer's memory, because doing so would put NT in jeopardy of crashing.

Working with WIN16 legacy applications

Essentially, the Windows On Windows (WOW) environment is really just a user-mode application. Therefore, the WOW application environment is not started until the first time a 16-bit Windows application is run. However, even if all 16-bit Windows applications are closed, the WOW application environment remains active until the user logs off Windows NT.

Running all WIN16 applications in the same VDM provides maximum compatibility with the native Windows 3.1 environment. However, this compatibility has a cost: It forces the WOW VDM to have the same weaknesses as Windows 3.1, as follows:

✔ It allows WIN16 applications to access memory that belongs to other WIN16 applications or to WOW, with potentially disastrous effects.

✔ It allows a single WIN16 application that does not yield control of the processor to effectively crash all other WIN16 applications.

✔ Even so, a crashed WIN16 application does not affect the other VDMs, nor does it affect applications running under other subsystems.

All 16-bit Windows applications running in the WOW share a common address space. The WIN16 VDM can be preemptively multitasked with other processes running on Windows NT; however, the threads within the WIN16 VDM (16-bit application programs) cannot be multitasked.

Running 16-bit applications

You can specify that each 16-bit application run in its own VDM to protect the applications against a 16-bit VDM that crashes. You have a couple of ways to make this specification:

- **Running the 16-bit app from the command line:** Specify which priority you want to use and whether you want to run the VDM in its own memory space by using the Start.exe command and a variety of switches.

- **Running the 16-bit app from the Start menu:** When you choose the Run command, you can check the Run in Separate Memory Space box.

The Start.exe command follows this pattern:

START ["title"] [/Dpath] [/I] [/MIN] [/MAX] [/SEPARATE I /SHARED]

[/LOW I /NORMAL I /HIGH I /REALTIME] [/WAIT] [/B] [command/program] [parameters]

See Table 16-1 for options.

Table 16-1	Command Line Switches for Start.exe
SEPARATE	Start 16-bit Windows program in separate memory space
SHARED	Start 16-bit Windows program in shared memory space
LOW	Start application in the IDLE priority class
NORMAL	Start application in the NORMAL priority class
HIGH	Start application in the HIGH priority class
REALTIME	Start application in the REALTIME priority class

If a 16-bit application is run in its own memory space, it can take advantage of being preemptively multitasked and can be protected from running into other 16-bit apps.

NT Application Subsystems

Windows NT is a unique operating system that's far more flexible than it's given credit for. Windows NT practically bends over backward to support some of the crazy applications on the market today. That's where NT application subsystems fit into the big picture. These various application subsystems mimic other operating environments so that all types of 16- and 32-bit applications can run under Windows NT.

You can think of this relationship between application subsystems and environment subsystems as a form of client/server relationship. The subsystems (servers) provide services that applications (clients) utilize. Client and servers communicate by using messages that they send via the Windows NT executive.

- ✔ OS/2: OS/2 applications

- ✔ WIN32: 32-bit Windows applications

- ✔ WIN16 APP: Supports 16-bit Windows applications or WOW (Windows On Windows)

- ✔ DOS APP: Supports MS-DOS applications

- ✔ POSIX: Meets the requirements for the government procurement standard FIPS (Federal Information Processing Standards)

For Windows NT to protect itself, each subsystem runs as a separate user-mode process so that it can't crash other subsystems or the executive. If a process running in the executive (kernel or Ring 0) crashes, the entire system will crash. Applications are all run as user-mode processes for the same reason.

Table 16-2 gives you a quick rundown of the benefits of application subsystems.

Table 16-2	Benefits of Application Subsystems
Benefit	**Description**
Compatibility	Users can continue to use applications written for other OSs.
Extensibility	Subsystems can be added later.
Maintainability	Subsystem changes and Windows NT changes don't affect other parts of Windows NT.
Reliability and robustness	Subsystems run in separate address spaces, so they're safe from each other.

The Windows subsystem WIN32 runs all the 32-bit applications in their own memory spaces so that no matter what 32-bit application crashes on your NT Workstation, none of the other applications will crash Windows NT. This feature makes for a very stable and secure operating environment.

Windows NT is a symmetric multiprocessing (SMP) operating system, which means that the processor schedules thread priority and makes sure that each application (process or thread) is receiving enough of the processor's time. Because 32-bit applications are made up of multiple threads, each process can be handled by Windows NT and can be preemptively multitasked, which ensures peak performance and stability.

Processes Prioritization

Windows NT is a symmetric multiprocessing (SMP) system, meaning that it assumes that all the processors are equal and that they all have access to the same physical memory. The following list explains what having SMP means in Windows NT:

- ✔ NT can use one or more processors in a computer as long as the processors are of the same type and are similarly configured.

- ✔ All processors are allowed to run a mixture of application and operating system code. In fact, different parts of the operating system can (and often do) run on different processors at the same time. This is a good thing because you don't have one thread or process burning up the processor for a task, while every other process or thread just waits around doing nothing.

- ✔ Because Windows NT uses Symmetric Multiprocessing, your processes all get different priorities, unless you specify otherwise. You can take a detailed look at processes if you open up Task Manager. Take a look at Figure 16-1 for an example of what I mean.

- ✔ Windows NT can run any thread on any available processor regardless of what process, user or Executive, owns the thread.

What does this mean for you? If you have more than one processor, Windows NT will perform better because of the way NT handles processes and threads. Instead of having each process or thread hog the processor, NT schedules the processor so that each thread or process can get enough time with the processor to finish the application. So the more processors that you have, the more work your workstation can do. Simple enough.

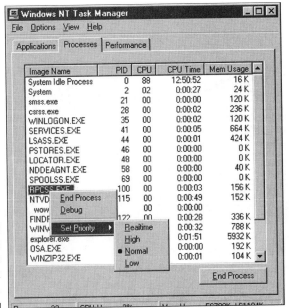

Figure 16-1:
Windows
NT Task
Manager.

POSIX

You won't find any questions on the exam about POSIX, but you may find a couple of POSIX facts to be good background information.

POSIX is still a Windows NT environmental subsystem. NTFS has several features that were included to support POSIX. Therefore, in order to have a system that is the most POSIX.1-compliant, you must use NTFS as your file system.

In Betas 1 and 2, the POSIX subsystem is automatically loaded at logon and then immediately paged out, but it remains active. The POSIX subsystem is not paged back into memory until it is needed to run a POSIX

application. The only way to restart the POSIX subsystem, in the case of a crash, is to shut down and restart the system.

In the final product, the POSIX subsystem will not start until a POSIX application is started. Once the POSIX subsystem is started, it will remain loaded but paged out when not in use, until the system has been shut down and restarted. The only way to restart the POSIX subsystem, once again, is to shut down and restart the system. Logging off and then logging on again will not restart the POSIX subsystem.

Here is a summary of processes and threads in case the concepts aren't clear. (See Figure 16-2.)

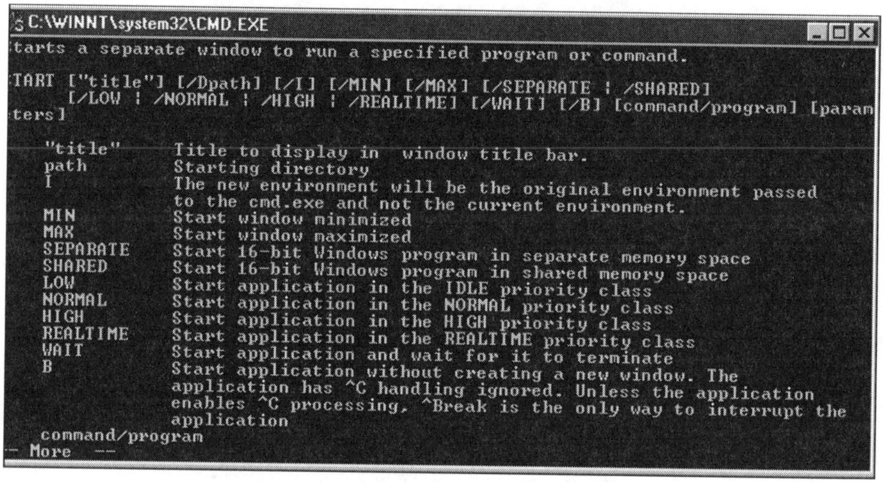

Figure 16-2:
Looking at processes on the NT Workstation.

```
C:\WINNT\system32\CMD.EXE                                      _ □ ×
tarts a separate window to run a specified program or command.

TART ["title"] [/Dpath] [/I] [/MIN] [/MAX] [/SEPARATE : /SHARED]
        [/LOW : /NORMAL : /HIGH : /REALTIME] [/WAIT] [/B] [command/program] [param
ters]

     "title"    Title to display in  window title bar.
     path       Starting directory
     I          The new environment will be the original environment passed
                to the cmd.exe and not the current environment.
     MIN        Start window minimized
     MAX        Start window maximized
     SEPARATE   Start 16-bit Windows program in separate memory space
     SHARED     Start 16-bit Windows program in shared memory space
     LOW        Start application in the IDLE priority class
     NORMAL     Start application in the NORMAL priority class
     HIGH       Start application in the HIGH priority class
     REALTIME   Start application in the REALTIME priority class
     WAIT       Start application and wait for it to terminate
     B          Start application without creating a new window. The
                application has ^C handling ignored. Unless the application
                enables ^C processing, ^Break is the only way to interrupt the
                application
     command/program
 -- More --
```

Processes

  ✔ A private memory address space in which the process's code and data are stored

  ✔ An access token against which Windows NT makes security checks

  ✔ System resources such as files and windows (represented as object handles)

  ✔ At least one thread to execute the code

Threads

  ✔ A processor state including the current instruction pointer

  ✔ A stack for use when running in user mode

  ✔ A stack for use when running in kernel mode

Be aware that multiple threads make up a process.

For the exam, you have to remember that a thread is the smallest schedulable unit in the system. You can kill a thread by terminating the last executing thread. Expect a test question on the size of threads.

All threads are based on a 32-level (they use the 0-31 numbering scheme) priority scheme. This runs from 0, which is the lowest priority, all the way to level 31, which is the highest.

✔ The threads with the highest number have the highest priority and will be running at any given time. Threads with a priority of 31 will be run before any others, while threads with a priority of 0 will run only if no other threads are ready.

✔ The range of priorities is divided in half, with the upper 16 reserved for real-time threads and the lower 16 reserved for variable priority threads.

✔ Windows NT determines which threads are given priority, and this fluctuates a great deal so that no thread is hogging the processor.

You can use Task Manager to take a peek at what processes are running on your NT Workstation and see how they're behaving. If any processes are crashing or out of control, you can kill a process from here.

Threads and scheduling

Here are the pertinent facts to know about threads:

✔ Remember that a thread is the smallest unit in the microkernel. This simple statement may be the answer to a question.

✔ Every time you launch an application, the kernel dispatcher schedules a thread based on a 32-level priority scheme (0 to 31). The threads that are ready and have the highest priority are guaranteed to be running at any given time (that's one thread on a single-processor system).

✔ Threads with a priority of 31 run before any others, whereas threads with a priority of 0 run only if no other threads are ready.

✔ The range of priorities is divided in half, with the upper 16 reserved for Realtime threads and the lower 16 reserved for variable-priority threads.

✔ If you want a certain thread or process to receive more or less attention from the processor, you can schedule your thread at a different priority, either at the command line or from the Task Manager. See Table 16-3.

Table 16-3	Different Thread Priorities
Priority	**Description**
Real-time	Threads run at the same priority for their entire lifetime. They are commonly used to monitor or control systems that require action to be taken at very precise intervals. These threads run at higher priorities than all variable priority threads, which means that they must be used sparingly.

(continued)

Table 16-3 *(continued)*

Priority	Description
High	Consume more processor time than the Normal or Low settings for your processes. This is a much safer option than running your threads at Real-time. Use this option if you need your application to receive a performance boost.
Normal	All applications are run from this priority level.
Low	This is the lowest setting that threads can run under, and they receive the lowest priority and processor time compared to all other processors. You can use this option if you have an application that is not very important to the work you're doing.

Remember that a thread is the smallest part of the microkernel. You can have multiple threads that make up a process.

The four priority levels are

- ✔ Real-time
- ✔ High
- ✔ Normal
- ✔ Low

Real-time priority runs at the same speed as the kernel and can be very dangerous because if the thread or process crashes at Real-time, it could crash the kernel. See Lab 16-1 for instructions on changing a priority level of a process.

Lab 16-1   Changing the Priority Level of a Process on Your Windows NT Workstation

1. **Press Ctrl+Alt+Delete to bring up Task Manager.**

2. **Click the Task Manager button to bring up Task Manager.**

3. **Click the Processes tab.**

4. **Highlight a specific process on your workstation and right-click the process.**

5. **Go to the Set Priority option and specify either Real-time, High, Normal, or Low.**

6. **You'll be prompted by a dialog box asking if you want to continue. If you're sure, press the Yes button.**

Memory protection

Windows NT is designed to be a secure, multithreaded, multiprocessing operating system that doesn't crash. How can it prevent crashes? By protecting itself.

A large part of this protection is protecting the executive's (kernel) memory (code and data) from direct access by applications, by assigning the executive's memory a privileged status. Code in the NT executive has adequate privilege to access the NT executive's memory, but code in normal applications is denied this privilege.

Windows NT applications have access to up to 4GB of memory — that is, the application has a 4GB virtual address space (virtual memory). The memory at each virtual address has a privilege level associated with it:

✔ Memory in the upper 2GB of the address space can be accessed only by privileged (kernel-mode) code (that is, code in the NT executive).

✔ Memory in the lower 2GB of the address space can be accessed by unprivileged (user-mode) code (such as normal applications) *and* by privileged code.

Because the NT Kernel resides exclusively in the upper 2GB of memory, it is protected from direct access by normal applications. Thus, promiscuous applications cannot accidentally crash your workstation, and misbehaving applications cannot intentionally steal system information or modify the system's behavior (like a program a hacker might code). Believe me, Windows NT does all it can to protect itself from outside harm.

Applications also have to be protected from each other. Windows NT ensures that one application can't access another application's memory unless *both* applications cooperate. Suppose that two processes try to read the memory at the same virtual address. Each process has its own address-translation tables, so the virtual address may translate to physical address 20 for one process and physical address 2000 for the other process. The only way the applications can talk to one another is if special arrangements are made for the two processes to share memory, they will always access different pages of physical memory, even if they use the same virtual addresses. This is the most secure and stable route to use as opposed to using the same memory spaces. When you start using the same memory spaces, applications begin to crash!

Prep Test

1 If you have four MS-DOS applications on your NT Workstation, each running in its own memory space, and one application crashes, how many of your MS-DOS applications are affected?

A ○ One

B ○ Two

C ○ Three

D ○ Four

E ○ None

2 What are the various levels of thread priorities that you can specify on your NT Workstation? (Choose all that apply.)

A ❏ Real-time

B ❏ Low

C ❏ High

D ❏ Special

E ❏ Normal

F ❏ Kernel

G ❏ Medium

H ❏ Executive

3 What does VDM stand for in a Windows NT Environment?

A ○ Virtual DOS Machine

B ○ Visual Derma Module

C ○ Virtual Digital Machine

D ○ Visual Digital Module

4 What are some benefits of memory protection with Windows NT? (Choose all that apply.)

A ❏ More efficient.

B ❏ Protects the NT executive from applications.

C ❏ Protects applications from each other.

D ❏ Performance monitoring.

E ❏ Compatible with multiple processors.

5 Which are valid Windows NT subsystems? (Choose all that apply.)

A ❑ POSIX

B ❑ WIN32

C ❑ OS/2

D ❑ MS-DOS

E ❑ UNIX

D ❑ NetWare

6 Holly wants to change the priority of some existing threads on her Windows NT Workstation. Where can she do this?

A ○ Windows NT Diagnostics

B ○ Task Manager

C ○ User Manager

D ○ Server Manager

E ○ Windows NT Explorer

7 How many different levels can threads be scheduled to under Windows NT?

A ○ 32

B ○ 21

C ○ 30

D ○ 14

8 What options do you have if you want to run your 16-bit applications in their own memory spaces? (Choose all that apply.)

A ❑ Command line

B ❑ User Manager

C ❑ Windows NT Diagnostics

D ❑ Start⇨Run

9 What are the benefits of running your 16-bit application in its own memory space? (Choose all that apply.)

A ❑ Won't crash other 16-bit applications.

B ❑ Runs at Real-time priority.

C ❑ Preemptively multitasked.

D ❑ Much faster.

10 Jerry wants his messaging application to receive the most time with the processor so that it runs well. He schedules this app to run at Realtime. Now he can't unlock his workstation, and nothing will work. What happened?

A ○ Thread crashed and also crashed the kernel.

B ○ Threads can't be scheduled at Real-time.

C ○ Nothing. Just wait.

D ○ He's recompiling the kernel.

Answers

1 *E.* With each MS-DOS application running in its own VDM, a crashed application doesn't affect any other applications. If each DOS application was not
running in its own memory space, all four would be affected. *See "Virtual
DOS Machines (VDMs)."*

2 *A, B, C, E.* You can specify the level at which your application runs by using
the command-line Start command or by using the Task Manager. *See
"Threads and scheduling."*

3 *A.* A Virtual DOS Machine is a protected memory space created to emulate
the 80286 MS-DOS operating system. Each VDM is protected from other
VDMs. *See "Working with DOS legacy applications."*

4 *A, B, C, E.* Also, memory protection is much more stable and keeps it from
crashing if an application fails. *See "Memory protection."*

5 *A, B, C, D.* The WIN32, POSIX, MS-DOS, and OS/2 subsystems are all environments that Windows NT emulates so that different applications can run
effectively. *See "NT Application Subsystems."*

6 *B.* If you want to change the priority of a process on your workstation, you
can pull up the Task Manager, click the Processes tab, right-click a process
that is running, and change the priority to Real-time, High, Normal, or Low.
See "Threads and scheduling."

7 *A.* Windows NT offers 32 levels of priorities, which you can choose at the
command line or in the Task Manager. *See "Threads and scheduling."*

8 *A, D.* You can specify that an app run in its own memory space with the
Start.exe command or from the Start menu's Run command. *See "Running
16-bit applications."*

9 *A, C.* When running in its own memory space, a 16-bit application will not
crash another and can be preemptively multitasked. *See "Running 16-bit
applications."*

10 *A.* If you run a thread or process at Real-time and that thread crashes,
you crash your kernel and, therefore, your workstation. *See "Threads and
scheduling."*

Legacy and 32-Bit Apps

Chapter 17

Printing: Putting It Down on Paper

Exam Objectives

▶ Installing and configuring printers

▶ Choosing the appropriate course of action when a print job fails

*N*etwork printing with Windows NT is different from other systems because of all the odd terms that are specific to Windows NT. To understand Windows NT printing, you first have to understand the terminology.

The Windows NT print model is designed to be as simple and trouble-free as possible. Under Windows NT, all you have to do is install the necessary printer, and your NT print server automatically uploads the correct print driver to your NT Workstation. This concept works extremely well when you have NT Workstation clients and an NT print server on your network.

Printing isn't covered as heavily on the NT Workstation exam as on the other exams. The Workstation exam looks more at the benefits of networking, including resource sharing for file and printer resources. Most of the printing-related questions deal with NetWare printing and print schedules and priorities.

Quick Assessment

Installing and config-uring printers

1 What tool do you use to add a new printer in NT?

2 What are the six tabs available under the Properties option for an NT printer?

3 Associating multiple print devices with a single printer is known as a _____.

4 True/False: You have to manually install a print driver on your Windows NT Workstation when printing to a Windows NT print server.

5 If your print device stops producing output, what is the first thing you should try?

6 True/False: In Windows NT lingo, a *print device* is actually the physical printer.

7 Name the four security options for setting permissions on printers.

8 When configuring a user or group's printer priority, _____ is the lowest priority, and _____ is the highest.

Choosing the appropriate course of action when a print job fails

9 True/False: By default, a user cannot delete a print job after it's submitted to the printer.

10 For a user to delete print jobs other than his or her own, what type of access for the specified NT printer must the user have?

Answers

1   *Add Printer.* See "Installing a local printer (print device)."

2   *General; Security; Ports; Scheduling; Device Settings; Sharing.* See "Configuring Printers."

3   *Printing pool.* See "Installing a local printer (print device)."

4   *False.* See "Printing Overview and the NT Print Model."

5   *Stop and restart the spooler service.* See "Troubleshooting Printer Problems."

6   *True.* See "Printing Overview and the NT Print Model."

7   *Full Control; Manage Documents; Print; No Access.* See "Security."

8   *0;99.* See "Scheduling."

9   *False.* See "Security."

10   *Manage Documents or Full Control.* See "Security."

Printing Overview and the NT Print Model

The exam questions about printing are surprisingly complex. Focus your studying on these five main areas: spooler settings, print clients, print-pool creation, security, and scheduling.

Network printing is a snap with Windows NT. With just a few clicks of the mouse while sitting at your NT Workstation, you connect to your NT print server, and the print server automatically sends the correct driver down to your workstation, without any user intervention. Just specify which printer you want to use. Pretty cool.

The Windows NT print model attempts to make printing on your network as simple as possible, as long as your network is mainly NT clients connecting to an NT print server.

Here are some Windows NT print-related terms that you should know:

- **Print device** is a piece of hardware, usually a printer. Why it's not referred to as simply a *printer* is a mystery. Just know that when you send a document to your print device, the physical printer produces the output.

- **Printer** is actually the software interface between a print device and the operating system — the print driver that you install when you are creating a local printer. Your printers are defined and managed in the Printers folder. Here is where you can change printing software (your print driver).

- **Print server** is the network server on which shared printers are defined. Client computers submit their print jobs to print servers for processing and management. All the print drivers are located on the print server so that when you add a printer to your workstation, NT automatically downloads and installs the print driver for you.

  The network print server controls all the documents that are sent to the print device. Here, you can implement security and printer pools and make device-setting changes for your printer.

- **Print driver** is the middleman that allows the operating system to communicate with a specific type of print device (the physical printer). The print driver is specific to the type of printer that you have installed or are connecting to over the network.

If you're connecting to a Windows NT print server over the network, the print server sends the correct print driver to your NT Workstation and installs the driver so that you can begin printing. You don't even have to reboot your system. This process is very fluid and seamless as long as both the client and the server are NT computers.

✔ **Printer pool** is a multiple physical print device associated with a single printer. For example, if you had multiple Hewlett Packard 5Si's, you could set up a printer pool with this type of printer. When you setup a printer pool, you have to use the same printer. This printer pool consists of the same printer added several times with different characteristics (such as priorities or schedules) for each printer that was added to the pool. This can be used to separate a group from manipulating the printers or keeping other documents from being printed during working hours.

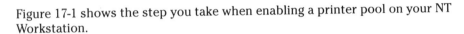

✔ Make sure that you understand how to implement a printer pool for your NT Workstation. Also make sure that you know that you have to use the same printer and you can set up options such as priorities and schedules between printers!

Figure 17-1 shows the step you take when enabling a printer pool on your NT Workstation.

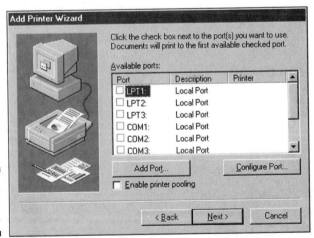

Figure 17-1:
Enabling a
printer pool.

Managing Printers

The NT printing process begins when a client attempts a connection with a printer, and ends when a print device receives processed data and produces a printed document.

For the exam, the most important step of this process to focus on is Step 1, the initial client connection. This chapter gives you the rest of the steps for context, but you don't need to memorize them for the exam.

1. Whenever a new network printer is added to a client machine, and any time a client machine attempts to send a print job to a print server (workstation), the client will first check the version of the print driver on the server if the client is running NT or Windows 95. If the workstation has a more recent driver, the client will download the driver from the NT workstation into memory. If the version is the same or earlier, the client will use its local print driver. This version of checking and automatic downloading can only occur with NT clients and Windows 95 clients attaching to an NT server.

2. The print job is sent to the client's local spooler via a remote procedure call (RPC), which then forwards the job to the workstation's spooler. This step does not occur if the client and server are the same computer.

3. The server-side spooler passes the document to the router, which then determines the data type and passes the information to the appropriate print processor on the local print provider.

4. The print processor analyzes the type of data and determines if further processing is required before returning the document to the local print provider.

5. If a separator page is to be used, this is the point in the process where the page is created and attached to the beginning of the print job.

6. The print job is passed to the print monitor, which determines when the job should print and which port it should print through.

7. And "Walla!" The print device receives processed data and produces a printed document.

Now that you're a whiz at setting up new printers, look at some of the management functions you're likely to see on the exam: pausing printing, setting default printers, setting document defaults, purging print documents, setting up network sharing of your printer, and setting a printer's properties.

You open the printer-management function by either

✔ Double-clicking the Printer icon in the Printers folder (under Start⇨Settings)

✔ Double-clicking the Printer icon in the System Tray (at the opposite end of the Start menu)

Managing print jobs

For the exam, you should know how to manage print jobs sent to your printer in case you have a problem printing, a problem with the printer, or an issue with print permissions.

You manage all your print jobs from the Printers folder (under Start⇨ Settings) on your NT Workstation. Double-click the printer that you want to manage, and you can control such things as

- ✔ Deleting print jobs
- ✔ Purging documents
- ✔ Pausing the printer
- ✔ Taking the printer offline
- ✔ Managing printer properties

For information about managing device settings, see "Configuring Printers," later in this chapter.

Installing a local printer (print device)

If you have a print device (or a printer for you and me) connected to your NT Workstation, you have to configure the necessary port so that Windows NT can communicate with your print device (the physical printer).

You can also configure the port if you are managing a TCP/IP port that you installed with the Microsoft TCP/IP Printing Service. You have to install this service in order to create a TCP/IP port on your NT Workstation.

See Lab 17-1 for the steps involved in installing a local printer for your NT Workstation.

Remember that you need to use the My Computer option when installing the printer, if you have a printer physically connected to your workstation.

Make sure that you know the difference between connecting to a printer and creating a printer! Remember that only when you create a printer do you have to install the Print Driver manually! When you connect to a printer (located on an NT Print Server), the driver is automatically downloaded and installed on your workstation!

Lab 17-1   Creating a Local Printer

1. **Choose Start⇨Settings⇨Printers and double-click Add Printer.**

2. **Specify My Computer.**

3. **Specify the port that you're going to use (if you need to configure your port, you can do that here, as well).**

4. **Specify the type of printer you're using (manufacturer).**

   If you're using a new printer or a new print driver, you can specify that as well.

5. **Select the name for your print device and choose whether it will be the default printer.**

6. **Specify whether to share the printer on the network.**

   If you're sharing the printer, you need to pick a share name and the print drivers that will be installed on your workstation.

7. **Print a test page to check that you've installed your printer correctly.**

Windows NT now installs the drivers that you specified for your network clients.

Connecting to a remote printer

Connecting to a remote printer is nothing more than connecting to the network share-point of that printer or mapping a drive with your UNC naming convention. After you connect to your remote printer (that is, if it's an NT Server), your print server will download the driver to your workstation. You can get a feel for this process in Lab 17-2 where you'll connect to a remote printer on a network.

Lab 17-2   Connecting to a Remote Printer

1. **Choose Start⇨Settings⇨Printers and double-click Add Printer.**

2. **Specify Network Print Server.**

3. **Specify the port that you're going to use (if you need to configure your port, you can do that here, as well).**

4. **Navigate to where the print device is located. Or specify the location of the printer via the UNC name (\\\\ServerName\\Printer).**

Windows NT now downloads and installs the correct printer driver for you.

Configuring Printers

You control your print configuration from the Properties menu of the printer that's connected to your workstation (just right-click the printer in the Printers folder and choose Properties). Become familiar with the six tabs of the Properties dialog box, described in the following sections.

General

The General tab enables you to specify the options that Table 17-1 describes. This tab has the most commonly changed settings for your printer.

Table 17-1	General Tab
Option	*Description*
Comment	What you want to say about the printer.
Location	You can make up a location so that people can find the printer on your network.
Driver	Lets you know what print driver you have installed.
Print Processor	Details what data type you are going to use (WinPrint is the default).
Separator Page	A separator page places a blank or text page between print jobs to keep them separate.
Print Test Page	You can print a test page to make sure that you've configured everything correctly.

Ports

If you are going to be physically connecting a printer to your NT Workstation, you need to configure the ports so that you can print to the print device. You can configure the ports for your NT Workstation when you're connecting a local printer with the Add Printer wizard, which prompts you for a port to use for your local connection. See Table 17-2.

You can also configure the port if you are managing a TCP/IP port that you installed with the Microsoft TCP/IP Printing Service. You have to install this service in order to create a TCP/IP port on your NT Workstation. TCP/IP-based printing clients, particularly UNIX clients, can print to NT print servers that are running the Microsoft TCP/IP Printing Service (LPD). Clients submit print jobs by using the LPR command, and a client can view the TCP/IP printer queue by using the LPQ command.

Table 17-2	Ports Tab
Option	*Description*
Add	Add a new port to your NT Workstation (LPT1, COM1, TCP/IP, and so on).
Delete	Remove a printer port (LPT1, COM1, TCP/IP, and so on).
Configure	Edit the port that is highlighted on your NT Workstation.
Enable Printer Pooling	Set up a printer pool.

Scheduling

On the Workstation exam, you need to find solutions to scenarios involving different functional user groups who need to be able to use the same print device in a method allowing access based on the types of jobs submitted. This situation is where *print priority* and *availability* come in. Both priority and availability are set under the Scheduling tab of the printer properties. The following are some highlights you'll want to focus on for the scheduling sections you may see on the exam:

- ✔ Your priorities can range from 1 to 99, with 1 being the lowest priority and 99 the highest.

- ✔ You set priorities in the printer properties and then set user rights to define who accesses the printer.

    Priorities are assigned to *printers,* not to *users.*

- ✔ A single printer cannot have multiple priority assignments. For each new priority you want to assign to a print device, you must create a new printer definition and then set security and access privileges through that printer's security dialog box.

- ✔ Availability does not prevent a user from submitting a print job to a printer at any given time. Rather, availability settings cause submitted print jobs to be held in the spooler until the time falls within the availability constraints. The spooler then forwards the held jobs to the print device.

- ✔ You can define multiple printers with similar availability settings but different priorities. When the print jobs go active within the availability constraints, the system looks at the priorities of the multiple printers and completes all the jobs in the print queue of the higher-ranked printer before starting on any of the jobs in the queue of the lower-ranked printer.

As you can see in Figure 17-2, you have the option of configuring the availability of your printers through scheduling.

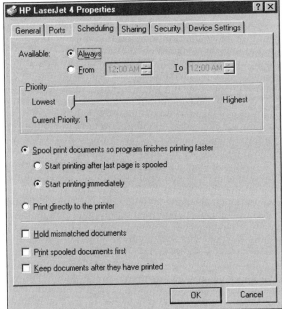

Figure 17-2:
Configuring
printer
scheduling
on your NT
Workstation.

For the exam, make sure that you know how to schedule different printer priorities for a printer pool.

Sharing

On the Sharing tab, you control whether you share your printer. More important, you configure which print drivers are installed on the workstation. If a Windows NT or Windows 95 client connects to your workstation to print and the correct print driver is installed, NT sends down and installs the print driver for the client.

If you're using a Windows NT Workstation as a print server, you can have only ten concurrent connections at once. Don't let them trick you into thinking you have unlimited connections!

You can see in Figure 17-3 the process for sharing your printer on your network.

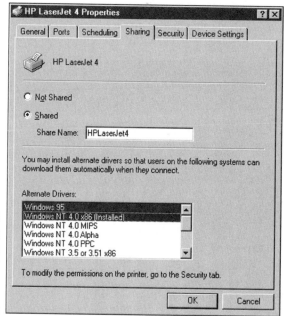

Figure 17-3:
Sharing
your printer
on the
network.

Security

As the administrator of your workstation, you can control the security options — particularly the permissions — for your printer. You have to manage print permissions from your workstation so that the right users can control documents that are sent to the printer. Table 17-3 describes these permissions.

Table 17-3	Security Tab
Option	*Description*
Print	Allows users to print documents and manage queued documents they have sent to the printer.
Manage Documents	Allows user to manage documents in the queue, regardless of who sent them. Document management includes pausing, restarting, resuming, and deleting existing documents.
No Access	User is denied all access to the printer or print queue.
Full Control	User is allowed to create, manage, and delete printers or documents.

Device Settings

The Device Settings tab enables you to control the actual properties of the print device: the paper tray to use, available memory settings, fonts, duplex printing, and so on. You don't have to know about this setting for the exam because it's mainly specific to an individual printer. Just make sure that you know where you have to go to change device settings.

In Figure 17-4, you can see what options are available through the Device Settings for your printer.

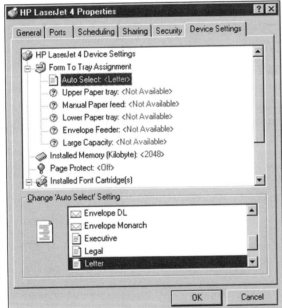

Figure 17-4:
Configuring Device Settings for your printer.

Troubleshooting Printer Problems

You probably won't see too many questions about troubleshooting printing problems. If you do, the question is likely to focus on fixing printing problems for print jobs residing on an NT print server.

In the real world, however, print problems can arise from any number of components in the printing process, such as the application that submits the print request, the client platform submitting the print request, a print device's mechanical components, and the network configuration of a network interface print device.

However, the exam does not focus on these issues.

What you *do* need to know for the exam is the spooler service. If you have trouble with the spooler and restarting the spooler doesn't fix your problem, here are some troubleshooting questions to ask yourself:

- ✔ Is the printer plugged in and powered up?

- ✔ Is the printer online or ready? If not, is it reporting an error condition?

- ✔ Are you using the proper type of cable for your printer connection? Is the cable attached securely at both ends?

- ✔ Do you have the latest version of the printer driver? Most manufacturers provide a service and support section on their Web sites where you can obtain updated device drivers.

- ✔ Are you printing to the correct printer port?

- ✔ Can you print a test page? If so, the application may be causing your print problem.

- ✔ Does the drive or partition that you're spooling to have enough space? If not, you can change the spooler location through the Windows NT Registry.

HKEY_LOCAL_MACHINE\System\CurrentControlSet\System\Print\ Printers\DefaultSpoolDirectory

Prep Test

1 Jim is creating a printing pool with two different print devices so that print jobs sent by users from the Human Resources group can be printed on either device. Which of the following statements best describe a printing pool? (Choose all that apply.)

A ❑ All print devices must use the same type of printer port.

B ❑ All print devices must be using TCP/IP printing.

C ❑ All print devices must be able to use a common driver.

D ❑ You can direct certain print jobs to a specific print device in the printing pool without the need to define a second printer.

E ❑ All print devices in the printing pool must be connected to the same print server.

2 Which security permission enables the user to control only the jobs that the user sends to the printer?

A ○ Full Control

B ○ Manage Documents

C ○ Print

D ○ No Access

3 Your NT Workstation belongs to a small workgroup with two user groups: Consultants and Accountants. You have to make sure that any documents submitted by the Consultants group are printed before documents submitted by the Accountants group. Which of the following must you do to accomplish this task? (Choose all that apply.)

A ❑ Create a separate printer for users of the Managers group and configure the printer to start printing immediately.

B ❑ Create a separate printer for users of the Managers group and set the print priority to 1.

C ❑ Create a separate printer for the users of the Managers group and set the print priority to 99.

D ❑ Create a separate printer for users of the Peons group and set the print priority to 1.

E ❑ Create a separate printer for users of the Peons group and set the print priority to 99.

4 What is the difference between the Print permission and the Manage Documents permission for a printer?

A ○ Manage Documents permissions allow users to submit jobs to printers, as well as manage documents submitted by any other user. Print permissions allow users to submit jobs to a printer, but only allows them to manage their own document.

B ○ Manage Documents permissions allow users to submit jobs to a printer, as well as manage documents submitted by any other user. Print permissions only allow users to submit a job to a printer.

C ○ Manage Documents permissions allow users to manage documents in a print queue, but does not allow them to submit their own jobs to a printer. Print permissions allow users to submit their own print jobs.

D ○ Manage Documents permissions allow users to manage print jobs they have submitted to the printer. Print permissions allow users to submit jobs to a printer.

5 By default, what permission do members of the Administrators group have on a newly created NT printer?

A ○ No Access

B ○ Print

C ○ Manage Documents

D ○ Full Control

6 The users that belong to your workgroup have sent several jobs to the print server, but the print device has produced no output. You enter the print queue and cannot delete the print jobs. What must you do to correct this problem?

A ○ Manually delete the files in the spool folder.

B ○ Stop and restart the spooler service.

C ○ Create a new printer that points to the same print device, and drag and drop all the jobs in the old print queue to the new print queue.

D ○ Stop and restart the server service.

7 When you try to connect to your Windows NT print server, you are prompted for the print driver for the print device. What could be the problem that is causing you to be prompted for this driver?

A ○ Incorrect driver on the print server.

B ○ No Access on the printer.

C ○ Spool directory is corrupt.

D ○ Scheduling priority is 0.

8 Jane wants to manage all the printers that are connected to her NT Workstation so that she can control access in her workgroup. Where can she manage the printers?

A ○ User Manager
B ○ Print Manager
C ○ Control Panel⇨Printers
D ○ Print Server

9 What is the permission that allows for managing all documents that are sent to the printer regardless of who sent them, but restricts access to printer properties?

A ○ Full Control
B ○ Manage Documents
C ○ Print
D ○ Special Access

Answers

1 *C, E.* To successfully implement a printing pool, all printers must be able to use a common driver and must be connected to the same print server. However, you can use different types of printer ports, such as one local port (LPT1) and one network port. When implementing a printing pool, all print devices act as a single physical unit, and directing a print job to a specific device without creating an additional NT printer isn't possible. *See "Installing a local printer (print device)."*

2 *C.* With the Print permission, users can send and manage the documents that they send to the printer only. They can view all other documents sent to the printer but cannot control them. *See "Security."*

3 *C, D.* Printer priority is set in the Scheduling tab for printer properties. The highest priority is 99, and the lowest is 1. *See "Scheduling."*

4 *A.* Manage Documents allows a user to manage any jobs that are submitted to the printer, but does not allow a user to manage the properties of the printer itself. *See "Security."*

5 *D.* Administrators that create the printer have Full Control over the printer and can make any changes to scheduling, sharing, ports, and properties and manage any documents that are sent to the printer. *See "Security."*

6 *B.* Resume from the Documents menu attempts to pick up printing where the device left off. Restart prints a document from the beginning, but you must restart the document before it is deleted from the spooler. *See "Troubleshooting Printer Problems."*

7 *A.* If you have installed the correct print drivers on your NT Workstation, Windows 95 and Windows NT clients should not be prompted to install necessary driver. *See "Connecting to a remote printer."*

8 *C.* To manage the printers that are connected to your NT Workstation, choose Control Panel⇨Printers. Here, you can control all the printer properties. *See "Configuring Printers."*

9 *B.* If you have Manage Documents permission, you can manage all documents that are sent to the printer, but you cannot change any printer properties, such as device settings. *See "Security."*

Part VII
Monitoring, Optimizing, and Troubleshooting

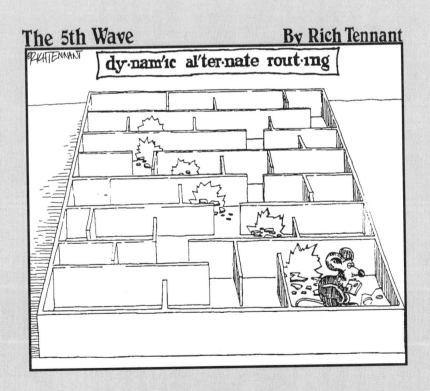

The 5th Wave · By Rich Tennant

dy·nam'ic al'ter·nate rout·ing

In this part . . .

Sooner or later, you run into a performance bottleneck on your NT Workstation. With the concept of Moore's Law (the theory that hardware resources double every 18 months), keeping your hardware up-to-speed is almost impossible. However, instead of panicking and calling someone for help, you can do all the troubleshooting yourself, with the help of Performance Monitor and a variety of system tools included on your NT Workstation. Performance Monitor tracks any resource that you specify — such as memory, processor, or hard disk — and sends back detailed information about the resource's performance. (Be sure to focus on this resource monitoring for the exam.)

Although your NT Workstation is just about tuned to perfection, not all computers or networks are the same. So you may have to tune and optimize your NT Workstation to meet a given situation.

Sometimes computers make mistakes. Another law that you may be familiar with is Murphy's Law: If something can go wrong, it probably will. And something always seems to go wrong at the worst possible time. Your job is to either prevent the worst from happening or troubleshoot the problem with minimum downtime. Something going wrong on the workstation isn't so bad, as long as you can fix the problem in a quick and reasonable manner.

The exam tests you on a variety of on-the-job scenarios. To prepare for these types of questions, be sure to know what to do (which tool is appropriate in a given situation) if the boot process fails, a print job fails, the installation process fails, an application fails, or a user can't access a resource or modify the Registry. Sound like a lot? Don't worry. Just turn the page, and you can see what you need to know!

Chapter 18

Workstation Monitoring and Performance

- -

Exam Objectives

▶ Monitor system performance by using various tools

▶ Identifying and resolving a given performance problem

▶ Optimize system performance in various areas

- -

*T*his chapter details the processes and counters to watch for when you are monitoring the performance on your NT Workstation, as well as information about how to increase the performance. For the exam, you need to know what tools to use to monitor your system's performance, how to identify and resolve performance problems, and how to optimize performance in a given area.

Here are some of the items that the exam concentrates on and that this chapter covers:

- ✔ Memory optimization, such as configuring your pagefile and using Performance Monitor to monitor your paging on your workstation.

- ✔ Troubleshooting problems associated with a bad processor or poor performance on your workstation, usually involving a scenario that gives you processor counters to check to see if a problem requires an upgrade.

- ✔ Disk performance issues, such as which utility to use in a given situation and what counters actually warrant an upgrade, as well as issues with physical and logical disk performance — the exam makers love to try to trick you with those questions.

- ✔ Improving application performance on an NT Workstation, which involves using some Windows NT tools, such as Performance Monitor and Task Manager (and a little common sense).

Quick Assessment

Optimize system performance in various areas

1 To help monitor your workstation, you can use _____.

Identify and resolve a given performance problem

2 You may have a hardware _____ if you are seeing poor performance on your NT Workstation.

3 _____ is a term that defines the use of multiple processors.

4 Windows NT 4.0 Workstation is a _____ operating system that can take advantage of more than one processor.

5 A great way to increase performance on your NT Workstation is to add more _____.

6 Name the four types of thread priorities.

7 Multiple threads make up a _____ in Windows NT.

Monitor system performance by using various tools

8 You can monitor different objects by specifying detailed _____ on your workstation.

9 Name the three most important resources that you have to monitor on your workstation.

10 Name three processor counters that you can monitor.

11 You can use the command-line utility _____ to monitor physical activity on the disk.

Answers

1   *Performance Monitor.* See "Monitor System Performance By Using Various Tools."

2   *Bottleneck.* See "Bottlenecks."

3   *Multiprocessing.* See "Optimizing Processor Performance."

4   *Symmetric multiprocessing.* See "Optimizing Processor Performance."

5   *RAM.* See "Optimizing Memory Performance."

6   *Real-time; High; Normal; Low.* See "Processes Prioritization."

7   *Process.* See "Processes Prioritization."

8   *Counters.* See "Object counters."

9   *Processor; memory; hard disk.* See "Monitor System Performance By Using Various Tools."

10   *% Processor Time; % Privileged Time; % User Time.* See "Object counters."

11   *Diskperf.* See "Monitoring physical disk performance."

Monitor System Performance By Using Various Tools

Performance monitoring on your NT Workstation can be an easy process from the get-go, or it can be a nightmare, depending on how you look at it. For starters, you're blessed with a wonderful tool that reports, in detailed form, almost any type of data that you specify, in Performance Monitor — also known as Perf Mon. (See Figure 18-1.) The downside is that Performance Monitor is an absolute monster! You have to get used to how Perf Mon actually works before you can start retrieving valuable information from your computer. But after you do, you'll be glad that you stuck with it. Performance Monitor can be your best friend when you get the hang of it. If you are going to remember anything about monitoring resources on your NT Workstation, try to remember the "Big Three." The Big Three are the three most common places where hardware resources fail:

- Memory
- Processor
- Hard Disk (physical drives and logical drives)

I also go over what counters you should be aware of and what to look for when things go wrong.

Identifying and Resolving a Given Performance Problem

Okay, suppose you're starting to get used to using Perf Mon and you begin seeing some performance problems. So what do you monitor on your NT Workstation? And why would you monitor them? How would you monitor them? Not to worry. There are labs later in the chapter to help you get comfortable with monitoring resources on your workstation. For more information on troubleshooting, check out Chapter 19.

When you use Performance Monitor, it's most important to get *accurate* data from your reports. To do this, you want to make sure that you get a baseline before you begin testing for bottlenecks. To get an accurate baseline, you should run Performance Monitor during *both* peak and off-peak hours. You must watch for bottlenecks and then decide which object counters to set up and watch in Performance Monitor.

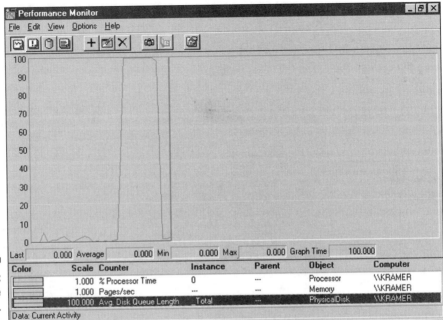

Figure 18-1:
Performance
Monitor.

Bottlenecks

Imagine trying to fit a square block in a round hole. That is what your NT Workstation is trying to do when it runs out of a needed resource, such as memory, processor, or hard disks resources. Bottlenecks can really make life terrible on your NT Workstation.

Although bottlenecks can be hard to troubleshoot, they don't have to destroy your workstation. You can think of bottlenecks as your NT Workstation's way of telling you that something is wrong. If you suspect that you have a bottleneck, your job is to troubleshoot and diagnose the problem.

Some exam questions ask you to troubleshoot individual bottlenecks on your NT Workstation, such as how to decide what resources need replacing. This is where your experience with Performance Monitor helps.

Keeping a close eye on your NT Workstation will help you troubleshoot any problems you may be having. When something goes wrong on your NT Workstation, it could be a number of different areas that need fixing. Being aware of how your NT Workstation is behaving helps you decide what is wrong with your computer. Check out Figure 18-2 for an example of using Performance Monitor to troubleshoot problems on your NT Workstation.

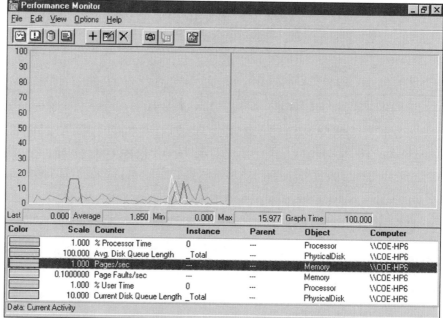

Figure 18-2:
Using
Performance
Monitor to
troubleshoot
problems
on the
desktop.

The test will ask you to identify and troubleshoot different hardware problems on your NT Workstation. The areas that you have to be concerned about for the test are processor, memory, and hard disks. The following list includes these hardware areas and some common problems associated with each type of hardware.

Memory (you need to add more RAM):

  ✔ Poor performance within applications or with having multiple applications open at once

  ✔ Slow performance

  ✔ Constant paging

Processor (add one or more processors):

  ✔ Slow performance when running intensive applications, such as SQL Server or Exchange

  ✔ Lots of number crunching or heavy compiling

Hard disk (need a faster seek time for hard disk or another hard disk adapter):

  ✔ Bad adapter or slow access time to hard disk

  ✔ Increased page faults

Object counters

With Performance Monitor, you can collect, average, and display all different types of data on your workstation from various objects collected on your NT Workstation. All you have to do is specify which counters that you want to monitor, and then you can begin the troubleshooting process. When I mention an "object," I am referring to something, such as processor, memory, physical hard disk, or logical drive. It all depends on what hardware resource you are referring to. A counter for that object defines the type of data that is available for a particular type of object, such as % **Processor Time** for Processor or % **Disk Time** for Logical Disk.

With this use of performance counters, you can collect data on almost any aspect of hardware and software performance on your workstation. This allows for a great degree of detail to monitor for bottlenecks, hardware failures, or needed upgrades. You can think of your object counters as a great pool of information, waiting to be tapped into. You can see in Figure 18-3 what object counters are available on your NT Workstation. All you have to do is set up the object counters on your workstation for the area that you suspect is causing the bottleneck. After you do that, all you have to do is sit back and wait!

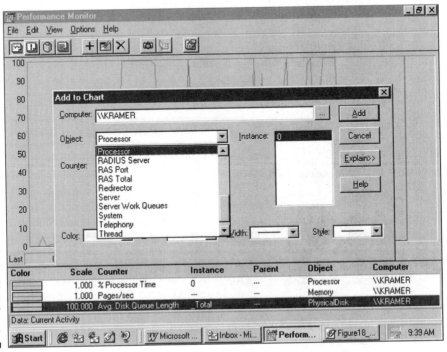

Figure 18-3: Object counters on your NT Workstation.

For this exam, you won't be tested on setting up or using Performance Monitor, but you will be tested on *which* object counters you should use and when to recognize *when* a resource on your computer is causing a bottleneck. That is what to watch out for and memorize for the exam.

Monitoring memory performance

Here are some counters to use in Performance Monitor for memory issues. Keep an eye on these counters if you suspect that your workstation is having memory problems.

- ✔ **Memory Available Bytes** displays the amount of free virtual memory.

- ✔ **Memory Pages/sec** provides the number of pages read from the disk or written to the disk to resolve memory references to pages that were not in memory at the time of the reference.

  As a rule, you can assume that if the *average* of this counter is consistently greater than 10, then memory is probably becoming a bottleneck in the system. After this counter starts to average consistently at 20 or above, performance is significantly degraded, and disk thrashing is probably occurring.

Monitoring processor performance

Troubleshooting processor performance on your NT Workstation (as shown in Figure 18-4) is a matter of selecting the necessary counters. Make sure that you memorize these counters because you will need to know them for the exam. Also, you may be asked whether to upgrade to a faster processor or even add another processor. Table 18-1 presents a list of counters to monitor if you are having any problems with your processor.

Table 18-1	Processor Counters
Counter	*Description*
% Processor Time	This measures the amount of time the processor is busy. When a processor is consistently running over 75 percent processor usage, the processor has become a system bottleneck. Analyze processor usage to determine what is causing the processor activity. This is accomplished by monitoring individual processes. If the system has multiple processors, then monitor the counter system: % Total Processor Time. Check out Figure 18-4 for an example of monitoring the performance of your processor.

Counter	Description
% Privileged Time	This measures the time the processor spends performing operating system services.
% User Time	This measures the time the processor spends performing user services, such as running a word processor.
Interrupts/sec	This is the number of interrupts the processor is servicing from applications or from hardware devices.
System: Processor Queue Length	This is the number of requests the processor has in its queue. It indicates the number of threads that are ready to be executed and are waiting for processor time.
Server Work Queues: Queue Length	This is the number of requests in the queue for the selected processor. If you have a queue length of over two, you are in trouble.

Monitoring physical disk performance

The number of physical disks in your NT Workstation is the number of hard disks that are being used. If you have five hard disks, you have five physical disks.

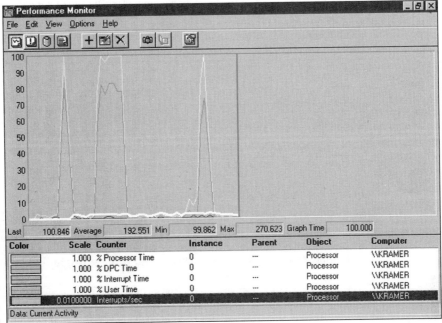

Figure 18-4:
Trouble-shooting
processor
performance.

If you want to monitor physical disk performance, you can run the command-line utility Diskperf.exe. This can be turned on when you are ready to begin monitoring physical disk performance, but it's important to know that a 10 percent to 15 percent performance hit is tacked on when Diskperf.exe is running. Diskperf.exe activates your physical disk counters so that you can use them with Performance Monitor. Because of the performance hit, it's not a good idea to keep this utility running all the time unless necessary. Otherwise, you may see degradation in other areas of your NT Workstation that may be confused as a bottleneck. You can see the command-line switches for Diskperf.exe in Figure 18-5.

Table 18-2 shows the command-line switches for Diskperf.exe.

Table 18-2	Diskperf.exe Command-Line Switches
Switch	*Description*
-Y[E]	Sets the system to start disk performance counters when the system is restarted.
E	Enables the disk performance counters used for measuring performance of the physical drives in striped disk set when the system is restarted. Specify -Y without the E to restore the normal disk performance counters.
-N	Sets the system disable disk performance counters when the system is restarted.
\\computername	Is the name of the computer you want either to see or to set disk performance counter use for.

For the exam, you'll want to remember that you have to turn on the physical disk performance counters for Performance Monitor with Diskperf.exe. You have to monitor logical disk performance with Performance Monitor only.

Remember that to activate the physical counters on your NT Workstation, you have to run Diskperf.exe from the command line!

Monitoring logical disk performance

The number of logical disks in your NT Workstation is the number of hard disks that Windows NT recognizes as drive letters. If you have C, D, and E drives in your NT Workstation, you have three logical disks. You could have five physical hard disks in your NT Workstation but only three logical disks.

Table 18-3 lists the counters to use when you want to monitor your logical disks.

Table 18-3	Counters for Monitoring Logical Disks
Counter	**Description**
% Disk Time	Indicates the amount of time that the disk drive is busy servicing read and write requests. If this number is consistently close to 100 percent, the disk is being used very heavily. Monitoring of individual processes can help determine which process or processes are making most of the disk requests.
Disk Queue Length	Indicates the number of pending disk I/O requests for the disk drive. If this value is consistently over 2, it indicates congestion.
Avg. Disk Bytes/Transfer	The average number of bytes transferred to or from the disk during write or read operations. The larger the transfer size, the more efficiently the system is running.
Disk Bytes/sec	The rate at which bytes are transferred to or from the disk during write or read operations. The higher the average, the more efficiently the system is running.

Check out Figure 18-5 for an example of monitoring logical disk performance.

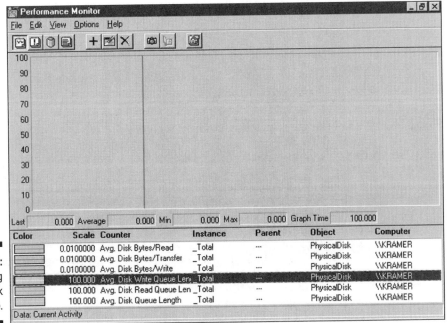

Figure 18-5:
Monitoring
logical disk
performance.

Optimizing Memory Performance

Making sure that you have optimized the NT Workstation memory correctly plays a large part in how well your computer runs. Memory optimization means

 ✔ Optimizing your pagefile

 ✔ Choosing the best place to put your pagefile

 ✔ Making sure that you have enough memory to run all your applications

If you run out of memory for your applications, your NT Workstation begins to use up virtual memory or moves portions of active processes to disk in order to reclaim physical memory. If this situation occurs often, performance suffers, and you experience what is called *paging*.

Optimizing the pagefile

To optimize performance on your NT Workstation, you have to optimize your pagefile so that you won't use up all of your good memory (physical memory, not virtual memory) and paging is kept as low as possible. Just remember that it uses up resources to process all the paging on your workstation.

Here is a summary of memory optimization with respect to pagefile:

Pagefile Size	Physical RAM + 11
Pagefile Location	Keep off of System Partition
Pagefile Location	Put your pagefile on multiple partitions
Pagefile Problems	Watch out for excessive paging!

Most of the questions that concern memory optimization are usually answered by "Adding more RAM" to the system. This is a standard question that you should expect. You'll even see it on other NT tests.

Essentially, your pagefile and virtual memory are the exact same thing. The size that you set for your pagefile on your NT Workstation determines how much virtual memory you have available for your applications. The Microsoft standard for virtual memory settings is to add the amount of physical RAM that you have installed on your NT Workstation and then add eleven. Check out Figure 18-6 as an example of how to configure your virtual memory on your NT Workstation. If you still aren't sure how to configure your virtual memory settings, Lab 18-1 will walk you through the steps to correctly configure your settings.

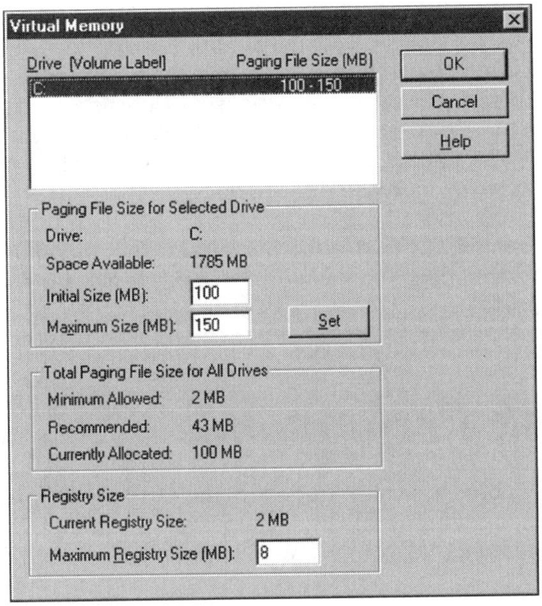

Figure 18-6:
Configuring
virtual
memory.

Lab 18-1   **Setting Up Your Virtual Memory**

1. Go to Start Menu⇨Settings⇨Control Panel.

2. Double-click the System icon.

3. Click the Performance tab.

4. Set up your pagefile according to how much memory you have.

5. Make sure that you click the Set button so that your changes are saved.

6. Reboot your computer for the changes to take effect.

Optimizing Processor Performance

The type of processor that you have installed on your NT Workstation has a huge effect on performance. If you have a Pentium 60 on your workstation and then upgrade to a 400 MHz Pentium II, you naturally see a major performance improvement. This only makes sense. Considering that hardware is becoming relatively cheap, it's not a major upgrade to get a faster processor or even add a second or third if your hardware supports it.

Another major benefit of Windows NT Workstation's support for symmetric multiprocessing (SMP) is that you can have multiple applications running at the same time with each sharing processor overhead. This essentially means that one application cannot hog all the processor time and cause slow performance if you have other applications open at the same time. To take advantage of SMP, you can add a second processor so that two processors work in tandem and really increase performance.

The bigger the processor, the better the performance. It only makes sense. For even better performance, you can add extra processors if your hardware configuration supports it.

Optimizing Disk Performance

Monitoring disk performance can require looking at several different areas. Controller type and the number of controllers have the most effect on the type of disk performance that your NT Workstation has.

Here are a couple of paths to follow for increasing disk performance on your workstation:

✔ Implement RAID, if you have the hardware resources. With RAID, you can implement disk striping (RAID 3) or disk striping with parity (RAID 5). Disk striping across your hard disks improves disk performance on your workstation.

For the exam, make sure that you understand each type of RAID that you can implement and the hardware resources (particularly the number of physical disks) that each type requires. Table 18-4 gives you this information.

✔ Another path to choose when trying to increase performance on your hard disks is making sure that your hard disk's access time is relatively low. The faster the access time to your hard disk, the faster and better the performance will be on your workstation.

Table 18-4	RAID Configurations	
RAID Number	*Number of Hard Disks Required*	*Type of RAID*
RAID 1	2	Disk mirroring
RAID 3	2 to 32 hard disks	Disk striping without parity
RAID 5	3 to 32 hard disks	Disk striping with parity

Make sure that you know how many physical disks you need to implement various levels of RAID. You may want to review Table 18-4 right before the exam.

Troubleshooting disk performance is a combination of monitoring your disk performance and knowing what to do when you are having a problem. In most situations, you need to upgrade to a new hard disk that has a quicker seek time or possibly add another hard disk adapter. If you are seeing a lot of paging to your hard disk, you should add more RAM to keep your NT Workstation from having to use virtual memory.

✔ Add more disk drives in a RAID environment, which spreads the data across multiple physical disks and improves performance, especially during reads.

✔ Offload processing to another system in the network (users, applications, or services).

Application Performance

Application performance has many different variables that may affect performance. These many variables take the form of processor, memory, hard disks, and paging. You can improve application performance by

✔ Reducing the number of applications that you have open, which reduces the resources that your NT Workstation has to allocate to such performance-hogging applications as Peer Web Services, Remote Access Service, and e-mail services.

✔ Scheduling memory-intensive applications during off-peak hours. You can use the AT scheduler that ships with Windows NT. For example, you may want to use the scheduler for tape backups because it doesn't make much sense to do a tape backup while a system is being heavily utilized by users.

✔ Distributing memory-intensive applications and processes across multiple machines. For example, if you are running Systems Management Server on the same machine as SQL Server, you may want to consider moving SQL Server to another system.

Processes Prioritization

Windows NT is a symmetric multiprocessing (SMP) system, meaning that it assumes that all of the processors are equal and that they all have access to the same physical memory. The following list explains what having SMP means in Windows NT:

- ✔ NT can use one or more processors in a computer as long as the processors are of the same type and are similarly configured.

- ✔ All processors are allowed to run a mixture of application and operating system code. In fact, different parts of the operating system can (and often do) run on different processors at the same time. This is good because you don't have one thread or process burning up the processor for a task while every other process or thread just waits around doing nothing.

- ✔ Because Windows NT uses SMP, your processes all get different priorities unless you specify otherwise. You can take a detailed look at processes if you open up Task Manager. Take a look at Figure 18-7 for an example of what I mean.

- ✔ Windows NT can run any thread on any available processor regardless of what process — user or executive — owns the thread.

If you have more than one processor, Windows NT performs better because of the way NT handles processes and threads. Instead of having each process or thread hog the processor, NT schedules the processor so that each thread or process can get enough time with the processor to finish the application. So the more processors you have, the more work your workstation can do.

```
C:\WINNT\system32\CMD.EXE                                              _ □ ×
tarts a separate window to run a specified program or command.

TART ["title"] [/Dpath] [/I] [/MIN] [/MAX] [/SEPARATE ¦ /SHARED]
      [/LOW ¦ /NORMAL ¦ /HIGH ¦ /REALTIME] [/WAIT] [/B] [command/program] [param
ters]

    "title"      Title to display in  window title bar.
    path         Starting directory
    I            The new environment will be the original environment passed
                 to the cmd.exe and not the current environment.
    MIN          Start window minimized
    MAX          Start window maximized
    SEPARATE     Start 16-bit Windows program in separate memory space
    SHARED       Start 16-bit Windows program in shared memory space
    LOW          Start application in the IDLE priority class
    NORMAL       Start application in the NORMAL priority class
    HIGH         Start application in the HIGH priority class
    REALTIME     Start application in the REALTIME priority class
    WAIT         Start application and wait for it to terminate
    B            Start application without creating a new window. The
                 application has ^C handling ignored. Unless the application
                 enables ^C processing, ^Break is the only way to interrupt the
                 application
    command/program
 -- More --
```

Figure 18-7: Looking at processes on the NT Workstation.

Processes

Remember these requirements for processes:

- ✔ A private memory address space in which the process's code and data are stored
- ✔ An access token against which Windows NT makes security checks
- ✔ System resources, such as files and windows (represented as object handles)
- ✔ At least one thread to execute the code

Threads

Remember these requirements for threads:

- ✔ A processor state, including the current instruction pointer
- ✔ A stack for use when running in user mode
- ✔ A stack for use when running in kernel mode

Be aware that multiple threads make up a process.

Expect a test question on the size of threads. A thread is the smallest schedulable unit in the system. You can kill a thread by terminating the last executing thread.

All threads are based on a 32-level priority scheme, 0 being the lowest priority and 31 the highest.

- ✔ The threads with the highest number have the highest priority and are running at any given time. Threads with a priority of 31 run before any others, whereas threads with a priority of 0 run only if no other threads are ready.
- ✔ The range of priorities is divided in half, with the upper 16 reserved for real-time threads and the lower 16 reserved for variable-priority threads.
- ✔ Windows NT determines which threads are given priority, and this status fluctuates a great deal so that no thread is hogging the processor.

You can use Task Manager to take a peek at what processes are running on your NT Workstation and see how they are behaving. If any processes are crashing or out of control, you can kill a process from here. See Table 18-5 for an explanation of the different priorities available to run the processes on your NT Workstation. And take a look at Figure 18-8 to see the Processes tab in Task Manager.

Table 18-5	Thread Priorities
Priority	**Description**
Real-time	Run at the same priority for their entire lifetime. They are commonly used to monitor or control systems that require action to be taken at very precise intervals. These threads run at higher priorities than all variable-priority threads, which means that real-time threads must be used sparingly.
High	Consume more processor time than the Normal or Low settings for your processes. This is a much safer option than running your threads at Real-time. Use this option if you need your application to receive a performance boost.
Normal	All applications are run from this priority level.
Low	This is the lowest setting that threads can run under, and they receive the lowest priority and processor time compared to all other processors. You can use this option if you have an application that is not very important to the work you're doing.

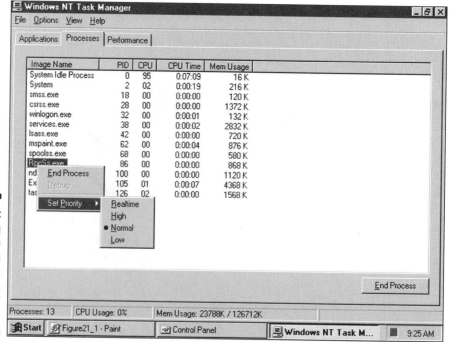

Figure 18-8:
Diagnosing
a file
system
cache
problem on
the NT
Workstation.

Remember that a thread is the smallest part of the microkernel. You can have multiple threads that make up a process.

Prep Test

1 What is the smallest unit that can be scheduled with the microkernel?

A ○ Thread

B ○ Process

C ○ Queue

D ○ Segment

2 You are experiencing excessive paging on your NT Workstation when running several applications at once. What should you do to improve performance?

A ○ Add a processor

B ○ Use NTFS

C ○ Add more RAM

D ○ Add another hard disk

3 If you want to monitor CPU utilization, which NT tool should you use?

A ○ Auditing

B ○ Performance Monitor

C ○ Windows NT Diagnostics

D ○ Protocol Analyzer

4 What kind of thread runs in the kernel or the priority of the operating system?

A ○ Real-time

B ○ High

C ○ Normal

D ○ Low

5 If you have 96MB of physical RAM, what should be the size of your pagefile?

A ○ 100

B ○ 206

C ○ 48

D ○ 107

6 What are some ways to optimize the pagefile on your computer? (Choose all that apply.)

A ❑ Keep the pagefile on the boot partition.

B ❑ Remove the pagefile from the system partition.

C ❑ Make the pagefile size equal to physical RAM plus 11.

D ❑ Keep the pagefile on multiple partitions.

7 Which two memory counters can you check if you are having problems with memory on your workstation?

A ❑ Memory Available Bytes

B ❑ Pagefile %'

C ❑ Memory Pages/sec

D ❑ Paging Size

8 If you want to monitor physical disk activity on your NT Workstation, what do you have to run?

A ○ Performance Monitor

B ○ Diskperf.exe

C ○ Windows Diagnostics

D ○ User Manager

9 When monitoring disk performance on your NT Workstation, you see that the Disk Queue Length is constantly over 2 for an extended period of time. What should you do?

A ○ Add more memory.

B ○ Add another processor.

C ○ Upgrade your processor.

D ○ Increase your paging file.

10 While monitoring processor performance on your workstation, you notice that your processor occasionally spikes above 75 percent. What should you do?

A ○ Upgrade your processor.

B ○ Add another processor.

C ○ Add more memory.

D ○ Do nothing.

11 What are the three most important objects that you can monitor on your NT Workstation?

A ❑ Processor

B ❑ Hard disks

C ❑ Bandwidth

D ❑ Memory

12 Which counters can you use to monitor your processor utilization? (Choose all that apply.)

A ❑ % Privileged Time

B ❑ % User Time

C ❑ Interrupts /Sec

D ❑ Disk Queue Length

13 What is a disadvantage of running Diskperf.exe to monitor physical disk performance on your NT Workstation?

A ○ Takes too long.

B ○ Performance degradation.

C ○ Inaccurate.

D ○ You could just use Performance Monitor.

14 What counters should you monitor if you are having trouble with your hard disks? (Choose all that apply.)

A ❏ Disk Queue Length

B ❏ % Disk Time

C ❏ % Access Time

D ❏ Managed Queue Length

15 What are the options for improving performance on your workstation when the resource is the processor? (Choose all that apply.)

A ❏ Add a second processor.

B ❏ Upgrade to Pentium Overdrive.

C ❏ Upgrade to a faster processor.

D ❏ Add more RAM.

16 What is the best method for using Performance Monitor on your NT Workstation?

A ○ Run Performance Monitor only at night.

B ○ Run Performance Monitor during peak and off-peak hours.

C ○ Run Performance Monitor during peak hours only.

D ○ Run Performance Monitor at random times during the work day.

Answers

1 *A.* A thread is the smallest unit of the microkernel. You can kill a thread by going into Task Manager and killing the active thread. *See "Processes Prioritization."*

2 *C.* Adding more RAM to your NT Workstation solves many problems, such as excessive paging and poor performance for your applications. *See "Optimizing Memory Performance."*

3 *B.* You can use Performance Monitor for monitoring many different counters on your NT Workstation, including memory, processor, and hard disk. *See "Object counters."*

4 *A.* A thread scheduled at real-time runs with the priority at kernel level, which is dangerous because if the thread running at the kernel level crashes, you could bring down the whole operating system. *See Table 18-5.*

5 *D.* When calculating the size of your pagefile, add 11 to the amount of physical RAM in your system. *See "Optimizing the pagefile."*

6 *B, C,* and *D.* To optimize your pagefile on your system, you should keep the pagefile off the system partition and, if possible, on multiple partitions. *See "Optimizing the pagefile."*

7 *A, C.* These counters are used predominantly to keep track of the amount of memory on your system. You can find them in Performance Monitor under the Memory object. *See "Monitoring memory performance."*

8 *B.* If you want to monitor physical disk performance on your NT Workstation, you have to run Diskperf.exe to activate the physical counters for Performance Monitor. *See "Monitoring physical disk performance."*

9 *A.* When you are monitoring your disk performance on your workstation with the Disk Queue Length counter, it may occasionally spike over 2. But if it does so frequently or consistently, you need to add more memory. *See Table 18-3.*

10 *D.* Occasional spiking over 75 percent utilization is normal. If you are experiencing repeated utilization over 75 percent, you have a bottleneck for your processor. *See Table 18-1.*

11 *A, B,* and *D.* When monitoring performance on your NT Workstation, you should make sure that you take a detailed look at memory, processor, and hard disk. These areas often cause bottlenecks on your workstation. *See "Monitor System Performance By Using Various Tools."*

12 *A, B.* % User Time measures the time the processor spends performing operating system services, and % Privileged Time measures the time the processor spends performing user applications. *See Table 18-1.*

13 *B.* Running Diskperf.exe on your workstation degrades performance 10 – 15 percent. *See "Monitoring physical disk performance."*

14 *A, B.* % Disk Time indicates the amount of time that the disk drive is busy servicing read and write requests. If this value is constantly close to 100 percent, the disk is being used very heavily, and you may want to upgrade. Disk Queue Length indicates the number of pending disk I/O requests for the disk drive. If this value is consistently over 2, you have a bottleneck that needs troubleshooting. *See Table 18-3.*

15 *A, C.* If you are having trouble with processor performance, you can either add a second processor or upgrade to a faster processor to fix the problem. *See "Optimizing Processor Performance."*

16 *B.* To receive the most accurate data from your NT Workstation's Performance Monitor, you should run tests in both peak and off-peak hours to determine a baseline for performance. *See "Monitor System Performance By Using Various Tools."*

Chapter 19

Troubleshooting without Guilt

Exam Objectives

▶ Monitor system performance by using various tools
▶ Identify and resolve a given performance problem
▶ Choose the appropriate course of action to take when an application fails
▶ Implement advanced techniques to resolve various problems

*O*ops. Some area of your computer isn't working. Everyone's had a problem like that, but the $64,000 question is, "Do you know how to fix the problem?" The hardest part is finding the tool to use — you can search and search for the right answer, but without the proper tools, you're out of luck.

Your job is to recognize what the problem is, figure out which tool to use to fix the problem, and restore NT Workstation to a state of operability. That's what troubleshooting is all about and what the exam wants to know: Can you diagnose the problem and fix your NT Workstation?

Hardware problems are easier to diagnose than software problems on your NT Workstation, but they're also harder to fix unless you have a graveyard of spare hardware devices. For the exam, you don't have to try to diagnose hardware problems, but you do need to know how to look for bottlenecks or hardware failures. (**Hint:** Performance Monitor, which is also covered in Chapter 18.)

You really need to know how to troubleshoot software problems in NT Workstation. The exam expects that you can recognize problems with the boot process, applications, security configurations, and so on, and fix the problem.

To make your life a little easier, Windows NT gives you access to a group of tools and safeguards in case your NT Workstation runs into trouble. With a little help from your ERD, Performance Monitor, and Windows NT Diagnostics, you can get your NT Workstation running perfectly in no time at all.

Quick Assessment

Monitor system performance by using various tools

1 For a quick summary of information on your NT Workstation, you can open _____.

2 A(n) _____ is used to help repair the workstation if your workstation crashes.

3 Quick. . . . The three logs in the Event Viewer are _____, _____, _____.

4 Name six tabs from the Windows NT Diagnostics tool.

Identify and resolve a given performance problem

5 True/False: You can boot up with your ERD if you're having problems with your NT Workstation.

6 Most problems with new computers deal with _____.

7 Name the three main hardware problems to watch out for on the exam.

8 _____ gives you detailed information about stop errors, service failure, and audits.

Choose the appropriate course of action when an application fails

9 To troubleshoot 16-bit applications, you should run them in their own _____.

10 If you're missing Ntoskrnl.exe, you need to double-check your _____ file.

Implement advanced techniques to resolve various problems

11 Name four of the tools that you use to troubleshoot your NT Workstation.

Answers

1   *NT Diagnostics.* See "Windows NT Diagnostics."

2   *Emergency Repair Disk.* See "The Boot Process: Restoration and ERD."

3   *Security; Application; System.* See "Event Viewer."

4   *Resources; Environment; Network; Display; Memory; Drivers; Version; System; Services.* See Table 19-2.

5   *False.* See "The Boot Process: Restoration and ERD."

6   *Hardware incompatibility.* See "Hardware."

7   *Memory; processor; hard disk.* See "Hardware."

8   *The Event Viewer.* See "Event Viewer."

9   *Memory spaces.* See "DOS."

10   *Boot.ini.* See Table 19-1.

11   *NT Diagnostics; Event Viewer; ERD; Performance Monitor.* See "Windows NT Diagnostics," "Event Viewer," "The Boot Process: Restoration and ERD," and Chapter 18.

Installation

You can run into many different problems when installing NT 4.0. The first place to start is with your hardware requirements. Do you have enough hardware resources to install NT 4.0? If so, you can go on to the next step, which is to check the Hardware Compatibility List (HCL) — see the next section of this chapter for more about hardware. Check out Chapter 4, if you forget the hardware requirements for Windows NT 4.0 Workstation.

Sometimes when installing NT 4.0, you can specify generic drivers if NT doesn't recognize any of your new hardware. This option can save you some time and anguish if your hardware isn't on the HCL.

Hardware

For the exam, you won't be asked to sit down and look inside a computer. But you are expected to know how to look for hardware problems, which you do with a little common sense and a handy tool known as the Performance Monitor. We cover using Performance Monitor to uncover bottlenecks and other problems in Chapter 18.

The exam doesn't test you on hardware problems that require specific hardware tools to troubleshoot, such as a bad Intel motherboard or a power supply on the fritz. Concentrate on IRQ conflicts and the big three: memory, processor, and hard disk. Review Chapter 18 carefully!

New computers

Most problems that occur with new computers deal with hardware-incompatibility issues. The way that hardware turns over and with all the technological features that keep popping up, it's tough to stay afloat.

To help make life easier for you and your new computer, Microsoft provides the Hardware Compatibility List (HCL), which you use to check the hardware configuration of your computer and make sure that all your hardware is compatible with Windows NT 4.0 Workstation. If Microsoft hasn't tested your hardware for compatibility, you may have to wait until working drivers are available, or find some new hardware that *is* compatible with NT 4.0. See Figure 19-1 for an example of the Hardware Compatibility List located on Microsoft's Web site at www.microsoft.com. You can find an updated copy of the HCL on the Microsoft Web site, in Microsoft TechNet, or in the Microsoft setup newsgroups on the Net.

DOS

Yep, you still have to know how to deal with those lovely 16-bit applications in today's 32-bit world. Because Windows NT has some minor problems running 16-bit applications, you may run into some problems with DOS applications. Check out Chapter 16 for more details on this subject.

Make sure that a troublesome16-bit application is running in its own memory space, which prohibits the DOS application from affecting any other 16-bit applications on the workstation. If your 16-bit apps aren't running in their own memory spaces and one crashes, *all* the 16-bit apps crash. (Of course, this crash doesn't affect your 32-bit apps.) But if the 16-bit apps are running in their own memory spaces, one crash doesn't affect the other 16-bit apps.

BIOS problems

BIOS problems on your workstation usually deal with computers that don't work properly with new hardware. To fix this problem, you can upgrade the BIOS of your computer by downloading a new BIOS from your hardware manufacturer's Web site or bulletin board.

Figure 19-1: Checking out the Hardware Compatibility List.

Hardware conflicts (IRQs)

You may not see any questions about hardware interrupts, but reviewing your list of IRQs before the exam is always a good idea. Unfortunately, you don't have a cool utility like the Device Manager within Windows NT to check for IRQ problems. You can use Windows NT Diagnostics to verify your IRQs, but the information you get doesn't describe the conflict. See Table 19-1 for a quick list of the IRQs and their designations.

Table 19-1	List of IRQs
IRQ	**Designation**
2)	EGA / VGA (enhanced graphics adapter / Video Graphics Adapter)
3)	Only available (unless used for second serial port (COM2, COM 4) or bus mouse)
4)	COM1, COM3
5)	Available (might be used for second parallel port or sound card)
6)	Floppy-disk controller
7)	Parallel Port (LPT1)
8)	Real-time Clock
10)	Available
11)	Available
12)	Mouse (PS/2)
13)	Math coprocessor
14)	Hard disk controller
15)	Available

The best place to start, if you suspect any type of hardware conflicts on your workstation, is the event log (located in Event Viewer), to check for services failing to start.

Hard disk controllers

Your hard disk controller can affect many areas on your NT Workstation, such as disk-access time and paging. Unfortunately, you can monitor only your hard disks and not your hard disk controller with Windows NT. (If you have an OEM version of Windows NT 4.0, you may see some third-party applications that take a detailed look at how your hardware is running, but that option is mainly for NT Servers or high-end NT Workstations.)

Your only choice of action is to monitor your hard disk with the Performance Monitor to see whether you're having any trouble with paging or really slow disk access. Then you may want to invest in upgrading your hard disk controller or adding a second to take the load off the first one if you access your hard disk heavily. If you're having problems with your hard disk, you may need to upgrade your controller (or add more memory, if you're experiencing heavy paging).

The Boot Process: Restoration and ERD

Most of the troubleshooting questions on the exam involve the boot process. So put down that cup of coffee and pay close attention! The problem is that troubleshooting the boot process isn't easy — you'd have to crash your workstation to create the errors, and you probably don't want to do that, do you? Not to worry, though: This section of the chapter tells you which error messages to look for and what to do about them.

Table 19-2 tells you which fixes go along with the error messages that you're likely to see on the exam.

Table 19-2	Boot-Sequence Errors
Error	*Solution*
Windows NT could not start because the following file is missing or corrupt: \Winnt Root\System32\ Ntoskrnl.Exe. Please reinstall a copy of the above file.	Problem with Boot.ini.
Non-System disk or disk error. Replace and press any key when ready.	Bootsect.dos file is missing.
Your Windows NT Workstation computer will not boot properly. You suspect that the boot sector is corrupt or that some system files are missing.	Start the computer from the Windows NT Workstation setup disks and start the emergency repair process.

If your NT Workstation does end up crashing and burning, you may need to restore your workstation, which you do by using one of the following:

- The Last Known Good Configuration
- The Emergency Repair Disk (ERD)

Making yourself an ERD is the best way to recover from a serious failure on your NT Workstation. You just have to remember to actually make one! Lab 19-1 shows how.

Lab 19-1   Creating Your First ERD

1. **At the command prompt, type:** C:\Rdisk.exe

   You see the Repair Disk Utility dialog box.

2. **Click the Update Repair Info button and respond with yes when asked whether you want to create an ERD.**

3. **Insert a 3¹/₂-inch floppy disk and click OK to begin the process.**

The system copies the following files from C:\Winnt\System32\Repair to your floppy ERD:

- ✔ Autoexec.nt
- ✔ Config.nt
- ✔ Default._
- ✔ Ntuser.da_
- ✔ Sam._
- ✔ Security._
- ✔ Setup.log
- ✔ Software._
- ✔ System._

Figure 19-2 shows the step for creating your ERD for your NT Workstation.

You can't just put in your ERD if something goes wrong on your workstation. You have to boot to NT with your three setup floppies and *then* use your ERD to fix your corrupted workstation. After you've used your ERD, you can select the Inspect Registry Files option from the Repair menu.

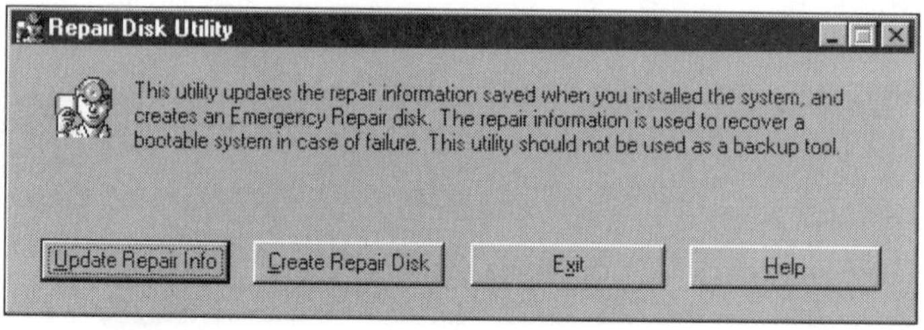

Figure 19-2:
Creating an
ERD for
your NT
Workstation.

Repair Disk Utility

This utility updates the repair information saved when you installed the system, and creates an Emergency Repair disk. The repair information is used to recover a bootable system in case of failure. This utility should not be used as a backup tool.

| Update Repair Info | Create Repair Disk | Exit | Help |

Keep in mind also that Windows NT is not your typical operating system, where you can just make a boot disk and use it to make everything okay again.

You can update the system information for your ERD by using the /S switch when you run Rdisk.exe.

Windows NT Diagnostics

The Windows NT Diagnostics tool, located in the Administrative Tools program group on your NT Workstation, is a collection of many tools in one convenient location. Instead of opening several applications at once, you can just open the diagnostics tool and get a quick summary of what's happening on your NT Workstation.

For more detailed information, you can open another application — such as Control Panel⇨Services, Control Panel⇨Display, or Disk Administrator — but for a quick look at your system, NT Diagnostics can't be beat.

Table 19-3 gives you details on what you do in each tab of the NT Diagnostics dialog box.

Table 19-3	Windows NT Diagnostics Tabs
Tab	*What to Use It For*
Version	Build number, service packs installed, registered owner
System	BIOS number, HAL, processor info
Display	Display driver, amount of video memory, type of adapter
Drives	Local drives on your system, including floppy, hard disk, and CD-ROM
Memory	Physical memory, virtual memory, kernel memory
Services	What services and devices are running and stopped on your NT Workstation
Resources	IRQ states
Environment	Number of processors, path, Windir, OS
Network	Quick summary of network information, such as transports, statistics, settings, and profile information

See Figure 19-3 for an example of what you can do with Windows NT Diagnostics.

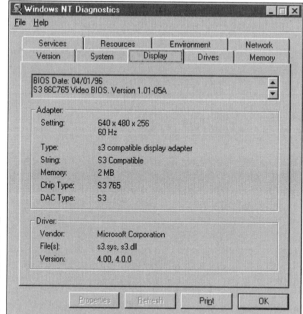

Figure 19-3:
Using
Windows
NT
Diagnostics.

Event Viewer

The Event Viewer can be your best friend when you're trying to trouble-shoot your NT Workstation on the fly. If you're suspecting any problems on your NT Workstation, you can just open up the Event Viewer to see what the issue is with an application. Inside Event Viewer, you'll find the application log and system log. These logs keep detailed information on how your applications are behaving and the different changes to the system.

See Figure 19-4 for an example of what you may see if you check out the Application Log on your Windows NT Workstation.

Also located within Event Viewer is the Administrator's secret weapon — the Security Log! The Security Log lets you keep detailed information on what is happening on the workstation, including security issues, such as permissions, user rights, and policies. Besides checking up on applications with Event Viewer, you can also find out about certain security events. See

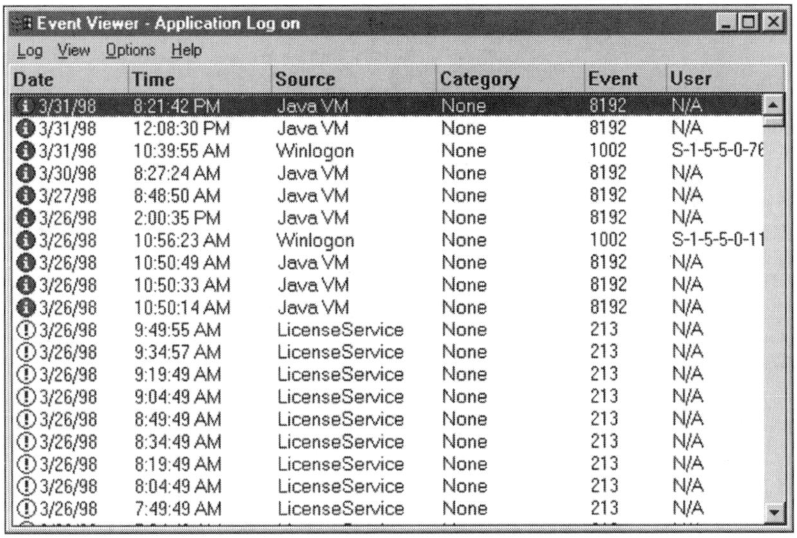

Date	Time	Source	Category	Event	User
3/31/98	8:21:42 PM	Java VM	None	8192	N/A
3/31/98	12:08:30 PM	Java VM	None	8192	N/A
3/31/98	10:39:55 AM	Winlogon	None	1002	S-1-5-5-0-78
3/30/98	8:27:24 AM	Java VM	None	8192	N/A
3/27/98	8:48:50 AM	Java VM	None	8192	N/A
3/26/98	2:00:35 PM	Java VM	None	8192	N/A
3/26/98	10:56:23 AM	Winlogon	None	1002	S-1-5-5-0-11
3/26/98	10:50:49 AM	Java VM	None	8192	N/A
3/26/98	10:50:33 AM	Java VM	None	8192	N/A
3/26/98	10:50:14 AM	Java VM	None	8192	N/A
3/26/98	9:49:55 AM	LicenseService	None	213	N/A
3/26/98	9:34:57 AM	LicenseService	None	213	N/A
3/26/98	9:19:49 AM	LicenseService	None	213	N/A
3/26/98	9:04:49 AM	LicenseService	None	213	N/A
3/26/98	8:49:49 AM	LicenseService	None	213	N/A
3/26/98	8:34:49 AM	LicenseService	None	213	N/A
3/26/98	8:19:49 AM	LicenseService	None	213	N/A
3/26/98	8:04:49 AM	LicenseService	None	213	N/A
3/26/98	7:49:49 AM	LicenseService	None	213	N/A

Event Viewer - Application Log on

Log   View   Options   Help

Figure 19-4: Checking out the Application Log in the Event Viewer.

Figure 19-5 for an example of what populates your Security Log in Event Viewer. If you have auditing enabled on your workstation, you can check up on what's going on by opening the Security Log in the Event Viewer, where you can find this detailed information:

- Who's logging on
- Who's accessing which files (remember that you need NTFS to audit files and folders)
- Other security issues, such as policies and user rights

See Chapter 8 for more about auditing.

You must be an administrator or a member of the Administrators local group to view the security log.

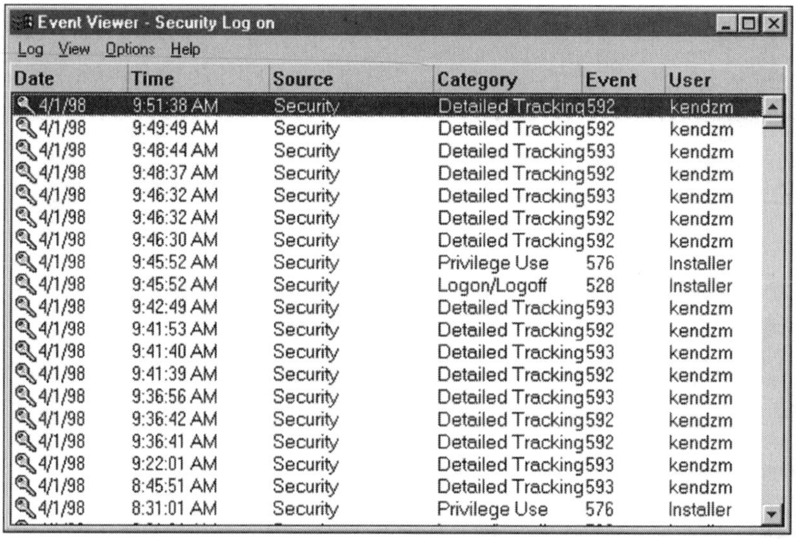
Event Viewer - Security Log on
Log View Options Help
Date Time Source Category Event User
4/1/98 9:51:38 AM Security Detailed Tracking 592 kendzm
4/1/98 9:49:49 AM Security Detailed Tracking 592 kendzm
4/1/98 9:48:44 AM Security Detailed Tracking 593 kendzm
4/1/98 9:48:37 AM Security Detailed Tracking 592 kendzm
4/1/98 9:46:32 AM Security Detailed Tracking 593 kendzm
4/1/98 9:46:32 AM Security Detailed Tracking 592 kendzm
4/1/98 9:46:30 AM Security Detailed Tracking 592 kendzm
4/1/98 9:45:52 AM Security Privilege Use 576 Installer
4/1/98 9:45:52 AM Security Logon/Logoff 528 Installer
4/1/98 9:42:49 AM Security Detailed Tracking 593 kendzm
4/1/98 9:41:53 AM Security Detailed Tracking 592 kendzm
4/1/98 9:41:40 AM Security Detailed Tracking 593 kendzm
4/1/98 9:41:39 AM Security Detailed Tracking 592 kendzm
4/1/98 9:36:56 AM Security Detailed Tracking 593 kendzm
4/1/98 9:36:42 AM Security Detailed Tracking 592 kendzm
4/1/98 9:36:41 AM Security Detailed Tracking 592 kendzm
4/1/98 9:22:01 AM Security Detailed Tracking 593 kendzm
4/1/98 8:45:51 AM Security Detailed Tracking 593 kendzm
4/1/98 8:31:01 AM Security Privilege Use 576 Installer

Figure 19-5: Checking out the Security Log in the Event Viewer.

Prep Test

1 Certain startup problems can be corrected by running the emergency repair process. Which of the following tasks can be accomplished by the emergency repair process? (Choose all that apply.)

A ❏ Verifying Windows NT system files

B ❏ Inspecting the startup environment

C ❏ Inspecting the boot sector

D ❏ Making an ERD

2 You share your Windows NT Workstation computer with several coworkers. You have just updated the Emergency Repair Disk by running Rdisk.exe with the /s switch. A complete backup of all system files, including the Registry, was done one week ago. Now a sudden system crash occurs, and the user-accounts database is lost. No one can log on to Windows NT. Which steps do you need to take? (Choose all that apply.)

A ❏ Boot to your NT Boot disk.

B ❏ Boot the computer by using the Windows NT Workstation setup disks and run the emergency repair process.

C ❏ Select the Inspect Registry Files option from the Repair menu.

D ❏ Use Last Known Good Configuration.

3 Laura V. wants to get a quick display of her system resources, such as memory, drives, services, and network information. However, she doesn't want to open several applications at once. Which tool should she use?

A ○ Event Viewer

B ○ Performance Monitor

C ○ Event Log

D ○ NT Diagnostics .

4 You are receiving several stop errors when you shut down your NT Workstation. Where can you view these errors to help troubleshoot them?

A ○ Event Viewer

B ○ Performance Monitor

C ○ Emergency Repair Disk

D ○ NT Diagnostics

5 After rebooting his workstation, Max receives the error message `Non-System disk or disk error; Replace and press any key when ready`. Which file is missing or needs to be replaced on the workstation?

A ○ Bootsect.dos

B ○ Boot.ini

C ○ Ntldr

D ○ NetBootDD.sys

6 Lorna B. just bought a brand-new computer with Windows 95 installed. However, because she likes Windows NT so much, she formats her workstation and tries to load Windows NT. However, when she tries to install NT, she keeps getting errors. What could she have done to eliminate her installation problems?

A ○ Run Setup.exe

B ○ Used Windows NT Diagnostics

C ○ Checked the Hardware Compatibility List before installation

D ○ Changed motherboards

7 How can you prevent your 16-bit applications from crashing one another if one of them crashes?

A ○ Run each in its own memory space.

B ○ Use NT Diagnostics.

C ○ Run CrashPrevent.exe.

D ○ Use the Event Viewer.

8 Which files are not located on your Emergency Repair Disk? (Choose all that apply.)

A ❑ Autoexec.bat

B ❑ Registry

C ❑ Config.nt

D ❑ Sam._

E ❑ BillGates.log

F ❑ Setup.log

G ❑ Device.log

H ❑ Regedt32.exe

I ❑ Ansi.sys

9 What are the two options for recovering from an NT Workstation system failure?

A ❑ ERD

B ❑ Windows NT Diagnostics

C ❑ Last Known Good Configuration

D ❑ Recover.exe

Answers

1 *A, B,* and *C.* If you boot with the three Windows NT setup floppies and run the emergency repair process, you can verify Windows NT system files, inspect the startup environment, repair a damaged Registry, or inspect the NT boot sector. Also remember that you cannot boot to your ERD. *See "The Boot Process: Restoration and ERD."*

2 *B, C.* By starting the emergency repair process, you can get to the menu that allows you to fix a damaged Registry on your NT Workstation. *See "The Boot Process: Restoration and ERD."*

3 *D.* Windows NT Diagnostics allows you to get quick system information on a variety of system resources, such as services, network, environment, memory, version, and display. *See "Windows NT Diagnostics."*

4 *A.* If you are receiving any stop errors on your NT Workstation, you can view them in the Event Viewer. *See "Event Viewer."*

5 *A.* The Bootsect.dos file is missing or corrupt. Max will also not be able to boot to MS-DOS. *See Table 19-1.*

6 *C.* Before installing Windows NT on any new piece of hardware, check the Hardware Compatibility List to make sure that your hardware will work with Windows NT 4.0 Workstation. *See "Hardware."*

7 *A.* By running your 16-bit applications in their own memory spaces, you can keep them from crashing one another (normally, they share the same memory space). *See "DOS."*

8 *A, B, E, G, H,* and *I, . See "The Boot Process: Restoration and ERD."*

9 *A, C.* If your workstation crashes, you have two options: use Last Known Good Configuration or use the recovery process with your ERD. *See "The Boot Process: Restoration and ERD."*

Part VIII
The Part of Tens

In this part . . .

This part of the book contains top-ten lists of useful information to help you emerge victorious from the Workstation NT 4.0 exam. Chapter 20 is crammed with proven test-day tips from those in the know — successful test-takers. These tips include valuable organizing and study tips to use as you're preparing for the exam. Chapter 21 lists the best online exam-preparation resources recommended by MCSEs — including myself!

Chapter 20

Don't Panic! And Other Test-Day Tips

In This Chapter

▶ Preparing for the exam without panicking

▶ Gaining moral support from a study group or a test-taking friend

▶ Making the study process as easy as possible

▶ Using all the study resources at your disposal

▶ Spending the night before the exam

You spent the last couple of days or weeks or months preparing for the NT Workstation exam, and you seem ready to take it. But are you *really* ready? If that question makes you nervous, relax. This chapter tells you how to be sure that you're ready to ace that exam when the Big Day comes. These common-sense tips have worked well for us over the years, so they're sure to help you, too.

You've already taken the first and most important step toward passing the exam: buying this book. If you've got a good grasp of all the topics covered in these pages, you'll do fine. Don't forget to check out Chapter 21, which gives you some great online resources to help you prepare for the exam. These Internet sites are well worth the time you spend browsing through them. Take advantage of the exam warriors who are willing to share their experiences and expertise with you over your modem!

Don't panic! You *will* pass the exam. A little positive reinforcement goes a long way.

> ✔ You've put in countless hours preparing for this exam.
>
> ✔ You've run through this book's lab exercises and absorbed all the tables of information (right?).
>
> ✔ You know how to pass this exam.

Just take a deep breath and go do it!

Join a Study Group

The Microsoft exams are by no means easy. Forming a study group with people who are going through the same process as you is a great help. You can

- Share personal experiences related to the exams and the subject matter.
- Find out about the study materials and methods that other people use.
- Bounce practice questions around.
- Bond with people who understand what you're going through.

Knowledge is power. The more of it you grasp, the better off you are.

Organize Your Study Notes

Work smarter, not harder. You're making the study process even more difficult when you have a small tree's worth of notes that you carry around and spend all your time sorting through.

Organize your notes into an outline form. Better yet, make them mirror the exam preparation guide (see "Go over the Exam Preparation Guide with a Fine-Tooth Comb" in this chapter) so that you have the answers right in front of you, in the Microsoft-prescribed order. This will help your study efficiency and help you memorize the necessary answers for the exam.

Use Flash Cards

For the questions that give you the most trouble, write each on a flash card (question on the front, answer on the back) and then run through the flash cards several days over the course of your studying. You'll be surprised at how the answers sink in. Trust us — flash cards work.

Memorize with Phonetics

Memorizing simple phrases where the first letter of each word stands for a piece of a complicated concept *(mnemonics)* is sometimes easier than memorizing the complicated concept on its own terms.

For example, the OSI Model consists of seven deadly layers: application, presentation, session, transport, network, data link, and physical. Take the first letter of each word and make a phrase: <u>A</u>ll <u>P</u>eople <u>S</u>eem <u>T</u>o <u>N</u>eed <u>D</u>ata <u>P</u>rocessing. Not quite as hard to remember that way, is it?

Go over the Exam Preparation Guide with a Fine-Tooth Comb

The Microsoft Web site offers the essential Preparation Guide for Exam 70-073 (www.microsoft.com/mcp/exam/stat/sp70-073.htm), which lists the topics covered on the Windows NT 4.0 Workstation exam. Take advantage of this guide; it should be your bible. Be sure to know the ins and outs of every item listed on that page — which is exactly what this book gives you — and don't waste time studying what the exam doesn't test you on.

Check out Microsoft TechNet

The Microsoft TechNet CD-ROM set has all the technical information you need about Microsoft products: articles, resource kits, knowledge base, tech support, drivers, service packs, white papers, and case studies. Just enter your query in the TechNet engine, and you get instant information from every source you can imagine.

You can find a lot of great information on the Microsoft TechNet CD-ROM in the section MS BackOffice and Enterprise Systems\Windows NT Workstation. Here you can find the Resource Kits, Technical Notes, and Tools and Utilities, as well as Product Facts. These are all great resources when you're stuck on a difficult exam question.

Microsoft TechNet has bailed this book's authors out of more tough situations than we'd like to remember. The subscription costs $300 if you're not an MCSE (as an MCSE, you get a free subscription).

Using the MS Windows NT Workstation 4.0 Resource Guide

With the NT Workstation Resource Guide, you learn the technology and prepare to take the exam at the same time. You can find everything you need to know about Windows NT in the kit; having all this information in a single volume makes finding NT answers much easier for you. This valuable tool is your one-stop shop for NT information.

Take the Exam with a Friend

Taking the exam with a friend who's also pursuing MCSE status is a great morale booster and the last line of defense before you go take your test — who else can you bounce a question off of at the midnight hour?

Being with a friend can also relieve some of the tension just before the exam. You can't be serious all the time!

Don't Cram

Don't cram? Are we serious? Yep. Pace yourself through the exam- preparation process; give yourself enough time to get ready to take the exam. If you try to cram for this exam, you're leaving yourself open to mistakes and long, sleepless nights.

If you need more time, no problem! Call Sylvan or Virtual University Enterprises (VUE) and reschedule your exam for another day. You don't get special bonus points for passing one week earlier. All that matters is that you pass.

You can contact Sylvan Prometric by calling 1-800-755-EXAM or checking out their Web site at `http://www.sylvanprometric.com/testingcandidates/register/reg.asp`. You can reach Virtual University Enterprises (VUE) at 888-837-8616 and see their website at `http://www.vue.com`.

Get a Good Night's Rest

This tip may be the hardest: Get a good night's rest just before the exam. You may have a hard time falling asleep with all the NT information buzzing in your brain, but getting at least eight hours of sleep will make you more mentally awake when you take the exam. As long as you take the time to thoroughly understand all the topics covered in this book, you'll still remember it all on the day of the exam, without staying up all night cramming or worrying.

Chapter 21

Taking Advantage of the Net

. . . .

In This Chapter

▶ Going straight to the source, microsoft.com

▶ Finding out more about the Windows NT Workstation exam

▶ Sharpening your skill at working with Windows NT Workstation

▶ Exploring the Net for everything you never knew about the NT Workstation exam

. . . .

*T*he best part about being connected to the Internet is the amazing number of resources that you have right at your fingertips. A little searching, and a wealth of information is yours. Even better, you have this chapter, which leads you to ten of the best Web sites for NT Workstation certification candidates so that you can spend more time studying and less time looking for study guides.

Online resources fall into two types of study categories. The first category consists of resources to help you learn the technology, with no direct references to the exam. For example, the *Windows NT 4.0 Workstation Resource Kit* isn't specifically geared toward certification, but you can find many exam answers throughout the book. The second category is for any study resource specifically tied to exam certification. This study material tells you just as much about the technology as you need to know to pass the exam (this book falls into the second category, but it still gets down and dirty with the technology).

Take advantage of all the resources you have available — think of the two categories as cross-training for the exam.

Microsoft Home Page

microsoft.com

Ahh . . . the mother lode. The Microsoft home page is where it all starts, boys and girls. Aside from the certification and download pages, which other sections of this chapter cover, the Microsoft Web site offers detailed product listings, tech support for individual products, up-to-date information about each product, and just about any kind of information you can think of about all existing and legacy Microsoft products. Although Microsoft's Web site is HUGE, you can still find a lot of information about the exam through the Knowledge Base Support site and the various pages that detail the Microsoft Pages. All you have to do is search for the information that you're looking for and the door to the NT Workstation exam is wide open. You can access all these resources from the home page, which Figure 21-1 shows.

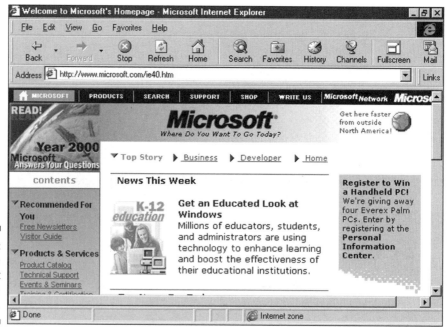

Figure 21-1:
The
Microsoft
Web site
home page.

Microsoft Training and Certification

`www.microsoft.com/train_cert`

The Microsoft Web site has a whole section dedicated to the training and certification of Microsoft Certified Professionals, with new exams, case studies, exam prep pages, and listings of existing exams — everything that you need for becoming and remaining an MCP. Figure 21-2 shows you this can't-live-without-it resource.

The Microsoft Preparation Guide for Exam 70-073 should be your study-guide map. Microsoft actually tries to make your life easier by telling you what the exam covers. You can click the link `www.microsoft.com/Mcp/exam/stat/SP70-073.htm` on the Training and Certification home page to look up the prep guide. Here you can find all the information that you need to know about what to study for the exam.

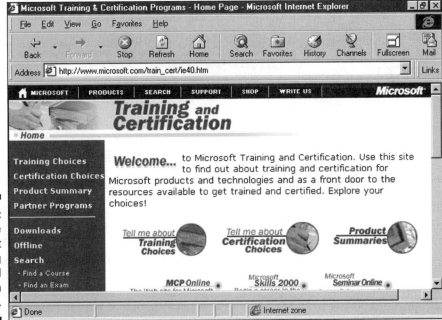

Figure 21-2: The Microsoft Training and Certification home page.

The Microsoft Training and Certification Download Page

`www.microsoft.com/train_cert/download/downld.htm`

The Microsoft Training and Certification page lets you download cool software utilities to help you study for the exams. Need a case study? A practice exam? How about a white paper? The download page, which Figure 21-3 shows, skips all the extra Web pages and gets down to the software applications. You can use this resource to find out more about the various tools that Windows NT 4.0 Workstation can take advantage of. Also, you can find documentation that explains the down-and-dirty technological details.

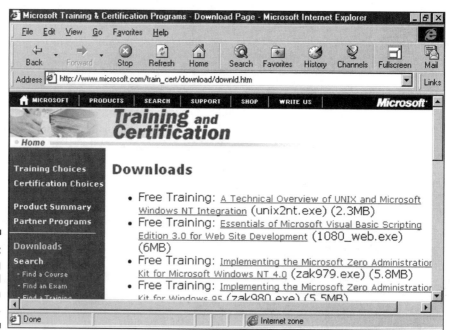

Figure 21-3:
Downloading training and certification software.

Microsoft Certified Professional Magazine Online

www.mcpmag.com

You can check out the latest issue of *Microsoft Certified Professional Magazine* online at this Web site, which Figure 21-4 shows. Find interesting articles concerning study-guide product reviews (even some written by this book's author), technology summaries, and the latest information about Microsoft Certified Professional exams.

This Web site has access to the technical forums, where you can check out or post your own messages concerning individual exams, study guides, and possible exam questions. Just like this book, this site is good for figuring out what to concentrate on and what to avoid when studying.

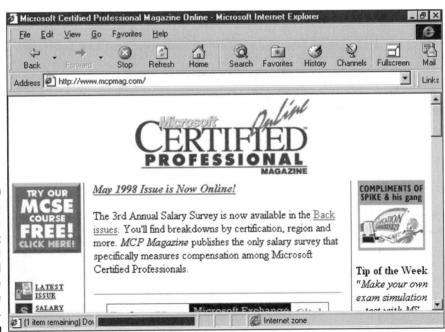

Figure 21-4:
The Microsoft Certified Professional Magazine Online home page.

Yahoo!

www.yahoo.com

The Yahoo! search engine is a good place to start when searching the Web for data about taking the exam or about becoming a Microsoft Certified Professional. Type a phrase in the search box shown in Figure 21-5, and off you go.

Here are some tips for search phrases:

- MCSE
- Braindump
- Exam Number (70-073)
- Certification
- MCP

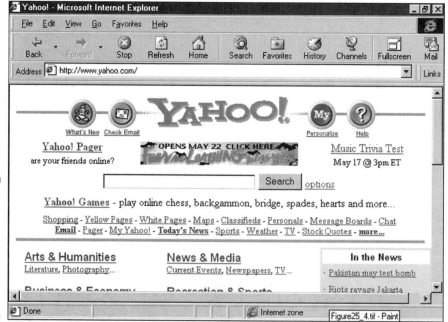

Figure 21-5: Using the Yahoo! search engine to find resources on the Web.

Transcender Corporation

www.transcender.com

The Transcender Corporation makes MCSE and MCSD practice tests that you can buy. These babies are the quick road to certification: You get three or four practice tests that mimic the Microsoft Certified Professional exam of your choice with about 50–70 questions a piece. These practice tests are a little expensive, but Transcender has no competition for them. They even come with a money-back guarantee if you don't pass the exam. Download sample practice tests right from the Web site (you can see the ordering link in Figure 21-6) or order them by mail. You'll find a Transcender Sampler on the CD in the back of this book.

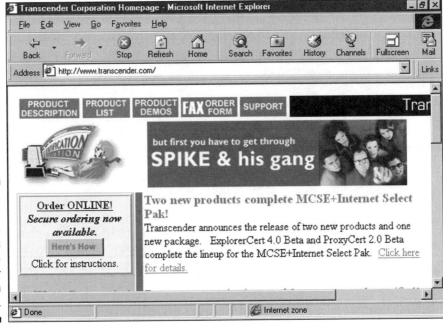

Figure 21-6: Purchasing practice tests from the Transcender Corporation home page.

Bookpool

www.bookpool.com

This Web site offers a huge selection of technical computer books of all different subjects including a great selection on Windows NT 4.0 Workstation. This Web site doesn't offer exam prep guides, but if you're looking for great books that talk and teach the technology, you can probably find them here and order them right from the site — pretty convenient. Figure 21-7 shows you a sample of the amazing discounts that Bookpool offers.

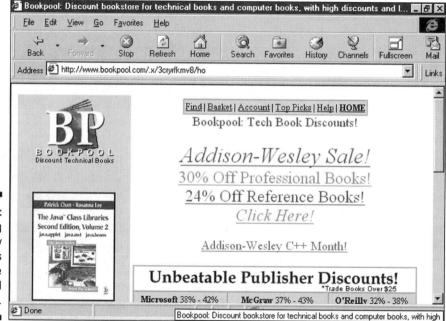

Figure 21-7: Finding more study resources at the Bookpool Web site.

Saluki Study Resources

`www.saluki.com/mcp`

Many computer professionals use Saluki study resources to help them study and pass various Microsoft Certified Professional exams. This Web site, shown in Figure 21-8, offers exam summaries, exam tidbits, and useful information concerning Microsoft certification. You may also find this site's message posting where MCSE hopefuls discuss exam topics that are useful in your study process — a great place to start studying.

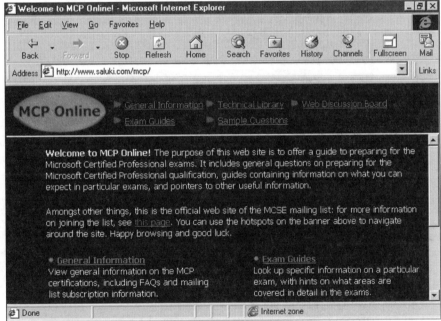

Figure 21-8:
Using
Saluki study
resources
on the Web.

MCSE Info Page

`www.metcorp.com/mcse`

This privately developed (that is, not sanctioned by Microsoft) Web site is full of excellent information and links to help you in your certification process. You can find recommendations for study guides, MCSE resources, and detailed exam information. No other private site can match this one, shown in Figure 21-9.

Figure 21-9:
MCSE Info
Home Page.

MCSE Connect!

www.mcse.com

If you want to see a site with a professional feel and an incredible number of links to other MCSE resources, check out the MCSE Connect! site, which Figure 21-10 shows. This site is a good place to find out more about the professional aspects of certification.

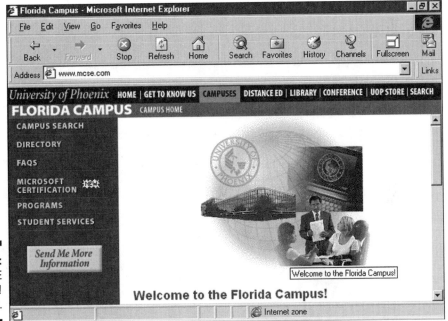

Figure 21-10: The MCSE Connect! home page.

Part IX
Appendixes

In this part . . .

The name of this part may be "Appendixes," but I wouldn't be surprised if you turned here first for some real juicy (and useful) stuff. Included are two sample exams such as you'll see come test time — more than 30 pages of questions to test your NT Workstation knowledge. You'll also find an appendix telling you about contents of the companion CD — which includes demo tests and a collection of test tips from the book.

Appendix A
Practice Exam 1

Practice Exam Rules

▶ 60 minutes

▶ 35 correct answers to pass

▶ 50 questions

1 Laura wants to begin rolling out Windows NT 4.0 Workstation in her corporate enterprise, but she doesn't know where to start. Which tools does she need to begin with? (Choose all that apply.)

A ❑ Unattend.txt

B ❑ Unique Database Files

C ❑ Windiff.exe

D ❑ Sysdiff.exe

2 During a Windows NT 4.0 Workstation rollout, which file do you need to use to create user-specific information, such as TCP/IP information or computer names?

A ○ Unattend.txt

B ○ Unique Database Files

C ○ Windiff.exe

D ○ Sysdiff.exe

3 Charlie is going to preinstall Microsoft Office 97 and Internet Explorer 4.0 as part of his Windows NT 4.0 rollout. Which file does he need to use to preinstall applications for a rollout?

A ○ Unattend.txt

B ○ Unique Database Files

C ○ Sysdiff.exe

D ○ LanScript.txt

4 Which application enables you to create Windows NT 4.0 Workstation Unattend.txt setup files?

A ○ Windows NT Setup Manager

B ○ Unattended Setup Manager

C ○ Windiff.exe

D ○ INFGen.exe

5 Your NT Workstation computer contains a shared folder on an NTFS partition. If you're accessing the folder remotely, what type of permissions would you have?

A ○ Same or more restrictive

B ○ Same or less restrictive

C ○ Same

D ○ No effect

6 Lorna has Full Control access on the \Human_Resources folder that resides on a remote NTFS partition. During the day, her network administrator changes her access permission to Read Only. Lorna has not logged off her NT Workstation all day. What type of access permissions does she have on the \Human_Resources folder if she tries to access it right now?

A ○ Full Control

B ○ No Access

C ○ Read Only

D ○ List

7 Carl needs access to the \SOW folder located on a remote server on an NTFS partition. He currently has No Access permission. He calls up the network administrator and is given Full Control on the share. However, when he tries to access the share, he still gets Access Denied. What is the problem?

A ○ He's not using Service Pack 3.

B ○ He hasn't logged off and logged back on.

C ○ The network administrator has made a mistake.

D ○ The network administrator needs to reboot the server.

8 Which Windows NT Setup switch specifies that you are going to be using an unattended setup file?

A ○ /B:Setup

B ○ /U:Unattend.txt

C ○ /NT

D ○ /Sysdiff.exe

9 Every time you log on to your Windows NT 4.0 Workstation, you are given a new _____ that specifies your access privileges.

A ○ Access token
B ○ Security list
C ○ Password key
D ○ Hashed password

10 Rita copies her Mortgage folder from an NTFS partition on her NT Workstation to an NTFS partition on her NT Server, which happens to be a PDC. What are her permissions for the \Mortgage folder on the NT Server?

A ○ Same as the target folder
B ○ Same as the original folder
C ○ Full Access
D ○ Change

11 David wants to set up permissions on his files and folders and at the same time use RAID 5 for fault tolerance on his workstation. What type of file system should he use?

A ○ HPFS
B ○ CDFD
C ○ FAT32
D ○ NTFS

12 Which file systems are not compatible with Windows NT 4.0 Workstation? (Choose all that apply.)

A ❑ NTFS
B ❑ FAT32
C ❑ FAT16
D ❑ CDFS
E ❑ HPFS

13 To dual-boot with Windows NT and Windows 95, which file system must you use to ensure a successful dual boot?

A ○ FAT16
B ○ NTFS
C ○ CDFS
D ○ FAT32

14 Which utility do you use to change the file system on an NT Workstation from FAT to NTFS?

A ○ Windisk
B ○ Convert
C ○ User Manager
D ○ Server Manager

15 How much memory do you need in order to install NT Workstation on a Pentium 60?

- A ○ 8MB
- B ○ 16MB
- C ○ 12MB
- D ○ 24MB

16 Which of the following computers can be upgraded to Windows NT 4.0 Workstation? (Choose all that apply.)

- A ❑ 486/33, 32MB RAM, 520 MB HD
- B ❑ Pentium 200, 12MB RAM, 4GB HD
- C ❑ Pentium 166, 8MB RAM, 1.1GB HD
- D ❑ 386/33, 32MB RAM, 400MB HD

17 Shelly wants to upgrade her Windows 3.1 computer to Windows NT. What does she have to do to make sure that all her program groups and icons are upgraded along with Windows NT?

- A ○ Install in the %WIN% folder.
- B ○ Run Upgrade.exe.
- C ○ Copy .Dat file to her System folder.
- D ○ Install in a new folder.

18 What do you have to do to remove Windows NT 4.0 Workstation from your computer? (Choose all that apply.)

- A ❑ Delete Windows NT system files.
- B ❑ Run the Sys.com command.
- C ❑ Run the Convert.exe command.
- D ❑ Delete *.dat from the workstation.

19 Which file system do you use if you want to implement fault tolerance and be able to set security on both files and folders on your workstation?

- A ○ NTFS
- B ○ FAT
- C ○ HPFS
- D ○ NFS

20 Where do you go to install and configure a MIDI-compatible device on your NT Workstation?

- A ○ Control Panel➪Multimedia
- B ○ Windows NT Diagnostics
- C ○ Control Panel➪System
- D ○ Control Panel➪Devices

21 You want to upgrade your Windows NT 3.51 Workstation to Windows NT 4.0. However, you are currently using a single HPFS partition on your 3.51 Workstation. What do you have to do to complete the upgrade? (Choose all that apply.)

A ❑ Convert to FAT.

B ❑ Convert to NTFS.

C ❑ Upgrade into the existing %WIN% folder.

D ❑ Upgrade in a new folder named \WINDOWSNT.

22 You have just installed a new video driver on your NT 4.0 Workstation. However, when you reboot your workstation, all you see is a black screen. What can you do to fix this situation? (Choose all that apply.)

A ❑ Boot to VGA mode.

B ❑ Use Last Known Good.

C ❑ Change your video driver to VGA.

D ❑ Use your ERD.

23 You want to make sure that your NT Workstation is as secure as possible. How can you configure your workstation to lock after 15 minutes so that no one has access to your workstation?

A ○ Configure the Security option in the Control Panel.

B ○ Use a password-protected screen saver.

C ○ Use the System Agent to protect the workstation.

D ○ Go to the Windows NT Security Panel.

24 Jeremy copies a file from one folder to another folder within the same NTFS partition. What happens to the security of the file?

A ○ The file retains its security permissions.

B ○ The file permission is Full Control.

C ○ The file permission is No Access.

D ○ The file inherits the permissions of the target folder.

25 Where do you configure the TCP/IP properties for your NT Workstation?

A ○ Control Panel⇨Protocols

B ○ Control Panel⇨Network

C ○ User Manager

D ○ Control Panel⇨TCP/IP

26 You just bought a new tape device so that you can back up your files. Where do you have to go to configure your tape device for backups?

A ○ Windows NT Backup

B ○ Control Panel⇨Tape Devices

C ○ Control Panel⇨SCSI Adapters

D ○ Control Panel⇨System

27 Where can you edit the delay for booting to Windows NT Workstation?

A ○ Ntldr

B ○ Ntdetect.com

C ○ Boot.ini

D ○ Ntbootdd.sys

28 You use your Windows NT 4.0 Workstation laptop computer at home and at the office. At home, you do not use a docking station; at work, you do. What can you do to make the transition easier from work to home?

A ○ Create a roaming profile.

B ○ Create two different users.

C ○ Create a local profile.

D ○ Create two hardware profiles, one for work and one for home.

29 Which file system allows for dual booting with Windows NT and Windows 95 and also supports long filenames?

A ○ NTFS

B ○ FAT

C ○ HPFS

D ○ CDFS

30 You need to make sure that you back up your local Registry on your workstation. What do you have to do for your backup configuration?

A ○ Make an ERD.

B ○ Select the drive containing the Registry, check the Backup Local Registry box, and run Windows NT Backup.

C ○ Back up the whole computer.

D ○ Run the Backup Local Registry command from Control Panel⇨System.

31 Somehow you accidentally lose your three Windows NT Setup disks. How can you re-create these setup disks?

A ○ Configure the Security option in the Control Panel

B ○ Setup /OX

C ○ Winnt.exe /OX

D ○ Winnt.exe /B

E ○ Winnt.exe /U

32 What is the smallest unit that can be scheduled with the microkernel?

A ○ Microthread

B ○ Thread

C ○ Microprocess

D ○ Process

33 What must you do to install and configure a UPS for your Windows NT 4.0 Workstation? (Choose all that apply.)

A ☐ Control Panel⇨UPS.

B ☐ Control Panel⇨Devices.

C ☐ Connect UPS with special serial cable.

D ☐ Configure LPT1 for UPS.

34 How do you install Windows NT 4.0 over Windows NT 3.51 Server on a computer with 386/66, 32MB of RAM, and 520MB HD?

A ○ Install into existing folder.

B ○ Install into new folder.

C ○ Winnt32.exe /s.

D ○ You cannot upgrade.

35 Which TCP/IP properties must be configured to communicate in a routed network? (Choose all that apply.)

A ☐ DNS

B ☐ WINS

C ☐ IP address

D ☐ Subnet Mask

E ☐ Default Gateway

F ☐ LMHOSTS

36 Which TCP/IP property sends remote packets to their destination network?

A ○ Domain Name Server

B ○ Windows Internet Naming Service

C ○ Default Gateway

D ○ Subnet Mask

37 Which type of server performs name resolution from IP addresses to NetBIOS names?

A ○ DNS

B ○ WINS

C ○ Router

D ○ DHCP

38 Which type of server dynamically assigns IP address information, such as Default Gateway, IP Address, Subnet Mask, WINS, and DNS?

A ○ DHCP server

B ○ WINS server

C ○ DNS server

D ○ Primary Domain Controller

39 Which feature of Remote Access Service allows for additional bandwidth if you have more than two links and two physical modems?

A ○ Bandwidth throttling
B ○ Call-Back
C ○ ISDN
D ○ Multi-link

40 Which protocol must you install if you want to create Virtual Private Networks?

A ○ ISDN
B ○ PPTP
C ○ VPN
D ○ ASDL

41 You're having trouble with your modem when logging on to your RAS server. Which file can you use to troubleshoot this process?

A ○ Device.log
B ○ RAS.log
C ○ DUN.log
D ○ Security log in the Event Viewer

42 You've been having problems, such as kernel stop errors with your Windows NT Workstation. Where can you get detailed information on your problems?

A ○ Windows NT Diagnostics
B ○ Event Viewer
C ○ Control Panel⇨System
D ○ Control Panel⇨Environment

43 You're moving a file from one folder to another on the same NTFS partition. What are the file permissions for the file?

A ○ Keeps its file permissions
B ○ Inherits its file permissions
C ○ Full Control to Everyone on the file
D ○ Owner of the folder has Full Control

44 You've been having problems with security on your NT Workstation. What do you have to do to keep track of security while you're away from the workstation, and where can you enable this? (Choose all that apply.)

A ❑ Enable NTFS security
B ❑ Enable auditing
C ❑ User Manager
D ❑ Windows NT security

45 Which Windows NT RAS security feature enables you to call back to a prespecified number?

A ○ MSCHAP

B ○ Virtual Private Networking

C ○ Callback

D ○ SLIP/PPP

46 Which features of Internet Information Server are not available with Peer Web Services? (Choose all that apply.)

A ❑ Virtual servers

B ❑ Bandwidth throttling

C ❑ Authentication

D ❑ NTFS security

47 Where can you configure virtual memory under Windows NT?

A ○ Control Panel⇨VMM

B ○ Control Panel⇨System

C ○ Windows NT Diagnostics

D ○ Windows NT Memory Manager

48 If you have 48MB of physical RAM installed on your NT Workstation, what is the optimum size of your pagefile?

A ○ 48

B ○ 96

C ○ 59

D ○ 100

49 What are two ways that you can optimize performance of your pagefile on your NT Workstation?

A ❑ Put your pagefile on a partition other than your boot partition.

B ❑ Keep the pagefile as small as possible.

C ❑ Don't use a pagefile.

D ❑ Keep the pagefile size equal to physical RAM + 11MB.

50 Which Registry tool can you use to search for certain Registry values on your NT Workstation?

A ○ Regedit16.exe

B ○ Regedit.exe

C ○ Regedt.32.exe

D ○ RegistryMaster.exe

Answers

1 *A, B,* and *D.* Unattend.txt files are the answer script for setup; Unique Database Files are used for machine-specific information; and Sysdiff.exe is used to preinstall applications as part of Windows NT Setup. *Objective: Create unattended installation files (Chapter 4).*

2 *B.* Unique Database Files are used to designate such machine-specific information as TCP/IP addressing, computer names, and any other information that you specify. The Unique Database File overrides any setting in the Unattend.txt file. *Objective: Create unattended installation files (Chapter 4).*

3 *C.* Sysdiff.exe enables you to preinstall applications as part of Windows NT setup. *Objective: Configure server-based installation for wide-scale deployment in a given situation (Chapter 4).*

4 *A.* Windows NT Setup Manager enables you to create an Unattend.txt file or Unattended Answer file through a GUI by answering a series of questions about your desired Windows NT build. *Objective: Create unattended installation files (Chapter 4).*

5 *A.* If you're remotely accessing a folder that resides on an NTFS partition, the security is the same or more restrictive. If you were local, the security would be the same or less restrictive. *Objective: Plan strategies for sharing and securing resources (Chapters 7, 8, and 11).*

6 *A.* Because Lorna hasn't logged off her Windows NT Workstation, the security changes have not taken effect. After she logs off and logs back on, she will be designated a new security token that details her new security permissions. *Objective: Plan strategies for sharing and securing resources (Chapter 7).*

7 *B.* Although the network administrator has reset the permissions for the directory, they won't take effect until Carl logs off and logs back on, at which time he will receive a new security access token that designates his security options. *Objective: Plan strategies for sharing and securing resources (Chapter 8).*

8 *B.* The /U:Unattend.txt switch, when run with Winnt.exe or Winnt32.exe, specifies an unattended answer script that will be used for unattended setup. *Objective: Create unattended installation files (Chapter 4).*

9 *A.* This access token is good until you log off your NT Workstation and are given a new access token. *Objective: Plan strategies for sharing and securing resources (Chapter 8).*

10 *A.* When you copy a file from one NTFS partition to another, your file permissions are inherited from the destination folder that you copied the file to. *Objective: Choose the appropriate file system to use in a given situation. File systems and situations include: NTFS, FAT, HPFS, Security, Dual-boot systems (Chapter 3).*

11 *D.* Some of the benefits of using NTFS are both file and folder security and the inclusion of fault tolerance. *Objective: Choose the appropriate file system to use in a given situation. File systems and situations include: NTFS, FAT, HPFS, Security, Dual-boot systems (Chapter 3).*

12 *B, E.* New to NT 4.0 is the incompatibility with HPFS. HPFS was recognized under NT 3.51, but not with NT 4.0. FAT32 is not compatible with NT 4.0, either, but will be with NT 5.0. *Objective: Choose the appropriate file system to use in a given situation. File systems and situations include: NTFS, FAT, HPFS, Security, Dual-boot systems (Chapter 3).*

13 *A.* Windows 95 cannot recognize NTFS locally. You have to use FAT16 so that Windows 95 will operate. *Objective: Choose the appropriate file system to use in a given situation. File systems and situations include: NTFS, FAT, HPFS, Security, Dual-boot systems (Chapter 3).*

14 *B.* If you want to convert your file system from FAT to NTFS, you can use the Convert.exe command. The proper syntax for this command is Convert.exe C: /FS:NTFS. (C: designates a standard drive letter but could be anything). *Objective: Choose the appropriate file system to use in a given situation. File systems and situations include: NTFS, FAT, HPFS, Security, Dual-boot systems (Chapter 3).*

15 *C.* You need at least 12MB of memory to install Windows NT 4.0 Workstation. However, 16MB is recommended. *Objective: Install Windows NT Workstation on an Intel platform in a given situation (Chapter 4).*

16 *A, B.* To install Windows NT 4.0 Workstation, you need the minimum of 12MB RAM, 486/33, and 120MB HD space. *Objective: Install Windows NT Workstation on an Intel platform in a given situation (Chapter 4).*

17 *A.* To ensure that all the user settings are transferred during the upgrade, she should upgrade into the existing Windows folder. *Objective: Install Windows NT Workstation on an Intel platform in a given situation (Chapter 4).*

18 *A, B.* To remove Windows NT from your system, you have to delete the Windows NT system files from your computer and run the Sys.com command to remove Ntldr from your boot partition. *Objective: Remove Windows NT Workstation in a given situation (Chapter 4).*

19 *A.* Using NTFS on your partitions enables you to set file and folder security as well as fault tolerance on your NT Workstation. *Objective: Set permissions on NTFS partitions, folders, and files (Chapters 8, 9).*

20 *A.* You install any MIDI or sound devices from the Multimedia icon in the Control Panel. *Objective: Use Control Panel applications to configure a Windows NT Workstation computer in a given situation (Chapter 6).*

21 *B, C.* If you want to upgrade from Windows NT 3.51, you have to first convert the HPFS partition to NTFS because NT 4.0 does not recognize HPFS. To preserve all your settings, install into the existing Windows NT folder. *Objective: Use Control Panel applications to configure a Windows NT Workstation computer in a given situation (Chapter 6).*

22 *A, C.* If you install an incompatible video driver, you can boot to VGA mode and change your driver to a compatible video driver. *Objective: Install, configure, and remove hardware components for a given situation. Hardware components include Network adapter drivers, SCSI device drivers, Tape device drivers, UPS, Multimedia devices, Display drivers, Keyboard drivers, Mouse drivers (Chapter 6).*

23 *B.* If you want to ensure that your NT Workstation locks after 15 minutes, specify a password-protected screen saver. *Objective: Install, configure, and remove hardware components for a given situation. Hardware components include Network adapter drivers, SCSI device drivers, Tape device drivers, UPS, Multimedia devices, Display drivers, Keyboard drivers, Mouse drivers (Chapter 6).*

24 *D.* When you copy a file from one folder to another on an NTFS partition, your file inherits the permissions of the target folder. *Objective: Set permissions on NTFS partitions, folders, and files (Chapters 8, 9).*

25 *B.* You configure all your TCP/IP properties from the Network icon in the Control Panel. *Objective: Add and configure the network components of Windows NT Workstation (Chapter 10) / Use various configurations to install Windows NT Workstation as a TCP/IP client (Chapter 13).*

26 *B.* If you receive a new tape device, you can configure your new device from the Tape Devices icon in the Control Panel. *Objective: Use Control Panel applications to configure a Windows NT Workstation computer in a given situation (Chapter 6).*

27 *C.* You can control how long the delay is for bootup within Boot.ini. *Objective: Use Control Panel applications to configure a Windows NT Workstation computer in a given situation (Chapter 6).*

28 *D.* If you have two different hardware configurations, you can create two different hardware profiles so that your transition between locations is quick and easy. *Objective: Set up and modify user profiles (Chapter 7).*

29 *B.* You need to use the FAT file system as long as you dual-boot with Windows 95. FAT also supports long filenames under Windows NT. *Objective: Set up a dual-boot system in a given situation (Chapters 4, 5).*

30 *B.* If you want to back up the local Registry on your NT Workstation, select the Backup Local Registry box under Windows NT Backup. *Objective: Use Control Panel applications to configure a Windows NT Workstation computer in a given situation (Chapter 6).*

31 *B.* The setup switch /OX can be run with either Winnt.exe or Winnt32.exe to re-create the three Windows NT Setup disks. *Objective: Choose the appropriate course of action to take when the boot process fails. (Chapter 5).*

32 *B.* The smallest scheduled unit under Windows NT is a thread. Multiple threads can make up a process. *Objective: Start applications at various priorities (Chapter 16).*

33 *A, C.* When you want to hook up a UPS, you have to configure your UPS under Control Panel⇨UPS *and* make sure that you hook up the special serial cable to your NT Workstation from the UPS. *Objective: Install, configure, and remove hardware components for a given situation. Hardware components include Network adapter drivers, SCSI device drivers, Tape device drivers, UPS, Multimedia devices, Display drivers, Keyboard drivers, Mouse drivers (Chapter 6).*

34 *D.* You can't upgrade, because the processor is only a 386/33. You need at least a 486/33 to install Windows NT. *Objective: Install Windows NT Workstation on an Intel platform in a given situation (Chapter 4).*

35 *C, D, E.* To communicate with a routed network, you need an IP address, a Subnet Mask, and a Default Gateway to route packets to remote networks. *Objective: Use various configurations to install Windows NT Workstation as a TCP/IP client (Chapter 13).*

36 *C.* A default gateway is used to route packets to and from remote networks. You need a default gateway if you are going to communicate on the Internet or to other networks by using TCP/IP. *Objective: Use various configurations to install Windows NT Workstation as a TCP/IP client (Chapter 13).*

37 *B.* A WINS (Windows Internet Naming Service) server is used for name resolution for IP addresses to Windows NetBIOS names. *Objective: Use various configurations to install Windows NT Workstation as a TCP/IP client (Chapter 13).*

38 *A.* If you are going to use a DHCP server, you don't have to specify any TCP/IP address information — your DHCP server takes care of that. *Objective: Use various configurations to install Windows NT Workstation as a TCP/IP client (Chapter 13).*

39 *D.* You can use multi-link to take advantage of multiple modems and physical lines to increase bandwidth. For example, if you have two 28.8 modems, you can achieve bandwidth of 57.6 Kbps by using multi-link on your NT Workstation. *Objective: Configure and install Dial Up Networking in a given situation (Chapter 15).*

40 *B.* You need to use Point-to-Point-Tunneling Protocol to create Virtual Private Networks. You can also use NetBEUI, TCP/IP, or IPX/SPX with PPTP to create VPNs. *Objective: Configure and install Dial Up Networking in a given situation (Chapter 15).*

41 *A.* You can use Device.log to troubleshoot any problems that you are having with your modems when you are trying to connect to a RAS server. *Objective: Configure and install Dial Up Networking in a given situation (Chapter 15).*

42 *B.* If you have any trouble with kernel stop errors, check out the Event Viewer system log. *Objective: Choose the appropriate course of action to take when an application fails (Chapter 16, 19).*

43 *A.* If you move a file from one NTFS partition to another, the file keeps its file attributes, including security information. *Objective: Set permissions on NTFS partitions, folders, and files (Chapter 8, 9).*

44 *B, C.* To keep track of security on your NT Workstation, you can enable auditing on NTFS partitions through the User Manager. *Objective: Plan strategies for sharing and securing resources (Chapters 7, 8, and 11).*

45 *C.* With Remote Access Service Callback security, you can specify a number that your dial-up server will call back so that you know exactly who is using your RAS server. *Objective: Configure and install Dial Up Networking in a given situation (Chapter 15).*

46 *A, B.* Peer Web Services is a diluted version of IIS and lacks some features, such as creating virtual servers and mandating bandwidth on your workstation. *Objective: Configure Microsoft Peer Web Services in a given situation (Chapter 14).*

47 *B.* You configure virtual memory settings from the System icon in the Control Panel. *Objective: Use Control Panel applications to configure a Windows NT Workstation computer in a given situation (Chapter 6).*

48 *C.* To configure your pagefile for your NT Workstation, add 11MB to your physical amount of RAM. *Objective: Optimize system performance in various areas (Chapters 5 and 18).*

49 *A, D.* These two steps optimize your virtual memory on your NT Workstation. *Objective: Optimize system performance in various areas (Chapters 5 and 18).*

50 *B.* Regedit is used to search for specific Registry values in a Windows Explorer interface. *Objective: Modify the Registry using the appropriate tool in a given situation (Chapter 6).*

Appendix B
Practice Exam 2

Practice Exam Rules
- ▶ 60 minutes
- ▶ 35 correct answers to pass
- ▶ 50 questions

1 Which protocol is mainly used to connect to Novell NetWare networks?

- A ○ TCP/IP
- B ○ NWLink Protocol
- C ○ DLC
- D ○ NetBEUI

2 What are two uses for the DLC protocol on your NT Workstation?

- A ❑ Connect to HP Jet Direct cards.
- B ❑ Connect to NT print servers.
- C ❑ Connect to the Internet.
- D ❑ Connect to mainframe computers via 3270 emulation.

3 What are two characteristics of the NetBEUI protocol?

- A ❑ Non-routable.
- B ❑ Fast protocol used mainly on smaller networks.
- C ❑ Connects to the Internet.
- D ❑ Exchanges routing information.

4 Which Registry tool is used to set permissions on individual Registry keys?

- A ○ Regedit.exe
- B ○ Regedt32.exe
- C ○ RegSecure.exe
- D ○ RegistryMaster.exe

5 What are three characteristics of the TCP/IP protocol suite?

A ❑ Used to connect to the Internet.

B ❑ Routable.

C ❑ FTP application.

D ❑ Non-routable.

E ❑ Used to connect to mainframe computers directly.

6 Which tool do you use to monitor performance on your NT Workstation with detailed counters?

A ○ Windows NT Diagnostics

B ○ Protocol Analyzer

C ○ Performance Monitor

D ○ Network Monitor

7 What are two benefits of running 16-bit applications in their own memory space?

A ❑ Won't crash other 16-bit applications.

B ❑ Much faster than 32-bit.

C ❑ Can be preemptively multitasked.

D ❑ Run in Kernel mode.

8 What are the four levels of thread priorities under Windows NT?

A ❑ Real-time

B ❑ Medium

C ❑ Low

D ❑ High

E ❑ Normal

F ❑ Fast

G ❑ Special

H ❑ Unique

9 Where can you specify that your 16-bit applications run in their own memory spaces? (Choose all that apply.)

A ❑ Start.exe from the command line

B ❑ Windows NT Diagnostics

C ❑ Control Panel⇨16-bit

D ❑ Start⇨Run⇨Run in Separate Memory Space

10 Which Registry key maintains machine-specific information about your NT Workstation?

A ○ HKEY_CURRENT_USER
B ○ HKEY_DYNAMIC_DATA
C ○ HKEY_LOCAL_MACHINE
D ○ HKEY_DEFAULT_USER

11 How many hard disks are required for disk striping with parity on your NT Workstation?

A ○ One
B ○ Two
C ○ Three
D ○ Four
E ○ Five
F ○ Six

12 Which of the following provides the fastest read/write performance time for your hard disk on your NT Workstation?

A ○ Disk striping with parity
B ○ Volume set
C ○ Disk striping without parity
D ○ Sector sparing

13 What must be installed on your NT Workstation to allow file and printer sharing on a NetWare network?

A ○ Client Service for NetWare
B ○ Gateway Service for NetWare
C ○ File and Print Services for NetWare
D ○ NetWare Client32

14 Karen has just configured and installed NWLink on her NT Workstation, but she still can't connect to any other computers running NWLink. What could be wrong?

A ○ Wrong internal network number
B ○ Incorrect frame type
C ○ RIP for IPX/SPX not installed
D ○ Client Service for NetWare not installed

15 How can you change your password on a NetWare 3.*x* Server from your NT Workstation if you have CSNW installed?

A ○ Ctrl+Alt+Delete, Change Password

B ○ Control Panel⇨CSNW

C ○ Control Panel⇨Security

D ○ Setpass.exe utility from the command line

16 Which file on your NT Workstation is used to map NetBIOS names to IP addresses?

A ○ HOSTS file

B ○ LMHOSTS file

C ○ Device.log

D ○ Spool.sys file

17 How can you change your password on a NetWare 4.*x* Server from your NT Workstation if you have CSNW installed?

A ○ Setpass utility from the command line

B ○ Control Panel⇨CSNW

C ○ Ctrl+Alt+Delete, Change Password, NetWare Server

D ○ Control Panel⇨NT Security

18 You want to connect to a network share over the Internet. What is the correct syntax for the domain name of SyngressMedia.com with the network share FrenchFries?

A ○ \\FrenchFries\SyngressMedia.com

B ○ \\SyngressMedia\FrenchFries

C ○ \\SyngressMedia.com\Syngress\FrenchFries.com

D ○ \\SyngressMedia.com\FrenchFries

19 What is the correct syntax for connecting to a network share over a LAN with the server name of Bubbles and the share name of \Timed?

A ○ \\Timed\Bubbles

B ○ \\Bubbles\Timed

C ○ \\Bubbles.com\Timed

D ○ Bubbles\\Timed

20 What is the extension of mandatory profiles under Windows NT?

A ○ .pol

B ○ .pro

C ○ .man

D ○ .dat

21 Under what printer property can you enable a printer pool?

A ○ Scheduling
B ○ Properties
C ○ Device Settings
D ○ Ports

22 If you are printing to a printer pool with the priorities of 10, 34, 68, and 98, which printer prints first if the jobs are all sent at the same time?

A ○ 10
B ○ 34
C ○ 68
D ○ 98

23 Where do you configure a memory dump in case you get a critical stop error on your NT Workstation?

A ○ Control Panel⇨Memory
B ○ Control Panel⇨System⇨Startup | Shutdown
C ○ Windows NT Diagnostics
D ○ User Manager

24 Which local group, by default, has permission to see the security log in the Event Viewer?

A ○ Power Users
B ○ Everyone
C ○ Backup Operators
D ○ Administrators

25 What should you do if your processor occasionally spikes above 85 percent when you monitor % Processor Time?

A ○ Add more memory.
B ○ Upgrade to a faster processor.
C ○ Add a new processor.
D ○ Do nothing.

26 What should you do to establish a baseline with Performance Monitor?

A ○ Run Perf Mon during peak hours.
B ○ Run Perf Mon during off hours.
C ○ Run Perf Mon at random times during the day.
D ○ Run Perf Mon during peak and non-peak hours.

27 When monitoring disk performance, you notice that your Current Disk Queue Length is constantly over 2. What should you do?

A ○ Upgrade hard disk.

B ○ Add another hard disk.

C ○ Use disk striping with parity.

D ○ Do nothing.

28 You have been monitoring your memory and notice that your pages/sec is constantly over 25 and your hard disk is paging constantly. What should you do?

A ○ Add more RAM.

B ○ Upgrade disk controller.

C ○ Add a separate processor.

D ○ Do nothing.

29 Where can you change the priority level of a process on your NT Workstation?

A ○ Task Manager⇨Process

B ○ Control Panel⇨Process

C ○ Windows NT Diagnostics

D ○ Control Panel⇨System

30 Where can you go to make sure that your logon scripts are run when you are part of NetWare network?

A ○ CSNW⇨Enable Logon Script Processing

B ○ CSNW⇨Setpass

C ○ GSNW⇨Scripts

D ○ Syscon

31 You have noticed that none of the documents being sent to your NT Workstation is printing. You try to purge the printer queue, but you are not having any luck. What can you do to fix this?

A ○ Delete the printer.

B ○ Install a new printer.

C ○ Stop and restart the spool service.

D ○ Delete all documents being sent to the printer.

32 Which printer permission enables you to control all documents being sent to the printer but restricts access to the printer's properties?

A ○ Full Control

B ○ Manage Documents

C ○ Print

D ○ No Access

33 Which command-line utility allows you to start applications at various priorities?

A ○ Run
B ○ Start
C ○ Priority
D ○ Begin

34 You want to audit any access to the printer attached to your Windows NT Workstation. Which type of auditing do you enable to see the activity for your printer?

A ○ File and Object Access
B ○ Security Policy Changes
C ○ Use of User Rights
D ○ Process Tracking

35 You want to make sure that you enable auditing for all the files on your NT Workstation. You have enabled auditing on your Workstation, but nothing is showing up in the security log. What is wrong?

A ○ Didn't enable File and Object Access.
B ○ Have to reboot the computer.
C ○ Not using NTFS.
D ○ Have to log off.

36 Where can you specify on your NT Workstation that users change their passwords every 21 days?

A ○ User Manager⇨Policies⇨Account
B ○ User Manager⇨Security
C ○ User Manager⇨Passwords
D ○ Control Panel⇨Passwords

37 Which local group on your NT Workstation has the power to create shares for folders and printers and to install software?

A ○ Users
B ○ Backup Operators
C ○ Account Operators
D ○ Power Users

38 You want to implement a policy on your NT Workstation. Where do you place this policy file so that anyone who logs on to the workstation receives this policy?

A ○ Logon script
B ○ NetLogon folder
C ○ Home folder
D ○ Spool folder

39 You have just gotten a new network interface card and need to configure the card. Where can you install and configure your NIC card?

A ○ Windows NT Diagnostics

B ○ Control Panel➪Network Cards

C ○ Control Panel➪Network

D ○ Administrative Tools➪Network

40 Which type of name resolution does a DNS server provide on a network?

A ○ NetBIOS names to IP addresses

B ○ FQDN to NetBIOS names

C ○ IP addresses to MAC addresses

D ○ HOST names to IP addresses

41 Which command-line utility can you use if you have Client Service for NetWare installed on your NT Workstation?

A ○ Map

B ○ Login

C ○ Syscon

D ○ Capture

42 You need to configure your modem so that you can install Remote-Access Service. Where do you install and configure your modem on your NT Workstation?

A ○ Control Panel➪RAS

B ○ Control Panel➪System

C ○ Administrative Tools➪Remote Access Admin

D ○ Control Panel➪Modems

43 Name the three Web services that are installed with Peer Web Services.

A ❏ FTP

B ❏ Gopher

C ❏ RSHELL

D ❏ WWW

E ❏ Winsock

F ❏ HTTP

44 Which browser role maintains the master copy of the network browse list but does not distribute the copy to browser clients?

A ○ Potential Browser

B ○ Master Browser

C ○ Backup Browser

D ○ PDC

45 Which protocol is mainly used to connect to the Internet?

- A ○ NetBEUI
- B ○ NWLink
- C ○ DLC
- D ○ TCP/IP

46 Where do you enable the Device.log file for troubleshooting your RAS connections?

- A ○ Control Panel⇨Modems
- B ○ Registry
- C ○ Administrative Tools⇨RAS Admin
- D ○ Control Panel⇨System

47 What is the location of the Device.log file on your NT Workstation?

- A ○ \Winnt \System32\RAS
- B ○ \Winnt\System32\Repl\Import\Scripts
- C ○ \Winnt\NTLogs\RAS
- D ○ \Winnt\Drivers\Logs

48 You want to run a diskless installation from your existing Windows NT 3.51 Workstation. What command do you need to use?

- A ○ Winnt.exe /b
- B ○ Winnt.exe /OX
- C ○ Winnt32.exe /B
- D ○ Winnt32.exe /U:Unattend.txt

49 Danielle is leaving the company and is going to be replaced by Arthur. What's the easiest way to give Arthur all of Danielle's network permissions and access?

- A ○ Delete Danielle's account and create a new one for Arthur.
- B ○ Rename Danielle's account in Arthur's name.
- C ○ Delete Danielle's user account and rename it in Arthur's name later on.
- D ○ Disable Danielle's account and add Arthur to all of Danielle's groups.

50 If all your 16-bit applications are running in separate memory spaces and one 16-bit application crashes, how will this crash affect the rest of your 16-bit applications?

- A ○ They will all crash.
- B ○ Two will crash.
- C ○ None will crash.
- D ○ Windows NT will crash.

Answers

1   *B.* The IPX/SPX protocol, or NWLink, is predominantly used to connect to Novell NetWare networks. If you see this protocol being used, look for a NetWare Server. *Objective: Implement Windows NT Workstation as a client in a NetWare environment (Chapter 12).*

2   *A, D.* The DLC protocol is mainly used to connect to HP printers using Jet Direct cards and to connect to mainframe computers through 3270 emulation. This protocol is not used for network communication. *Objective: Add and configure the network components of Windows NT Workstation (Chapter 10).*

3   *A, B.* The NetBEUI protocol has certain characteristics that separate it from other protocols: It is not routable and is mainly used for small LANs because of its speed. *Objective: Add and configure the network components of Windows NT Workstation (Chapter 10).*

4   *B.* Regedt32.exe is the only Registry tool that you can use to set permissions on individual keys in the Registry. Regedit.exe is used to search for specific values. *Objective: Modify the Registry using the appropriate tool in a given situation (Chapter 6).*

5   *A, B, C.* The TCP/IP protocol suite is very popular because of its use on the Internet, its routability, and its use of different applications, such as FTP and Telnet. *Objective: Use various configurations to install Windows NT Workstation as a TCP/IP client (Chapter 13).*

6   *C.* Performance Monitor is your best tool to monitor your workstation. You can set individual counters on your workstation for areas, such as memory, processor, and hard disks. *Objective: Monitor system performance by using various tools (Chapters 18, 19).*

7   *A, C.* If you run your 16-bit applications in their own memory space, you don't have to worry about each 16-bit app crashing the other applications. Also, they can be preemptively multitasked. *Objective: Choose the appropriate course of action to take when an application fails (Chapter 16, 19).*

8   *A, C, D, and E.* Most applications start out at Normal and are adjusted from the Task Manager. *Objective: Start applications on Intel and RISC platforms in various operating system environments (Chapter 16).*

9   *A, D.* You can specify that your 16-bit application be run in its own memory space through the command line or through the Start menu. *Objective: Start applications on Intel and RISC platforms in various operating system environments (Chapter 16).*

10   *C.* HKEY_LOCAL_MACHINE is the Registry key that controls all the machine-specific information about your computer. *Objective: Implement advanced techniques to resolve various problems (Chapter 19).*

11 C. If you implement disk striping with parity, you need at least three physical hard disks (a maximum of 32). This setup is RAID 5 and offers a great deal of fault tolerance. *Objective: Optimize system performance in various areas (Chapters 5, 18).*

12 C. Although disk striping without parity does not offer any fault tolerance, it does provide a good deal of speed for accessing your hard disk. *Objective: Optimize system performance in various areas (Chapters 5, 18).*

13 A. In order to use file and print services on a NetWare network, you need to have CSNW installed on your NT Workstation. *Objective: Implement Windows NT Workstation as a client in a NetWare environment (Chapter 12).*

14 B. A common problem when installing NWLink is that it does not detect the correct frame type. To fix this problem, you have to specify exactly what frame type you need to use. *Objective: Implement Windows NT Workstation as a client in a NetWare environment (Chapter 12).*

15 D. If you are connecting to a NetWare 3.*x* server, you can change your password with the Setpass.exe utility at the command line. *Objective: Implement Windows NT Workstation as a client in a NetWare environment (Chapter 12).*

16 B. LMHOSTS files are used to load remote NetBIOS computers into remote name cache to be resolved when you try to access them over the Internet or LAN. You can find this file in the \Winnt\System32\Drivers folder. *Objective: Choose the appropriate course of action to take when a user cannot access a resource (Chapters 5, 7).*

17 C. If you are connected to a NetWare 4.*x* Server and have Client Service for NetWare installed, you can change your password just as if you were changing it on a Windows NT Server. *Objective: Implement Windows NT Workstation as a client in a NetWare environment (Chapter 12).*

18 D. When mapping to a remote share over the Internet, you must have the \\DomainName.com\ShareName syntax correct. *Objective: Use various methods to access network resources (Chapters 9, 10).*

19 B. When mapping to a network share, you must specify \\ServerName\SharePoint. *Objective: Use various methods to access network resources (Chapters 9, 10).*

20 C. All mandatory profiles have the .man extension and can be placed in the \Netlogon folder. *Objective: Set up and modify user profiles (Chapter 7).*

21 D. You need to use the same printer driver and enable the printer pool from the Ports property tab. *Objective: Install and configure printers in a given environment (Chapter 17).*

22 D. In a printer pool, the printer with the highest priority processes the jobs first. *Objective: Install and configure printers in a given environment (Chapter 17).*

23 B. In case you have any critical stop errors on your NT Workstation, you can configure a memory dump so that you can examine exactly what went wrong and fix the problem. *Objective: Implement advanced techniques to resolve various problems (Chapter 19).*

24 *D.* Only members of the Administrators group have permission, by default, to look at the security log in the Event Viewer. However, in the User Manager, you can specify this user right for other groups and users. *Objective: Monitor system performance by using various tools (Chapters 18, 19).*

25 *D.* Occasionally spiking above 80 percent is normal; if it were a regular occurrence, you would need to upgrade. *Objective: Monitor system performance by using various tools (Chapters 18, 19).*

26 *D.* To establish a baseline with Performance Monitor, you should run Perf Mon at both peak and off-peak hours to develop a strategy for monitoring performance. *Objective: Monitor system performance by using various tools (Chapters 18, 19).*

27 *A.* If the Average Disk Queue Length is constantly over 2, the time may have come to upgrade the hard disk or disk controller on your NT Workstation. *Objective: Identify and resolve a given performance problem (Chapters 5, 18, and 19).*

28 *A.* If your hard disk is paging excessively, you can add more RAM so that your hard disk is not swapping virtual memory so often. *Objective: Optimize system performance in various areas (Chapters 5, 18, and 19).*

29 *A.* If you go to Task Manager⇨Processes, you can view or change the priority level of certain processes that are running on your NT Workstation. *Objective: Start applications at various priorities (Chapters 16).*

30 *A.* Part of the reason for using Client Service for NetWare is the compatibility with Windows NT. You can run your logon scripts from CSNW if you specify the option in the CSNW properties on your workstation. *Objective: Implement Windows NT Workstation as a client in a NetWare environment (Chapter 12).*

31 *C.* If you're having trouble getting your print device to process documents, you may have to stop and restart the spool service on your workstation as a last resort. *Objective: Choose the appropriate course of action to take when a print job fails (Chapter 17).*

32 *B.* The Manage Documents permission lets you control any documents that are sent to the printer, including those that belong to other users. *Objective: Choose the appropriate course of action to take when a print job fails (Chapter 17).*

33 *B.* You can use the Start switch to begin processes at different priorities from the command line. *Objective: Start applications at various priorities (Chapter 16).*

34 *A.* Under Windows NT, everything is considered an object, including printers. If you want to monitor your printer, enable File and Object Access. *Objective: Implement advanced techniques to resolve various problems (Chapter 19).*

35 *C.* If you try to audit the files on your workstation but aren't using NTFS partitions, you don't see any effect. *Objective: Set permissions on NTFS partitions, folders, and files (Chapters 8, 9).*

36 *A.* The Account Policy dialog box is where you specify such password-specific information as length, uniqueness, account lockout, and so on. *Objective: Create and manage local user accounts and local group accounts to meet given requirements (Chapters 7, 8, and 11).*

37 *D.* The local Power Users group on your NT Workstation has the ability to create and share documents on your NT Workstation and also to install software. *Objective: Create and manage local user accounts and local group accounts to meet given requirements (Chapters 7, 8, and 11).*

38 *B.* For a policy to be available to all users, you need to place the policy file in the NetLogon folder on the Domain Controller or your workstation. *Objective: Set up and modify user profiles (Chapter 7).*

39 *C.* You can configure all your network settings — such as protocols, adapters, services, and bindings — from the Network icon in the Control Panel. *Objective: Use the Control Panel applications to configure a Windows NT Workstation computer in a given situation (Chapter 6).*

40 *D.* A DNS Server provides name resolution for HOST names to IP addresses on a LAN or WAN. *Objective: Use various configurations to install Windows NT Workstation as a TCP/IP client (Chapter 13).*

41 *C.* Syscon is one of the available applications that can be run from the command line when CSNW is installed on your NT Workstation. *Objective: Implement Windows NT Workstation as a client in a NetWare environment (Chapter 12).*

42 *D.* You configure all your modems from Control Panel⇨Modems. Hardware components include Network adapter drivers, SCSI device drivers, Tape device drivers, UPS, Multimedia devices, Display drivers, Keyboard drivers, and Mouse drivers. *Objective: Install, configure, and remove hardware components for a given situation. (Chapter 6, 10).*

43 *A, B, D.* If you install Peer Web Services for your NT Workstation, you have the option of installing the FTP, Gopher, and WWW services. *Objective: Configure Microsoft Peer Web Services in a given situation (Chapter 14).*

44 *B.* The Master Browser on your network maintains the master browse list for the network and hands off the most up-to-date list to the Backup Browser. The Backup Browser then distributes this list to all the clients. *Objective: Add and configure the network components of Windows NT Workstation (Chapter 10).*

45 *D.* The TCP/IP protocol suite is predominantly used to connect to the Internet because of its wide support for FTP, Telnet, HTTP, and Gopher. *Objective: Configure Microsoft Peer Web Services in a given situation (Chapter 14).*

46 *B.* To enable the Device.log file, you need to manually edit the Registry for RAS troubleshooting. *Objective: Implement advanced techniques to resolve various problems (Chapter 19).*

47 *A.* If you have enabled RAS troubleshooting with the Device.log file, you can view the file in the \Winnt\System32\RAS folder. *Objective: Implement advanced techniques to resolve various problems (Chapter 19).*

48 *C.* To run a diskless installation, you need to run the /B switch from the Winnt.exe or Winnt32.exe setup. *Objective: Choose the appropriate course of action to take when the installation process fails (Chapter 5, 19).*

49 *B.* The easiest method is to just rename Danielle's account in Arthur's name instead of having to create a new account for Arthur with all of Danielle's security information. *Objective: Choose the appropriate course of action to take when a user cannot access a resource (Chapters 5, 7).*

50 *C.* If you run your 16-bit applications in their own memory spaces, you don't have to worry about them crashing your other applications. They're treated as their own individual applications and won't affect any other apps. *Objective: Choose the appropriate course of action to take when an application fails (Chapters 16, 19).*

Appendix C

MS Certified Professional Requirements

Microsoft offers a number of certifications that you can earn to accelerate your career. These certifications are the most in-demand certifications in the industry today, owing in large part to the overwhelming acceptance of the Microsoft Windows NT operating system. The following certifications all require passing computer-based exams that thoroughly test your ability to implement and support the product.

Many exams apply to more than one Microsoft certification. This appendix includes advice on choosing exams for basic certification requirements that can also apply to advanced certification.

MCP

On your way to your MCSE, you earn an additional acronym: MCP (Microsoft Certified Professional). Upon passing any qualifying exams, you achieve MCP status for that operating system.

Qualifying exams

Passing *one* of the these exams earns you MCP status while you work toward MCSE certification for Windows NT 4.0:

✔ Implementing and Supporting Microsoft Windows 95 (either Exam 70-064, active, *or* Exam 70-063, retired)

✔ Implementing and Supporting Microsoft Windows NT Server 4.0 (Exam 70-067)

✔ Implementing and Supporting Microsoft Windows NT Workstation 4.02 (Exam 70-073)

✔ Microsoft Windows for Workgroups 3.11 (Exam 70-048, available until September 1998; certified until September 1999)

Consider working on one of the preceding exams before taking other MCSE exams. MCP-qualifying exams are required for MCSE certification, so it makes sense to earn MCP status as soon as possible.

The Windows NT Server 4.0 exam (70-067) is required for MCP+I certification. If you're planning to try for MCP+I certification, consider taking the NT Server 4.0 exam to get started on the MCP+I requirements and earn MCP certification at the same time. (The MCP+I requirements are covered in this appendix.)

Microsoft plans to retire the Windows NT 3.51 exams when Windows NT 5.0 exams come out. These exams qualify you for MCP status for a year after they are retired:

✔ Implementing and Supporting Microsoft Windows NT Workstation 3.51 (Exam 70-042)

✔ Implementing and Supporting Microsoft Windows NT Server 3.51 (Exam 70-043)

Two other exams earn MCP status and count toward MCSD certification for developers:

✔ Microsoft Windows Architecture I (Exam 70-160)

✔ Microsoft Windows Architecture II (Exam 70-161)

As of March 1999, the retired Windows architecture exams, 70-150 and 70-151, do not count toward MCP or MCSD certification.

Benefits

Johnny, tell our lucky MCPs about their fabulous prizes!

✔ Authorization to use the Microsoft Certified Professional logos on your resume and other promotional materials, such as business cards.

✔ An official Microsoft Certified Professional certificate, suitable for flaunting.

✔ Access to a private area on the Microsoft Web site for Microsoft Certified Professionals. Here, you can find information on Microsoft products and technologies.

✔ A free subscription to *Microsoft Certified Professional Magazine,* which has a lot of great information on Microsoft products, new exams, new certification products, book reviews, and more.

✔ Invitations to Microsoft conferences and training events.

MCT

Microsoft Certified Trainers (MCTs) are certified, technically competent individuals who can deliver Microsoft Official Curriculum at Microsoft Authorized Technical Education Centers (ATECs). And they have another cool set of initials to add to their resumes.

Requirements

For the MCT designation, candidates must

✔ Pass the exam for the course they are teaching

✔ Prove their instruction presentation skills

You prove your presentation skills by attending approved instructional presentations or via instructor certification by any of the following vendors:

✔ Novell

✔ Lotus

✔ Santa Cruz Operation

✔ Banyan Vines

✔ Cisco Systems

✔ Sun Microsystems

Benefits

Benefits for becoming a Microsoft Certified Trainer are like the benefits of becoming an MCP:

- ✔ Use of the Microsoft Certified Trainer logos on your resume and other promotional materials, such as business cards.

- ✔ An official Microsoft Certified Trainer certificate.

- ✔ Access to a private area on Microsoft's Web site for Microsoft Certified Trainers, where you can exchange information with other MCTs and course developers.

- ✔ A free subscription to *Microsoft Certified Professional Magazine,* which can help you prepare for your courses.

- ✔ Invitations to Microsoft conferences and training events.

- ✔ Subscription to the *Microsoft Education Forum Newsletter,* which is available to all MCTs and Authorized Technical Education Centers (ATECs).

MCP+Internet

The Microsoft Certified Professional+Internet (MCP+I) certification documents your ability to plan, configure, and troubleshoot Windows NT Server systems for intranets and the Internet.

You can achieve MCP+I certification while you work toward MCSE status. All the MCP+I requirements count toward MCSE certification for Windows NT 4.0. The Windows NT Server 4.0 exam (70-067) also qualifies you for MCP status, so consider taking it first.

Qualifying exams

MCP+I certification requires an exam for each of the three subjects listed in Table C-1. Your only option is your choice of Internet Information Server versions.

Table C-1	MCP+I Exams	
Subject	*Newest Exams*	*Older Exams*
Internet Information Server	Implementing and Supporting Microsoft Internet Information Server 4.0 (Exam 70-087)	Implementing and Supporting Microsoft Internet Information Server 3.0 and Microsoft Index Server 1.1 (Exam 70-077)
TCP/IP	Internetworking with Microsoft TCP/IP on Microsoft Windows NT 4.0 (Exam 70-059)	
Windows NT Server	Implementing and Supporting Microsoft Windows NT Server 4.0 (Exam 70-067)	

Consider taking the IIS 4.0 exam (70-087) for the Internet Information Server requirement of MCP+I certification, because IIS 4.0 is the most recent version. When Microsoft decides that IIS 3.0 is obsolete, you may have to pass the IIS 4.0 exam to maintain your certification.

Benefits

In addition to receiving all of the benefits listed for becoming an MCP, upon attaining the MCP+Internet certification, you can market yourself with an MCP+Internet logo and add another certificate to your wall.

MCSE

Microsoft Certified Systems Engineer (MCSE) is one of the most respected certifications in the industry. The dominance of the Windows NT operating system in the market has created great demand for MCSEs skilled in planning, implementing, and troubleshooting Windows NT and the BackOffice suite of products.

Windows NT 4.0 certification requirements

To become a Microsoft Certified Systems Engineer for Windows NT 4.0, you are required to pass *six* Microsoft exams:

✔ Four core exams

✔ Two elective exams

Core exams

The MCSE core exam requirements for Windows NT 4.0 cover *four* subjects, listed in Table C-2. You must pass an exam for each subject. Your only option is your choice of desktop operating system.

Always try to take the newest exam for a subject. When Microsoft retires the older exam, you may have to pass a newer exam to maintain your certification.

Table C-2	MCSE Windows NT 4.0 Core Exams		
Subject	*Newest Exams*	*Older Exams*	*Retired Exams*
Desktop operating system	Microsoft Windows NT Workstation 4.0 (Exam 70-073) Implementing and Supporting Microsoft Windows 98 (Exam 70-098)	Implementing and Supporting Microsoft Windows 95 (either Exam 70-064, active, *or* Exam 70-063, retired)	Microsoft Windows for Workgroups 3.11 (Exam 70-048, available until September 1998; certified until September 1999) Microsoft Windows 3.1 (Exam 70-030, available until September 1998; certified until September 1999)
Network basics	Networking Essentials (Exam 70-058) or approved equivalent certification		
Windows NT Server (basic)	Implementing and Supporting Microsoft Windows NT Server 4.0 (Exam 70-067)		
Windows NT Server (advanced)	Implementing and Supporting Microsoft Windows NT Server 4.0 in the Enterprise (Exam 70-068)		

Microsoft recognizes that other certification programs cover the requirements of the Networking Essentials exam. After you pass any of the MCSE exams, Microsoft will give you credit for Networking Essentials if you have proof for any of these certifications:

- ✔ Novell CNE, Master CNE, or CNI
- ✔ Banyan CBS or CBE
- ✔ Sun Certified Network Administrator for Solaris 2.5 or 2.6

Elective exams

MCSE certification requires you to pass elective exams for *two* of the subjects listed in Table C-3. *Retired exams* aren't available, but they count toward certification if you passed them when they were current.

Make sure that your MCSE elective exams cover two different subjects in Table C-3. If you take two exams for the same subject, only one exam counts toward your MCSE requirements.

Some of the MCSE elective exams are *core* requirements for MCSE+Internet (MCSE+I) certification. If you're interested in that level of certification, consider fulfilling your MCSE elective requirements from these MCSE+I core requirements:

- ✔ Internetworking with Microsoft TCP/IP on Microsoft Windows NT 4.0 (Exam 70-059)
- ✔ Implementing and Supporting Microsoft Internet Explorer 4.0 by Using the Internet Explorer Administration Kit (Exam 70-079)
- ✔ Implementing and Supporting Microsoft Internet Information Server 4.0 (Exam 70-087) *or* Implementing and Supporting Microsoft Internet Information Server 3.0 and Microsoft Index Server 1.1 (Exam 70-077) (only *one* Internet Information Server exam counts toward your MCSE or MCSE+I certification)

Many of the MCSE elective exams *do not count* toward MCSE+I certification. When you select an MCSE exam, check whether it applies to MCSE+I. If it doesn't apply, consider selecting another exam. (MCSE+I requirements are covered in this appendix.)

Table C-3

MCSE Elective Exams

Subject	Newest Exams	Older Exams	Retired Exams
Exchange Server	Implementing and Supporting Microsoft Exchange Server 5.5 (Exam 70-081)	Implementing and Supporting Microsoft Exchange Server 5 (Exam 70-076)	Implementing and Supporting Microsoft Exchange Server 4.0 (Exam 70-075; certified until September 1, 1999)
Internet Explorer	Implementing and Supporting Microsoft Internet Explorer 4.0 by Using the Internet Explorer Administration Kit (Exam 70-079)		
Internet Information Server	Implementing and Supporting Microsoft Internet Information Server 4.0 (Exam 70-087)		Implementing and Supporting Microsoft Internet Information Server 3.0 and Microsoft Index Server 1.1 (Exam 70-077)
Mail	Microsoft Mail for PC Networks 3.2-Enterprise (Exam 70-037)		
Proxy Server	Implementing and Supporting Microsoft Proxy Server 2.0 (Exam 70-088)	Implementing and Supporting Microsoft Proxy Server 1.0 (Exam 70-078)	
Site Server	Implementing and Supporting Web Sites using Site Server 3.0 (Exam 70-056)		
SNA Server	Implementing and Supporting Microsoft SNA Server 4.0 (Exam 70-085)	Implementing and Supporting Microsoft SNA Server 3.0 (Exam 70-013)	
SQL Server administration	System Administration for Microsoft SQL Server 7.0 (Exam 70-028)	System Administration for Microsoft SQL Server 6.5 (Exam 70-026)	Microsoft SQL Server 4.2 Database Administration for Microsoft Windows NT (Exam 70-022)
SQL Server implementation	Implementing a Database Design on Microsoft SQL Server 7.0 (Exam 70-029)	Implementing a Database Design on Microsoft SQL Server 6.5 (Exam 70-027)	Microsoft SQL Server 4.2 Database Implementation (Exam 70-021)
Systems Management Server	Implementing and Supporting Microsoft Systems Management Server 2.0 (Exam 70-085)	Implementing and Supporting Microsoft Systems Management Server 1.2 (Exam 70-018)	Implementing and Supporting Microsoft Systems Management Server 1.0 (Exam 70-014)
TCP/IP	Internetworking with Microsoft TCP/IP on Microsoft Windows NT 4.0 (Exam 70-059)	Internetworking Microsoft TCP/IP on Microsoft Windows NT (3.5-3.51) (Exam 70-053)	

Windows NT 3.51 certification requirements

Microsoft plans to retire the Windows NT 3.51 exams when it releases the Windows NT 5.0 exams. Until then, you can earn an MCSE for Windows NT 3.51. The certification remains valid for a year after the exams are retired. At the end of that year, be prepared to requalify for a current version of Windows NT.

Table C-4 lists the required core subjects for MCSE certification on the Windows NT 3.51 track. You must pass an exam for each subject. (As with NT 4.0, the only NT 3.51 core option is your choice of desktop operating system.)

Table C-4	MCSE Windows NT 3.51 Core Exams		
Subject	*Newest Exams*	*Older Exams*	*Retired Exams*
Desktop operating system	Implementing and Supporting Microsoft Windows 98 (Exam 70-098)	Implementing and Supporting Microsoft Windows 95 (either Exam 70-064, active, *or* Exam 70-063, retired)	Microsoft Windows for Workgroups 3.11 (Exam 70-048, available until September 1998; certified until September 1999)
			Microsoft (Exam 70-030, Windows 3.1 available until September 1998; certified until September 1999)
Network basics	Networking Essentials (Exam 70-058) or approved equivalent certification		
Windows NT Workstation	Implementing and Supporting Microsoft Windows NT Workstation 3.51 (Exam 70-042)		
Windows NT Server	Implementing and Supporting Microsoft Windows NT Server 3.51 (Exam 70-043)		

MCSE for Windows NT 3.51 also requires two electives, just like they are described for the Windows NT 4.0 certification.

Don't bother with NT 3.51 certification. Microsoft intends to decertify the NT 3.51 exams, and they don't count toward MCSE+I. Unless you just need *one* NT 3.51 exam to finish your MCSE requirements on the NT 3.51 track, spend your time on NT 4.0.

Benefits

In addition to receiving all the benefits of becoming an MCP, upon attaining the MCSE certification, you enjoy these benefits:

- Marketing yourself with an MCSE logo
- Yet another certificate for your accomplishments
- Subscription to Microsoft TechNet
- Subscription to the Microsoft BETA evaluation program (a monthly distribution of new Microsoft products in development)

MCSE+Internet

This new designation is quickly becoming known as MCSE+I. This designates Microsoft Certified Systems Engineers who have extensive qualifications for Internet system management, including

- Web sites
- Browsers
- Commerce applications
- Intranets

MCSE+I requirements

Nine different exams are necessary for MCSE+I certification:

- Seven core exams
- Two elective exams

Here's how they add up.

Core exams

The MCSE+I core exam requirements for Windows NT 4.0 cover *seven* subjects, listed in Table C-5. You must pass an exam for each subject. Your only options are your choice of desktop operating system and version of Internet Information Server.

Table C-5	MCSE+I Core Exams		
Subject	*Newest Exams*	*Older Exams*	*Retired Exams*
Desktop operating system	Microsoft Windows NT Workstation 4.0 (Exam 70-073) and Implementing and Supporting Microsoft Windows 98 (Exam 70-098)	Implementing and Supporting Microsoft Windows 95 (either Exam 70-064, active, *or* Exam 70-063, retired)	Microsoft Windows for Workgroups 3.11 (Exam 70-048, available until September 1998; certified until September 1999)
			Microsoft Windows 3.1 (Exam 70-030, available until September 1998; certified until September 1999)
Internet Explorer	Implementing and Supporting Microsoft Internet Explorer 4.0 by Using the Internet Explorer Administration Kit (Exam 70-079)		
Internet Information Server	Implementing and Supporting Microsoft Internet Information Server 4.0 (Exam 70-087)	Implementing and Supporting Microsoft Internet Information Server 3.0 and Microsoft Index Server 1.1 (Exam 70-077)	
Network basics	Networking Essentials (Exam 70-058) or approved equivalent certification		
TCP/IP	Internetworking with Microsoft TCP/IP on Microsoft Windows NT 4.0 (Exam 70-059)		

(continued)

Table C-5 *(continued)*

Subject	Newest Exams	Older Exams	Retired Exams
Windows NT Server (basic)	Implementing and Supporting Microsoft Windows NT Server 4.0 (Exam 70-067)		
Windows NT Server (advanced)	Implementing and Supporting Microsoft Windows NT Server 4.0 in the Enterprise (Exam 70-068)		

Elective exams

MCSE+I certification requires you to pass elective exams for *two* of the subjects listed in Table C-6.

Make sure that your MCSE+I elective exams cover two different subjects in Table C-6. If you take two exams for the same subject, only one exam counts toward MCSE+I certification.

Table C-6   MCSE+I Elective Exams

Subject	Newest Exams	Older Exams
Exchange Server	Implementing and Supporting Microsoft Exchange Server 5.5 (Exam 70-081)	Implementing and Supporting Microsoft Exchange Server 5 (Exam 70-076)
Proxy Server	Implementing and Supporting Microsoft Proxy Server 2.0 (Exam 70-088)	Implementing and Supporting Microsoft Proxy Server 1.0 (Exam 70-078)
Site Server	Implementing and Supporting Web Sites using Site Server 3.0 (Exam 70-056)	
SNA Server	Implementing and Supporting Microsoft SNA Server 4.0 (Exam 70-085)	
SQL Server administration	System Administration for Microsoft SQL Server 6.5 (Exam 70-026)	
SQL Server implementation	Implementing a Database Design on Microsoft SQL Server 6.5 (Exam 70-027)	

Benefits

In addition to receiving all of the benefits listed for becoming an MCSE, upon attaining the MCSE+Internet certification, you can also market yourself with an MCSE+Internet logo and receive another certificate for your accomplishments.

Online References

If you want to find out more about the Microsoft certification programs, check out the Microsoft Training and Certification Web site:

```
www.Microsoft.com/Train_Cert/
```

Make it a practice to visit this site regularly: It's the definitive source for updated information about the Microsoft Certified Professional program. Microsoft updates and retires exams often enough that you need to make an effort to stay on top of the changes, and this Web site is your best center for the latest information on the certifications and the exams.

Appendix D
About the CD

On the CD-ROM:

▶ The QuickLearn Game, a fun way to study for the test

▶ Practice and Self-Assessment tests, to make sure that you're ready for the real thing

▶ Practice test demos from Transcender, QuickCert, and EndeavorX

System Requirements

Make sure that your computer meets the minimum system requirements listed next. If your computer doesn't match up to most of these requirements, you may have problems using the contents of the CD.

- ✔ A PC with a 486 or faster processor.
- ✔ Microsoft Windows 95 or later.
- ✔ At least 16MB of total RAM installed on your computer.
- ✔ At least 32MB of hard drive space available to install all the software from this CD. (You need less space if you don't install every program.)
- ✔ A CD-ROM drive — double-speed (2x) or faster.
- ✔ A sound card for PCs.
- ✔ A monitor capable of displaying at least 256 colors or grayscale.
- ✔ A modem with a speed of at least 14,400 bps.

Using the CD with Microsoft Windows

To install the items from the CD to your hard drive, follow these steps:

1. **Insert the CD into your computer's CD-ROM drive.**

2. **Click Start⇨Run.**

3. **In the dialog box that appears, type** D:\SETUP.EXE.

Replace *D* with the proper drive letter if your CD-ROM drive uses a different letter.

4. **Click OK.**

A license agreement window appears.

5. **Read through the license agreement, nod your head, and then click the Accept button if you want to use the CD — after you click Accept, you'll never be bothered by the License Agreement window again.**

The CD interface Welcome screen appears. The interface is a little program that shows you what's on the CD and coordinates installing the programs and running the demos. The interface basically enables you to click a button or two to make things happen.

6. **Click anywhere on the Welcome screen to enter the interface.**

Now you're getting to the action. The next screen lists categories for the software on the CD.

7. **To view the items within a category, just click the category's name.**

A list of programs in the category appears.

8. **For more information about a program, click the program's name.**

Be sure to read the information that appears. Sometimes a program has its own system requirements or requires you to do a few tricks on your computer before you can install or run the program, and this screen tells you what you may need to do, if necessary.

9. **If you don't want to install the program, click the Go Back button to return to the previous screen.**

You can always return to the previous screen by clicking the Go Back button. This feature enables you to browse the different categories and products and decide what you want to install.

10. **To install a program, click the appropriate Install button.**

The CD interface drops to the background while the CD installs the program you chose.

11. **To install other items, repeat Steps 7 through 10.**

12. **When you finish installing programs, click the Quit button to close the interface.**

You can eject the CD now. Carefully place it back in the plastic jacket of the book for safekeeping.

In order to run some of the programs on the *MCSE Certification For Dummies* CD, you may need to keep the CD inside your CD-ROM drive. This is a Good Thing. Otherwise, the installed program would have required you to install a very large chunk of the program to your hard drive, which may have kept you from installing other software.

What You'll Find

Here's a summary of the software on this CD.

Dummies test prep tools

QuickLearn Game

The QuickLearn Game is the *...For Dummies* way of making studying for the Certification exam fun. Well, okay, less painful. OutPost is a DirectX, high-resolution, fast-paced arcade game.

Answer questions to defuse dimensional disrupters and save the universe from a rift in space-time. (The questions come from the same set of questions that the Self-Assessment and Practice Test use, but isn't this way more fun?) Missing a few questions on the real exam almost never results in a rip in the fabric of the universe, so just think how easy it'll be when you get there!

The QuickLearn Game requires Microsoft DirectX 5.0 or later. If you have Windows 95 or Windows 98 without DirectX, you can download DirectX at `www.microsoft.com/directx/resources/dx5end.htm`. DirectX 5.0 does not run on Windows NT 4.0. When Windows NT 5 is released, it will run DirectX 6.0.

Practice Test

The Practice Test is designed to help you get comfortable with the MCSE testing situation and pinpoint your strengths and weaknesses on the topic. You can accept the default setting of 60 questions in 60 minutes, or you can customize the settings. You can pick the number of questions, the amount of time, and even decide which objectives you want to focus on.

After you answer the questions, the Practice Test gives you plenty of feedback. You can find out which questions you got right or wrong and get statistics on how you did, broken down by objective. Then you can review the questions — all of them, all the ones you missed, all the ones you marked, or a combination of the ones you marked and the ones you missed.

Self-Assessment Test

The Self-Assessment Test is designed to simulate the actual MCSE testing situation. You must answer 60 questions in 60 minutes. After you answer all the questions, you find out your score and whether you pass or fail — but that's all the feedback you get. If you can pass the Self-Assessment Test fairly regularly, you're ready to tackle the real thing.

Links Page

I've also created a Links Page, a handy starting place for accessing the huge amounts of information on the Internet about the MCSE tests. You can find the page, Links.htm, at the root of the CD.

Commercial demos

Transcender Certification Sampler, from Transcender Corporation

Transcender's demo tests are some of the most popular practice tests available. The Certification Sampler offers demos of all the exams that Transcender offers.

QuickCert, from Specialized Solutions

This package from Specialized Solutions offers QuickCert practice tests for several Certification exams. Run the QuickCert IDG Demo to choose the practice test you want to work on.

EndeavorX, from VFX Technologies

EndeavorX is a powerful new knowledge assessment application, with four different testing modes and a wide variety of question filters.

The first time you run EndeavorX, you need to import the exam set:

1. **Choose File⇨Import/Export to open the Administration dialog box.**

2. **Find the file** Microsoft Evaluation Exams for Import.mdb **and enter it in the Import Data From text box.**

3. **Click the Import button and select exactly what elements you want to import.**

   VFX also provides the file Novell Evaluation Exams for Import.mdb as a bonus.

4. **After you import the exams, use the Control Panel to select the test or the categories you want to work with and to set the other test parameters.**

When you install EndeavorX, I advise you to accept the default installation location and use the Typical installation option. If you choose to install the software on a drive or in a directory other than the default, EndeavorX can't find the question database.

If the physical installation and the registry settings don't match, one or more error messages may appear. If you get an error message, try the following steps to straighten things out:

(**or** To make sure that you don't get any error messages, follow these steps:)

1. **When the File Open dialog box opens looking for** EndeavorX.mdb, **navigate to the directory/drive where the software is installed.**

2. **Double-click on the** EndeavorX.mdb **file.**

   To update all the registry settings, proceed immediately to the EndeavorX Control Panel.

3. **Review all the settings, make any changes needed, and then click the OK button to close the Control Panel and save these settings.**

4. **If any tests have been imported, select a test and some combination of categories.**

5. **Select a default printing device.**

6. **Set the Font to any font installed on your system.**

   All font characteristics should be listed, as well as a sample of the font.

7. **Carefully examine the colors to ensure that the foreground and background colors contrast (for example, black on white).**

   Typically, the explanation text is offset as a different color than the question/answer text.

8. **For environmental settings, "uncheck" login, tips, and so on.**

   By default, only the Splash Screen and the Auto Advance are checked.

9. **Click OK to exit the EndeavorX Control Panel.**

If You've Got Problems (Of the CD Kind)

I tried my best to compile programs that work on most computers with the minimum system requirements. Alas, your computer may differ, and some programs may not work properly for some reason.

The two most likely problems are that you don't have enough memory (RAM) for the programs you want to use, or that you have other programs running that are affecting installation or running of a program. If you get error messages like Not enough memory or Setup cannot continue, try one or more of these methods and then try using the software again:

- ✔ **Turn off any antivirus software that you have on your computer.** Installers sometimes mimic virus activity and may make your computer incorrectly believe that it is being infected by a virus.

- ✔ **Close all running programs.** The more programs you're running, the less memory is available to other programs. Installers also typically update files and programs; if you keep other programs running, installation may not work properly.

- ✔ **In Windows, close the CD interface and run demos or installations directly from Windows Explorer.** The interface itself can tie up system memory or even conflict with certain kinds of interactive demos. Use Windows Explorer to browse the files on the CD and launch installers or demos.

- ✔ **Have your local computer store add more RAM to your computer.** This is, admittedly, a drastic and somewhat expensive step. However, if you have a Windows 95 PC or a Mac OS computer with a PowerPC chip, adding more memory can really help the speed of your computer and enable more programs to run at the same time.

If you still have trouble installing the items from the CD, please call the IDG Books Worldwide Customer Service phone number: 800-762-2974 (outside the U.S.: 317-596-5430).

Index

● *K* ●

● *Q* ●

(continued)

IDG Books Worldwide, Inc., End-User License Agreement

READ THIS. You should carefully read these terms and conditions before opening the software packet(s) included with this book ("Book"). This is a license agreement ("Agreement") between you and IDG Books Worldwide, Inc. ("IDGB"). By opening the accompanying software packet(s), you acknowledge that you have read and accept the following terms and conditions. If you do not agree and do not want to be bound by such terms and conditions, promptly return the Book and the unopened software packet(s) to the place you obtained them for a full refund.

1. **License Grant.** IDGB grants to you (either an individual or entity) a nonexclusive license to use one copy of the enclosed software program(s) (collectively, the "Software") solely for your own personal or business purposes on a single computer (whether a standard computer or a workstation component of a multiuser network). The Software is in use on a computer when it is loaded into temporary memory (RAM) or installed into permanent memory (hard disk, CD-ROM, or other storage device). IDGB reserves all rights not expressly granted herein.

2. **Ownership.** IDGB is the owner of all right, title, and interest, including copyright, in and to the compilation of the Software recorded on the disk(s) or CD-ROM ("Software Media"). Copyright to the individual programs recorded on the Software Media is owned by the author or other authorized copyright owner of each program. Ownership of the Software and all proprietary rights relating thereto remain with IDGB and its licensers.

3. **Restrictions on Use and Transfer.**

   (a) You may only (i) make one copy of the Software for backup or archival purposes, or (ii) transfer the Software to a single hard disk, provided that you keep the original for backup or archival purposes. You may not (i) rent or lease the Software, (ii) copy or reproduce the Software through a LAN or other network system or through any computer subscriber system or bulletin-board system, or (iii) modify, adapt, or create derivative works based on the Software.

   (b) You may not reverse engineer, decompile, or disassemble the Software. You may transfer the Software and user documentation on a permanent basis, provided that the transferee agrees to accept the terms and conditions of this Agreement and you retain no copies. If the Software is an update or has been updated, any transfer must include the most recent update and all prior versions.

4. **Restrictions on Use of Individual Programs.** You must follow the individual requirements and restrictions detailed for each individual program in Appendix D of this Book. These limitations are also contained in the individual license agreements recorded on the Software Media. These limitations may include a requirement that after using the program for a specified period of time, the user must pay a registration fee or discontinue use. By opening the Software packet(s), you will be agreeing to abide by the licenses and restrictions for these individual programs that are detailed in Appendix D and on the Software Media. None of the material on this Software Media or listed in this Book may ever be redistributed, in original or modified form, for commercial purposes.

5. **Limited Warranty.**

   (a) IDGB warrants that the Software and Software Media are free from defects in materials and workmanship under normal use for a period of sixty (60) days from the date of purchase of this Book. If IDGB receives notification within the warranty period of defects in materials or workmanship, IDGB will replace the defective Software Media.

   (b) **IDGB AND THE AUTHOR OF THE BOOK DISCLAIM ALL OTHER WARRANTIES, EXPRESS OR IMPLIED, INCLUDING WITHOUT LIMITATION IMPLIED WARRANTIES OF MERCHANTABILITY AND FITNESS FOR A PARTICULAR PURPOSE, WITH RESPECT TO THE SOFTWARE, THE PROGRAMS, THE SOURCE CODE CONTAINED THEREIN, AND/OR THE TECHNIQUES DESCRIBED IN THIS BOOK. IDGB DOES NOT WARRANT THAT THE FUNCTIONS CONTAINED IN THE SOFTWARE WILL MEET YOUR REQUIREMENTS OR THAT THE OPERATION OF THE SOFTWARE WILL BE ERROR FREE.**

   (c) This limited warranty gives you specific legal rights, and you may have other rights that vary from jurisdiction to jurisdiction.

6. **Remedies.**

   (a) IDGB's entire liability and your exclusive remedy for defects in materials and workmanship shall be limited to replacement of the Software Media, which may be returned to IDGB with a copy of your receipt at the following address: Software Media Fulfillment Department, Attn.: *MCSE Windows NT Workstation 4 For Dummies,* IDG Books Worldwide, Inc., 7260 Shadeland Station, Ste. 100, Indianapolis, IN 46256, or call 800-762-2974. Please allow three to four weeks for delivery. This Limited Warranty is void if failure of the Software Media has resulted from accident, abuse, or misapplication. Any replacement Software Media will be warranted for the remainder of the original warranty period or thirty (30) days, whichever is longer.

   (b) In no event shall IDGB or the author be liable for any damages whatsoever (including without limitation damages for loss of business profits, business interruption, loss of business information, or any other pecuniary loss) arising from the use of or inability to use the Book or the Software, even if IDGB has been advised of the possibility of such damages.

   (c) Because some jurisdictions do not allow the exclusion or limitation of liability for consequential or incidental damages, the above limitation or exclusion may not apply to you.

7. **U.S. Government Restricted Rights.** Use, duplication, or disclosure of the Software by the U.S. Government is subject to restrictions stated in paragraph (c)(1)(ii) of the Rights in Technical Data and Computer Software clause of DFARS 252.227-7013, and in subparagraphs (a) through (d) of the Commercial Computer–Restricted Rights clause at FAR 52.227-19, and in similar clauses in the NASA FAR supplement, when applicable.

8. **General.** This Agreement constitutes the entire understanding of the parties and revokes and supersedes all prior agreements, oral or written, between them and may not be modified or amended except in a writing signed by both parties hereto that specifically refers to this Agreement. This Agreement shall take precedence over any other documents that may be in conflict herewith. If any one or more provisions contained in this Agreement are held by any court or tribunal to be invalid, illegal, or otherwise unenforceable, each and every other provision shall remain in full force and effect.

Installation Instructions

● ●

*T*o install the items from the CD to your hard drive, follow these steps:

1. **Insert the CD into your computer's CD-ROM drive.**

2. **Click Start➪Run.**

3. **In the dialog box that appears, type** D:\SETUP.EXE.

   Replace *D* with the proper drive letter if your CD-ROM drive uses a different letter.

4. **Click OK.**

   A license agreement window appears.

5. **Read through the license agreement, nod your head, and then click the Accept button if you want to use the CD — after you click Accept, you'll never be bothered by the License Agreement window again.**

   The CD interface Welcome screen appears. The interface is a little program that shows you what's on the CD and coordinates installing the programs and running the demos. The interface basically enables you to click a button or two to make things happen.

6. **Click anywhere on the Welcome screen to enter the interface.**

   Now you're getting to the action. The next screen lists categories for the software on the CD.

7. **To view the items within a category, just click the category's name.**

   A list of programs in the category appears.

8. **For more information about a program, click the program's name.**

   Be sure to read the information that appears. Sometimes a program has its own system requirements or requires you to do a few tricks on your computer before you can install or run the program, and this screen tells you what you may need to do, if necessary.

9. **If you don't want to install the program, click the Go Back button to return to the previous screen.**

   You can always return to the previous screen by clicking the Go Back button. This feature enables you to browse the different categories and products and decide what you want to install.

10. **To install a program, click the appropriate Install button.**

    The CD interface drops to the background while the CD installs the program you chose.

11. **To install other items, repeat Steps 7 through 10.**

12. **When you finish installing programs, click the Quit button to close the interface.**

    You can eject the CD now. Carefully place it back in the plastic jacket of the book for safekeeping.

In order to run some of the programs on the *MCSE Certification For Dummies* CD, you may need to keep the CD inside your CD-ROM drive. This is a Good Thing. Otherwise, the installed program would have required you to install a very large chunk of the program to your hard drive, which may have kept you from installing other software.

IDG BOOKS WORLDWIDE BOOK REGISTRATION

We want to hear from you!

Visit **http://my2cents.dummies.com** to register this book and tell us how you liked it!

- ✔ Get entered in our monthly prize giveaway.

- ✔ Give us feedback about this book — tell us what you like best, what you like least, or maybe what you'd like to ask the author and us to change!

- ✔ Let us know any other ...*For Dummies*® topics that interest you.

Your feedback helps us determine what books to publish, tells us what coverage to add as we revise our books, and lets us know whether we're meeting your needs as a ...*For Dummies* reader. You're our most valuable resource, and what you have to say is important to us!

Not on the Web yet? It's easy to get started with *Dummies 101*®: *The Internet For Windows*® *95* or *The Internet For Dummies*®, 5th Edition, at local retailers everywhere.

Or let us know what you think by sending us a letter at the following address:

...*For Dummies* Book Registration
Dummies Press
7260 Shadeland Station, Suite 100
Indianapolis, IN 46256-3945
Fax 317-596-5498

BUSINESS AND
GENERAL
REFERENCE
BOOK SERIES
FROM IDG

COMPUTER
BOOK SERIES
FROM IDG